EBURY PRESS

THE PARENTS I MET

Mansi Zaveri is the founder and CEO of India's most trusted discovery platform for parenting and childcare, Kidsstoppress.com, which boasts a digital reach of 20 million people per month. She was also featured in Exchange4Media's Content 40 Under 40 list in 2020. In June 2011, this mom of two decided to combine her passion for digital medium and her parenting journey to become an entrepreneur, leaving behind her corporate life to empower parents to make informed choices.

Mansi is the voice of the New Age Indian parents and has emerged as one of the most popular influencers in the parenting and baby care space. With a whole lot of passion and hard work, she has built Kidsstoppress.com into an enormously successful brand that today hosts online courses for parents, kids and women entrepreneurs.

Her first book, *50 Indian Meal Plans*, ranked no. 1 on Amazon in Food and Encyclopaedias in 2020. The Kids Stop Press (KSP) Awards, which celebrates excellence in parenting and baby care, is her brainchild. A yoga student and sustainable living advocate, Mansi lives in Mumbai with her two daughters, husband and family.

ADVANCE PRAISE FOR THE BOOK

'As parents, we all want what's best for our kids. But sometimes what's "best" for us isn't necessarily best for them. This book gives a unique perspective and moments that we can all relate to. Lots of learning and love. A must-read!'—**Sameera Reddy, actor and creator**

'Interesting and refreshing, a book that will help parents find that peace they look for, the strength and even the satisfaction of knowing that those guilty pangs as a parent when balancing a hectic career is a shared experience, and personal goals don't make you a better or a more organized parent. The narrative features the parent, devoid of gender bias and that is its greatest strength.

'These anecdotes captured by you are about real people with real challenges and advantages, and real choices that they made, and their reflections allow you to reflect on your own journey.

'Parenting is personal and therefore this book allows the reader to be inspired rather than providing a mantra which is the most enjoyable aspect.

'An easy relatable style, the book has so many hidden strategies! Super effort, Mansi!'—**Fatema Agarkar, founder, Agarkar Centre of Excellence (ACE)**

'Mansi's book is a wonderful tribute, resplendent with touching stories. I've always believed that the greatest accomplishments come from people who harnessed the best of nature and nurture from the village that raised them. Parents dominated those first two decades. I love the premise of the investigation into these achievers, each on top of their game, and the hat tip to each of their parents'—**Karthik Reddy, co-founder and managing partner, Blume Ventures**

'This book is an "art-science" in parenting! I must congratulate Mansi for bringing together the art and science of parenting in one book. There are no perfect parents, but there can be perfection in parenting as parenting is a journey and never a destination, the quest for perfection is what keeps every parent excited and involved. Each and every parent featured here touched on the aspect of instinctive parenting, listening to your inner instincts when it comes to your child. And that is the elixir of parenting that Mansi has provided in this book.

'Her introduction resonates with all of us and each chapter brings a smile, some tears and many exclamations of "I can relate to this!"

'I congratulate her and Penguin Random House for this brilliant must-have book that will soon find its place in every parent's hands, minds and hearts'—**Dr Swati Popat Vats, president, Early Childhood Association**

'This book served as a reminder for me that parenting is about embracing our own journey, flaws and all. A relatable gem for any parent!'—**Masoom Minawala Mehta, fashion creator, investor and entrepreneur**

'*The Parents I Met* is a unique approach to speaking with the parents of children who have gone on to make their parents, families, societies and the nation proud. This book captures the emotions and hard work of the parents who generally do not get credit for doing a thankless job.

'This is an ode to all the parents out there. Raising children, in my opinion, is one of the toughest jobs. Thank you for documenting these heart-touching twenty-two stories.

Wishing you all the best'—**Manish Pandey, author, brand consultant and content creator**

'The book we parents didn't know we needed! A must-read if you want to inspire your kids to self-actualize. An inspirational, instructional and informative book about how to raise one's children as committed leaders and empaths for this age'—**Tisca Chopra, Indian actress, author and film producer**

'I absolutely loved reading this one! The preface and introduction itself got me hooked. I am a big fan of the Bhagavad Gita myself and I love how Mansi has used it. The whole narrative is so relatable and real.

'To my mind—it's a very authentic representation of parents to parents! Loved it!'—**Bhavna Mandon, marketing director, LEGO Group India**

'We know a parent's role is important, but what to do when and how much are elusive answers. The book's candid conversations offer real insights in a fun-to-read and engaging style. For those seeking a parenting guidebook, start here!'—**Kimberly Dixit, CEO and co-founder, The Red Pen**

'As a paediatrician, I know what it takes to be a parent. Parenting is one such journey that you can only learn when you are going through it. There cannot be a better person to write this book than Mansi Zaveri. Her experiences of being a mother and of constantly interacting with so many parents across India through Kidsstoppress.com have made her the epitome of honest parental advice and parental counselling. With this book, in which she has interviewed parents of people from different walks of life, she has shown her commitment towards the parenting community. This could become the Bible for future parents to learn from parents who have brought up amazing human beings who have made a difference in society. Please do not miss a single line of this amazing book'—**Dr Nihar Parekh, paediatrician**

The Parents I Met

Mansi Zaveri

An imprint of Penguin Random House

EBURY PRESS

USA | Canada | UK | Ireland | Australia
New Zealand | India | South Africa | China | Singapore

Ebury Press is part of the Penguin Random House group of companies
whose addresses can be found at global.penguinrandomhouse.com

Published by Penguin Random House India Pvt. Ltd
4th Floor, Capital Tower 1, MG Road,
Gurugram 122 002, Haryana, India

First published in Ebury Press by Penguin Random House India 2023

10 9 8 7 6 5 4 3

ISBN 9780143459743

Typeset in Sabon by Manipal Technologies Limited, Manipal
Printed at Replika Press Pvt. Ltd, India

www.penguin.co.in

To my parents

Contents

Preface

I have found so many answers to parenting and life in the Bhagavad Gita that I couldn't start this one without quoting something that deeply resonated with me.

> *mātā gurutarā bhūmeḥ pitā uccataraś ca khāt*
> *manaḥ śīghrataraṃ vāyoś cintā bahutarī nṛṇām*
>
> (Yudhishthira answered, 'The mother is heavier than the earth; the father is higher than the heaven; the mind is lighter than the wind and our thoughts are numbered more than grass.')

Growing up, I didn't have too many memories of my parents agreeing to what I wanted or vice versa. They were too busy providing for my sisters and me, and nurturing us. It didn't seem like parenting was a chore for them. It appeared more like a natural extension. I don't recall them talking to their friends about us applying to schools or what we ate, drank—were we fussy eaters? Nothing at all.

My earliest recollections involve my parents taking a stand for something they deeply believed in—education.

They picked an English-medium school for my older sister, in contrast to the Gujarati-medium schools attended by my cousins. I am sure, like most parents between the 1970s and 1990s, my parents believed that education, regardless of a person's gender, would be the defining factor in changing the world. All our parents, rather than spending money on us for clothes, shoes, parties or presents, made sure we had access to the best food and the best education possible—they never cut corners when it came to these two things.

There were no dedicated story times or bedtime routines. There was no option or idea of sleep training or co-sleeping. You learn to sleep on your own when you have to live in a joint family, which was the norm back then with many people living in a tiny house. My mother, who was raising four children on her own, hardly made it to bed on time. And then she had to get up early and start the day all over again. She prioritized family, work and sleep.

Even as she was braiding the hair of her four girls, she supervised our homework and checked in with us about our day. There was no moment our parents spent not playing catch-up. *For a parent, life was about multitasking then and it is about multitasking even now*.

All my life, I have watched my parents just 'do'. No one complained when they had more on their plate than their fair share. Until we have children, our parents always seem extreme in comparison. Today, as parents, we seek answers from them whenever we feel challenged in different situations every single day. We all seek a playbook to parenting of different people who, according to us, have done it right. I am sure you have come back from a conversation with a parent or read a book, saw a billboard with someone on it or scrolled through Instagram and thought 'I wish I knew what their parents did right.'

Now that I'm older, I can see that I had no idea how my formative years had influenced me the way they did. I can't pinpoint one thing. Was it the everyday things? You will question on your journey as a parent, the mundane, the routine things, the simple things that may seem very insignificant to you then but they could be your child's fondest memories.

For me, I wonder what it was that contributed to who I am today. Was it the long walks I took at Marine Drive with my dad, holding his hand as I asked him all the questions I could think of and he'd patiently answer? Or was it the time he took us horseback riding at the park, where he jogged right behind me just in case I fell as the horse rider took me for a ride?

Was it the holidays and train rides we took, where we shared food with fellow passengers and learned to protect ourselves and our belongings? *We grew up in a world that was real and not a bubble, like the one our kids are growing up in today—far from reality.*

Or was it teaching us table tennis on the dining table at home by placing two glasses and a stick to create the net? Was it getting up and staying up with us, or driving us to and from the exam centres so we could study in the car? Or maybe it was my mom, who managed to become financially secure by the time she was forty, despite having only completed high school.

Maybe getting up at ungodly hours to get everything done was keeping her from realizing her dreams. The problem could never be bigger than her. Her willpower was taller than any mountain I've ever seen. The seeds for my early rising habit (I was up by 5 a.m.) were planted by her when I was young. My father instilled in me the importance of a routine by working from 10.30 a.m. to 8 p.m., Monday through Saturday, and not getting home until after 9 p.m. This routine wasn't compromised if it was raining, we were unwell, there was a family function, or even during the Mumbai riots. These habits and restraints may have seemed mundane and boring at the time, but they were, without a doubt, instrumental in ensuring that my parents enjoyed a prosperous old age and that my mother would continue to do so, long after his passing.

Sure enough, I grew up in a home where my father treated my mother with the utmost respect and fully supported every professional and personal choice she made—from her decision to enter the workforce at the age of forty to her wanting to teach Hindi since she wasn't well versed in English. Since we were a nuclear family, he would prepare meals on the days my mother was away or needed rest (when she had her period, for example) and would pack our school dabbas while she did our hair. My dad has always said that a woman's worth is not solely measured by her ability to work in the kitchen, even though my mom is an excellent cook. To ensure that she could spend time with us and pursue her ambitions of working and being financially independent, he hired a cook to prepare all of our meals.

Girls should get an education because a path to financial independence is the greatest gift of all. The value of money and the importance of saving it were not mere lessons I picked up from books, but rather from watching my parents prioritize our education over material possessions and practise thrift in order to fund our annual summer vacation. Despite being able to live reasonably well, both of my parents never once made anything except books and education abundantly available. *Everything was in limited supply so maybe we valued it a lot more.* Dresses were stitched twice a year for Diwali and birthdays, and birthdays were celebrated at home with Camy Wafers, home-made pav bhaji and cake from Monginis. We would give out our favourite Bourbon biscuits or Jim Jam as return gifts and ah, the joy of eating that or taking it to school the next day was an achievement of a different level altogether.

I am baffled at how my parents could have four kids and still appreciate and support each of us despite our differences. How hard it must have been to avoid making comparisons between your four kids. And not compare us to the children from the extended family too? Yes, there was no social media pressure where you were competing and comparing with strangers, but there was social pressure where you were competing with your neighbour and cousins.

Looking back, I can't pinpoint a single event or realization that turned out to be formative, but there were certainly pivotal times in my life that will forever live in my memory.

As soon as you make the decision to become a parent, you begin to wonder if you're capable of becoming one. Questions such as 'How should I go about becoming a parent?' and 'How can I do this right?' start to consume you. You eventually reach a point where you realize you love someone more than yourself. Worries like whether you're doing a good job, whether you're keeping up with the 'Sharmas', or how to do it all like the parents you look up to, start to weigh on you.

When my daughter was three, I decided to launch Kidsstoppress.com because I felt, all parents, including myself, needed a guide to parenting. Food, feeding schedules, bedtime rituals, playtime strategies and toys, all needed to be just right. But that was the simple part—the part about being a role model who walked the talk seemed to be the least explored.

After ten years of running Kidsstoppress, interviewing thousands of Indian and international celebrities, raising two daughters on the cusp of teenage, and dealing with a global pandemic, I found myself wondering—what do parents of outliers, people who have stood for something and left an impact on the world, do differently than I am/we are doing? What have these outliers, these children, gone through in life to reach where they are today?

Whether our upbringing was good, bad, ugly or beautiful, I am confident that it played a significant role in shaping who we are today. Since we take so much with us from our past, it was instinctive to check in with those who lived then to see if they had any inkling that their descendants would one day exhibit characteristics typically associated with the exceptional.

Our self-portrait, as we present it to the world, is a polished and curated version of who we want to be, but our parents are the only people who ever get to see the real us. *They understand us more intimately than we know ourselves. They have known us even before we knew ourselves.*

Introduction

Absolutely nothing prepares you for being a parent.

You may assume, 'I will have so much money, this position, at this stage, at this age,' but having a child is the first stage in life where you have no control. You need to do it and do it selflessly.

The conversations I have had with the parents of outliers have brewed in my mind for over ten years. Every time a mother has a conversation with another parent or wonders if she is a good parent, she experiences doubt: 'Am I doing a good job of raising my kids—like my friends have?' My definition of success and how I measure it shifted dramatically when I had children in my twenties, as it does for all of us every decade or, in the case of major life events, half a decade.

This book slowly formed in me as I waited for my daughter to open her door after an argument; it came to me in playgroups, PTMs, parks, at birthday parties, during school application processes and also her adolescent years. One year, while out for dinner celebrating our anniversary, my husband and I talked about how we could do a better job of parenting. It even came up at a family gathering where my in-laws had a different take on things than mine.

There are moments in a parent's life when they do feel overwhelmed, knowing they are making life decisions, which can be scary. I don't know to date if the decision to change their school was right, I don't know if athletics was better than football, and I don't know whether the subjects I chose for them today will be relevant tomorrow.

I remember my anaesthetist, Dr Ketan Parikh, sharing with all the expectant mothers in his prenatal class a line that I haven't forgotten even after fifteen years of childbirth—every mother, tall or short, fat or thin, fair or dark, rich or poor, can feed *if she wants to* feed. Why is this important?

I was very fortunate to have been born in Mumbai in a non-abusive and loving family, with an abundance of wealth and love. I had siblings who mothered me, opportunities irrespective of my gender and was able to receive a great education. I know the world is unfair and not everyone gets these privileges. I have immense gratitude for it and so much respect for children who battle the odds and find their goals. In the early years of being a parent, life seems physically hard—there is this one extra human who needs to go through life, whom you need to carry with you. The sleepless nights, the raccoon eyes, the feeding, the pooping and puking saga, and the all-nighters you will pull, will not only test you but every relationship you've ever had as a man and woman. *Your marriage goes through a different phase altogether. You will put every difference aside to show up as parents.*

I know that physically and emotionally, for a woman, childbirth is hard. *It rearranges every cell in your body, quite literally.* I have so much respect for women who have pulled themselves out of post-partum depression, and their families and partners who have supported them through it. Each time as a parent when you've said, 'This can't happen to me,' it comes alive within you and sometimes within your child.

To all the parents who saw and addressed early signs of a learning disability in their child or embraced parenthood for a specially-abled child, you are brave. No one can feel your pain, love and joy because no one else has walked your path. For me, every time there was a situation that deviated from the normal, I would call and ask my dad, 'Why me?'

He would answer, 'Why not you?' He would tell me, 'It's you because you can handle this better than anyone else.'

Joys of Parenting

I don't know if there is anything that brings someone more joy than being a parent. Your child's first smile, the first time they open their eyes, their first day at school, the first race they run, their first report card, their first day at the beach, their first taste of chocolate—this is more special than anything else in the world. *Somewhere in the rigmarole of life and material achievements, we forget these precious moments and start chasing a mythical finish line. We start chasing that first place on the victory stand for our kids.*

When was the last time you celebrated your child's participation wholeheartedly with a double scoop of ice cream?

I still remember when I asked my three-year-old, 'What do you want to be when you grow up? A doctor, a doll, a teacher, a fireman?' and she said, 'I want to be the tiger who came to tea.'

I remember one fleeting conversation when a cousin passed away at a young age and someone said everyone can be replaced in their lives except a mother. Your office may replace you in thirty days, a partner may remarry, siblings have their own lives, a child has their youth to live, but it's only the parents for whom you will always be irreplaceable. They will miss you forever. *It's only with them that your umbilical cord is cut, but it remains strong, long after delivery, childhood, adolescence and puberty.*

My husband and I had a standard conversation starter ready whenever we were to meet a new group of parents: 'How was your labour experience?' That moment will forever be etched in the memory of every parent. Even fifteen years after that event, I still find myself thinking about that day with great fondness and remembering many specifics.

The love you feel for your child may be irrevocable because it is the only relationship in which you experience such profound physical pain and life-altering shifts. You are in it forever. It's probably the only relationship you'll never walk out of. Yes, you may have differences, but you can't move on.

It's the one relationship that brings cuddles and hugs, but it's also the one that pierces you more than the toys they leave lying around. Sometimes the things we say to our kids in good faith come back to us in the least expected ways. It is these experiences that make you tougher than any other.

As my mother likes to say, 'Being a parent, as opposed to giving birth, is like pushing out a coconut through your nostril; it gives you the courage and fearlessness to go through anything and any heights.' *I know what you mean, Maa.*

There will be nights when you sleep off crying in their beds after they have left for university, nights when you cry because they have said harsh words in an argument, nights when you are overthinking what their future will be, nights when you pace the hallway because they haven't come home yet, and nights when you cry because you haven't slept because they are babies and can't stop crying.

Even if you're the head of a major corporation and seem invincible, a child's tantrum can bring you to your knees and make you feel like a failure, no matter how many degrees you have.

With a child, you get to experience life from the beginning to the end all over again. You review the alphabet, create works of art and study geometry, algebra and statistics. You realize that you have no idea what happened after Jack broke his crown and Jill came tumbling after him. You learn to play football again and celebrate Holi, Diwali, Dussehra, Eid, Christmas and Halloween. If your child asks you to become a horse, you become a horse. *You realize that there is a new master in the house—the one that calls the shots on what time you sleep, how much space you sleep in, what you eat and how much you eat.*

In 2020, my husband and I were having a casual conversation about random things and the topic of this book came up. We started wondering, 'How did the parents of all these incredible people do it?' Is there something special that they did? How did they encourage them during the critical times? How could we best prepare our child for life outside the nest? Should we prioritize their grades and pick their friends?

How do you know when to back down or give in? How to be a rock for your kids when things fall apart? How to be forthright with them and never sugarcoat your mistakes? It was 27 April 2020, I had just celebrated my fortieth birthday and I told my husband that I was ready to find these answers.

We recorded the inspiration in the form of an iPhone note and a guest wish list. I'm relieved that we were able to transport the majority of them to reality.

Like the signature dish you perfected by crushing and grinding the masalas by hand instead of using a pre-packaged blend, sound advice takes time and effort to perfect but rewards you with a dish that is uniquely yours. Sourcing from such remarkable people has enriched my life because I now understand that parenting is pure hard work. The goal of this book is undoubtedly to cull out that signature blend, which, when crushed and ground with the ideal combination of someone's years of experience, will help the parents in their journey.

Everyone here is someone I admire—either personally or professionally—because of their work or their stories. Some of them I never would have expected to meet, but as fate would have it, we were meant to be in the same room.

I talked my family and friends into meetings, whether it was over email, at a conference, over the phone, through a direct message on Instagram, or in the ladies' room.

I didn't hold back on getting personal with the guests in this book because success in life is about knowing what you want and finding the people or forces that will help you get there.

A wise person once said, 'If you want different results, ask different questions,' and so I sit here drafting new questions, wondering if the ones I'll be asking the parents of children who are in their twenties, thirties and forties will still apply to the current generation. For me, the only satisfactory explanation is that parenting comes with no instruction manual. While the specific advice and expertise parents need vary by circumstance, they all share a common goal—navigating that difficult crossroads.

Just like the Ramayana and the Mahabharata, which have spawned multiple adaptations and animated series, the annual Ram Leela always sells out and leaves audiences feeling uplifted and inspired. *Similarly, although the challenges faced by each new generation will be unique, the fundamental principles by which they are to be overcome will remain constant.* This new generation has smartphones, Netflix and PlayStation 5 to keep them entertained, while we had only video games and cable TV.

A large part of who we are is shaped within the four walls called home. Much of who we are and how we came to think is a product of our upbringing and the culture in which we were immersed.

Having grown up in the 1980s, I can attest that it was common practice for parents in large Indian families to act as a shield between their children and their aunt, grandparent or uncle who always had an opinion on everything.

Nobody in the book has succeeded in life simply by bucking up and doing what they needed to do. Their parents were the unseen backstage orchestrators of a flawless performance. I asked each parent the same set of questions, and they've all been refreshingly open about the challenges they faced and the lessons they learned as a result.

They had their fair share of self-doubts while they were bringing up their children, but they listened to their gut and used it to steer them through rough waters.

Since there are so many possible parents of outliers and this first collection can only hope to capture a small subset of them, I have no doubt that this is not the last book on the subject. Parenting is one of the hardest decisions you will ever make and much of it cannot be undone, but there are endless stories here that will help you believe that there is no such thing as wrong or good or bad parenting—only the choices we make at that moment.

I am sure at least two out of the twenty-two stories will appeal to you and you will find your voice in those stories/ questions.

There will be times when you're at a different developmental stage and a different set of parents strike a much deeper chord. This book has no finite timeline, just like parenting. Being a parent changes you forever, but I pray that this book will have some impact on who you become and, more importantly, how you parent.

You are the best parent your child could ask for and I know you know it, so please stop doubting yourself.

Each of the featured individuals in this book was selected because they have blazed a trail that will be studied by future generations to learn 'how it's done'. I made a point of choosing people from a wide variety of backgrounds and while they certainly aren't the only 'outliers', you'll find that you develop a soft spot for them after reading their stories, just as I have.

At the end of each chapter, you will find an Instagram poll that we conducted on certain focus points that each guest's parents expressed. You could put a tick mark next to the option you agree with.

As someone who takes copious notes, I felt compelled to create a section that I'd like to see in more books. Flip to end of the book and happy note-taking!

If you loved the book or have something to share, please reach out to me on Instagram (@mansi.zaveri and @kidsstoppress) and check out my website (www.mansi.zaveri.com) for exciting future updates.

For extended conversations:

If you scan the QR code below, you'll be able to watch the exclusive conversations that are the foundations of these chapters.

1

Priyanka Chopra Jonas

'When you give them importance as children, they will learn self-worth as they grow up.'

Instagram: @priyankachopra
LinkedIn: Priyanka Chopra

Priyanka Chopra Jonas is an Indian actress and producer. The winner of the Miss World 2000 pageant, Priyanka is one of India's highest-paid actresses and has received numerous awards, including the Padma Shri in 2016. She was named as one of the 100 most influential people in the world by *TIME* in 2016, one of the world's 100 most powerful women by *Forbes* in 2017 and was in the BBC 100 Women list in 2022.

Her memoir titled *Unfinished* was published in 2021.

Her father, Dr Ashok Chopra, was a physician in the Indian Army and her mother, Dr Madhu Akhouri Chopra, is an Indian businesswoman, film producer and physician who has served in the Indian Army for several years.

In the course of the last few years, I have been asked on numerous occasions, 'Whom do you look up to?' or 'Whom do you admire?' My longtime role models have been my mom and Oprah, with Priyanka Chopra joining the group most recently. A global monarch who perpetually reinvents herself, she is responsible for making possible connections and pathways for countless people in the world. She could have followed the traditional path of Miss India, Bollywood and it could have stopped there, but it didn't. Her hunger to improve, master her craft and achieve her goals through hard work is incredibly inspiring. I've often pondered the question of what, exactly, did her mother do to raise such an opinionated daughter who is never scared to speak her mind?

Initially, I had arranged to speak with Dr Madhu Chopra via Zoom, but after our conversation, I knew I had to meet her in person. A remarkable parent, she somehow balanced her career, marriage and children at the same time.

Despite her initial doubts about whether her parenting practices from nearly three decades ago would still be relevant, she welcomed me with open arms and was happy to talk. Friendly as always, she paused to ask her assistant Zarin for a green tea in Gujarati, all the while considering which chai flavour would best prepare her for this exchange. She then took a sip and said, 'Mansi, what was important is that I didn't back down—that gave me immense confidence. That confidence emanates power and brings me respect from my kids even to this day. If they respect you, it becomes easy.'

She has fond memories of working night shifts at the army hospital, which were always a family affair because she had to bring her two children along, Priyanka and her brother Siddharth. 'I turned it into a game by telling

Priyanka, "Mom's on night duty, baby's on night duty," as she carried her toy backpack and squealed with excitement. I didn't fall into the trap of feeling guilty because my work gave me immense joy. The guilt crept in only once when she talked back to my father and that made me wonder, "Is it because I am working?" Even the fancy, well-planned tiffins of other kids who had stay-at-home moms couldn't make me feel guilty as I sent the same tiffins every day, like a paratha roll or jam sandwich. *I taught her to not compare these tiffins or feel deprived.* Parenting is not a day's job. It starts the day your baby is conceived and continues forever.'

I asked her if Priyanka had ever asked, 'Why can't you sit at home or why do you need to work?' and she said, 'No. She didn't know any other way and took this as normal.' Family was a huge support, with both sets of parents and relatives chipping in at every stage.

Dr Chopra continued, 'Both kids used to tag along. If mom had night duty, baby had night duty. She would pack her little bag to carry to the hospital because she knew she had to keep herself busy while I was away on duty. *You see, we didn't give them choices that didn't exist.*'

Dr Chopra then unapologetically admitted, 'I am a great parent.' To see a parent be so self-assured was refreshing. Especially when parents today second guess most of their decisions.

When Priyanka was preparing for Miss India, her entire family pooled their resources to buy her new footwear, a wardrobe and cosmetics. No one ever questioned who she was or why she would want to compete in a Miss India pageant. Some parents hope their children will follow in their footsteps and go into business with them or pursue a similar line of work, but Priyanka knew at the tender age of three that she did not want to become a doctor because she did not like the smell of hospitals and did not want to leave her child at home.'

She added, '*When your path is different from your kids, there is no tantrum and shouting but there is a conversation. You convince me or I convince you.*' The one time that we did push our wishes on a child who was a topper in her academics and extracurriculars, was when we asked her to sing and dance both. When her grades dipped, I backed off, but being a committed, competitive learner, she persevered. Her habit of seeking perfection in everything that she did was most evident when she helped her younger brother Siddharth learn his speech on Chacha Nehru. She corrected his work and sat all night rehearsing with him till he didn't even miss a single word.'

She continued, 'I think this is the temperament that has got her here and is keeping her here. Ours was a democratic house, and questions and curiosity were rewarded promptly. When Priyanka was in kindergarten and questioned why her name was missing from the name plate outside her house, her father, Dr Ashok Chopra, got it changed the next day and added "Priyanka Chopra-UKG."'

Dr Chopra went on to say, 'Dinner table conversations were animated ones, where *you could pour your heart out and no one would be judged. No one raised their voices or banged plates—it was not allowed in my household.* Our kids never saw us yell, fight or be violent—it started and ended in the bedroom, but even that was a discussion.'

'I was heartbroken when I sent her to boarding school at seven years old after she had talked back to my dad,' she confessed, 'but the end result of that decision was a polished, responsible pre-teen who could even parent me. She became so disciplined, much better than I could have ever done. Each leap of faith was made with my family as a safety net.'

When I asked her if she had had any indication that Priyanka was exceptional before she turned eighteen, she said, '*I knew my child was focused and never frivolous. She would make the most of every opportunity that was presented to her. You cannot be a great parent if you don't have a receptive child.*'

When I asked her how she managed to instil such a sense of hunger and determination in her children despite their privileged upbringing, she told me that teaching them to say 'no' was crucial, as was making them work for what they wanted.

She said, '*Don't be afraid to be that "bad parent." The word "no" carried great weight in the Chopra household. One parent's "no" would never be followed by a "yes" from the other. Their "whys," however, were never shunned but addressed with discussions and explanations of the consequences early on. My children knew from day one that their every action had a consequence and that would be theirs alone.*'

Dr Chopra would always tell them, '"*If you get into trouble, I will be there." That unconditional support gave them a lot of confidence to take a step back, re-evaluate their decision and find that middle path on most occasions.* For e.g. if noodle strap tops and short shorts would draw unwanted attention, she would choose to wear a shirt on the road till she reached the party.'

She continued, 'Parents are making a mistake if they feel guilty about telling their children "no." *We've never parented on demand. I firmly believe that parents need to be parents, not friends.* Everyone has only one set of parents versus 100 sets of friends. Your child is coming to you as a parent because they need love and guidance and because they look up to you. They need a parent to parent, to be kind, to be non-judgemental.'

Dr Chopra then went on to tell me about Priyanka's relationship with her father. 'Priyanka was very close to her father. He was that cosy corner for her and *while I was the bad cop, I wasn't unreasonable or harsh. She just had to convince me.* There was a small instance of a sleepover, when she wasn't allowed to go. I was happy to host it but she came to me and said "You want other mothers to trust you but you don't want to trust them," and that got me thinking—*maybe I did need to know them better, visit their houses, see their environments and trust my child.*'

As I soaked in the conversation with Dr Chopra and she ordered another cup of her green tea, I remembered what my mother had said when my elder one was fairly little. '*Raising a child also means being hated sometimes and as my mom would always tell me "If you've never been hated by your child, you haven't been a good parent."*'

We continued the conversation and it seemed like every line that Dr Chopra shared needed to be highlighted.

'What were the values that ring a bell even today in Priyanka's head?' I asked.

Dr Chopra quickly retorted that all her values have been learned through consequences, mainly the value to accept the reality and move on. '*Sob all you want, but tomorrow brings another chance to make tomorrow and the days ahead better than the day before.*'

She further explained how a parent's role evolves as the child grows up. 'Age-wise, 0–5 is dependent parenting and they trust you, 5–10 is curious parenting when it's important to address all their whys and get into conversations. You can't say, "I will explain when you grow up." The era of execution is ages 8–13. Where there is confusion, they will come up to you but ultimately, they will do what they want.'

'*Being a working parent is not an excuse*,' she said firmly, 'I would make time every day from 5–7 p.m. for the kids and 7–9 p.m. for us as a couple. I did make time for their homework and occasionally cook a meal, even though I am not such a great cook. They looked forward to this private time. All their questions would be answered and everything they wanted would be done. Our dinner table conversations brought us closer. You would never hear anyone say, "Get out of my house. Get lost."'

When I asked her if she had any advice for raising an independent woman who speaks her mind, she told me that 'It starts with the small things, like her name on the door. How should this room be? What should we cook when we have guests over? Which car should we buy? We need to listen to the children.' Children are not just children—they have a mind of their own too. As parents it is our job to nurture those opinions.

'*When you give them importance as children, they will learn self-worth as they grow up. We talked about everything from current events to our own lives over dinner. The stream of conversation was constant, plentiful and never ran dry. These brief discussions sparked a hunger for knowledge and made space for it in their minds.*'

Dr Chopra revealed, 'When she spoke so confidently at seventeen, addressing the Press Trust of India, everyone was surprised but I wasn't. I knew those dinner table conversations, her reading the newspapers and non-fiction books, and being aware of worldly things had given her this confidence. Talking about an ideal way to be versus walking that talk and implementing it is what we combined as a family.'

This was the first question that came to mind when I started writing questions for the book—for someone whose life is scrutinized by the second, how does one navigate the messy and the magical, and how do we parents prepare them for a world we've never thought of or seen before?

Dr Chopra promptly said, 'I told her "Insulate yourself, because they are doing their job and you need to do yours. No one, absolutely no one, can have an opinion about you. Your work and your life. Blinkers on and stick to your lane. *As long as you have that first circle of people around you and they are there for you, it doesn't matter.* Some days you need to clear things and some days they don't deserve your time."'

When I asked her about her views on handling competition since Priyanka has always been an overachiever who really conquered the world and redefined the universe, she said, '*I told her that "A fall is inevitable and you should dust off the failure very quickly because it's gone. Competition and failure are not going anywhere. The truth is, you can't do anything about it. But what you can do is work on yourself. What is important is how quickly you stand up and what you do about it." That is what separates a successful person from a failure.* Jo peeche gaya use chhod do *[Leave the things in the past where they belong].*'

Her response to my question about shielding your child from the perils of comparisons to others' successes was, '*Competition is good for you. There will be ten people at the same step as you. You can't push them back, but you can work on yourself to make yourself better, so when you take that step forward, you are better than them.* Individuals who strive for excellence never settle for mediocrity. If they are working on a school play or script for an acting assignment, they're going to give it their all. Priyanka is not one to settle for second best and she will always strive for more. That's just how she is—she always tries to improve upon the opportunities presented to her.'

Outliers are never afraid of competition; they accept it and better themselves.

Dr Chopra went on to say, 'As parents, you can't teach them without practising it. They need to see you do it. They need to see you play that part every single day. That's the way they will respect you, honour you and most importantly, listen to you. That means you've got to keep moving. You need to be one step ahead so they have someone to look up to. They are seeking answers from you and the questions change at every stage, from boyfriends to relationships to husbands-to-be. They need to have that confidence that they will get the answers from their parents.'

Our conversation moved from competition and failure to dealing with disappointment and self-doubt. As parents, we might have expectations but our kids have their own goals too. Sometimes they don't meet their goals and they are disappointed. How do you equip them to deal with their own expectations?

She recounted a moment when Priyanka sang a song for the talent round at Miss India and was very confident she would do well until someone else performed an original dance and Priyanka was shattered. 'She said, "I am not a model, I can't do anything, I can't sing, I can't act." She started to doubt her abilities and her reason for participating in Miss India, and wanted to go back. At that point, we encouraged her to let go of any expectations for her performance and instead focus on having a good time. We told her "You've come this far, *ab maze kar* [now have fun]."'

She added, 'The same rule applied when she came to the movies. She said, "I can't act, I can't dance." We said "Try it, you can always go back to school, but we never want you to have a 'what if' moment." Today, parents want to stretch themselves to give more, which puts more pressure on themselves and therefore, on the child. Children will find their way. If you keep pushing vehemently, they may do it until some point, but what about afterwards?'

Dr Chopra said, *'The parents' role is to give a gentle nudge but not push to add to the pressure.* Tell your kids what you can give and what you can't give. Reassure your kids, tell them "I am there for you, unconditionally, no matter what." Don't push them into a grinder where they can barely lift their heads up to know whether it's day or night. If you want a good human being, you'll have to do that.'

She added, 'As parents, we want our kids to walk a certain path and it's only human to react when they don't. Reacting by saying "I told you so" doesn't always cut it. Of course, I am not perfect, and I would remind them that "I told you what the consequence could be," but the easier option was to tell them, "This is how I would do it." Although the teenage years were an exception where reverse psychology worked, it was a short-lived phenomenon.'

As someone in her early forties, I truly believe that life is divided into three folds—education, career and family. I wondered what qualities helped Priyanka sail through each of these?

Dr Chopra answered, 'Priyanka had it hard when she came back from the US. With everything being different like the boards, she wasn't ready to settle into an army school and cope with all the pressure. She would wake up at 4 a.m and come back home after classes at 8 p.m every day. We saw the toll it took on her and asked her to take a gap year. We weren't scared of what the world would say. We wanted to make sure that we didn't hamper our daughter's self-esteem with a bad grade and that too, in twelfth, when the result was important.'

She informed me, 'We let her take that gap year and that's when Miss India happened. As parents, we aimed to relieve our kids of any unnecessary stress. *We wanted to give them responsibilities but not pressure.* Responsibility to make their decisions, about what to pack on road trips, what to do and where to go. We spent a lot of time with our children through travel and holidays and took a lot of road trips.'

Now she came to the second fold: 'As a professional, I think the one quality that helped her sail through was that of being principled and sticking to her path. I remember a director once sending a stylist with really flimsy and itsy-bitsy clothes for Priyanka, and I asked her, "What is this?." The stylist said it's the director's mandate that "*Chaddi dikhni chahiye* [The underwear should show]. It needs to be that skimpy." Priyanka refused to do it and refunded the signing amount because she understood that she couldn't work with a person who had this mindset about women. The director warned her that she would not be able to last in this industry if she refused his film but Priyanka said it was okay. She did lose 6–7 projects after that, but I am proud of her for sticking by what she stands for.'

She went on to add, 'Priyanka was a born leader. These skills were what she was born with and as parents, we just needed to hone them—whether it was as a squad leader or captain in the army club. At the dinner table, she would tell us about her achievements and her efforts, and we would make her feel even better about what she had achieved than she actually had. She has to have confidence in her head to know that she has it in her heart.'

This prompted me to ask, '*As parents, we all want success for our kids, but somewhere we are also worried that what if it disappears overnight. We get sleepless nights knowing this is not forever. Did you also have this fear, Dr Chopra?*'

'I accept that this career has a shelf life and I think she has known that all along, which is why she kept working and why she has so many other businesses.'

I was curious to know how their conversations had evolved from the teenage years to now. Had they become more complex?

She replied, '*When you dismiss the attention they need from you, they will give it back to you. Never tell them you don't have time for them.* Also, the teenage years are tough. I just conditioned myself to listen to this child and her frustrations. *As a parent of a teenager, you have to be their punching bag.* Priyanka had become such an attractive kid and she was getting so much attention that *uff* [stressful sigh], I was like "What prepares you to take care of this as a parent?" When she got all this attention even then, I asked her if she liked it and she said yes. I asked her "Whom do you want to be with?" and that one statement changed everything. It put her in a position of choice and even as a child, made her feel powerful. That power gave her the confidence.'

When I asked her about maintaining the balance between two kids from wildly different worlds, she said, 'Being the youngest of four sisters, I always felt the weight of trying to measure up. If Priyanka Chopra is your sister, I know how you feel. They both feel that I love the other more. As a parent, you have to understand that both your kids are different. To compare them is foolish but in that moment, you make that mistake and you end up comparing. For e.g.

Sid feels like his didi (elder sister) is such a huge personality and has unachievable success, how does one even compete? I tell him to take baby steps. I tell him "Priyanka is one of a kind. So are you. You can't be her and she can't be you."'

We concluded our conversation by talking about her next assignment and how Dr Chopra is a constant learner. We sealed it with a hug and an exchange of energy and calm that she brought to the conversation.

If you had a huge billboard on parenting, what message would it read?

'Get your child to be responsible for the things they need and their decisions too. Be responsible for everything that you own and take ownership of your actions.'

We asked parents on Instagram about their opinion on the following:

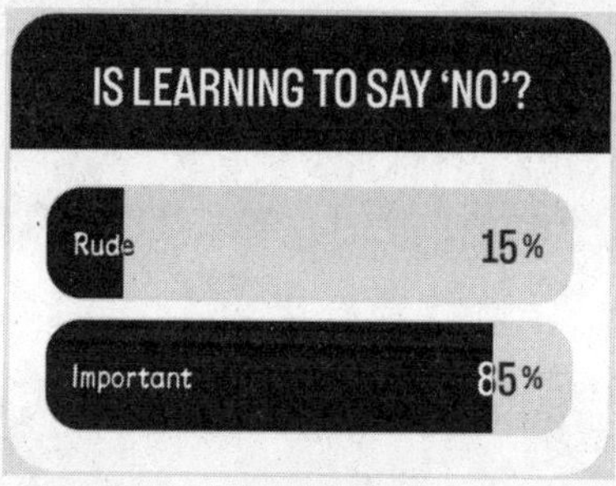

Learnings and Observations

1. Sometimes, you have to be your child's punching bag.
2. Take the pressure off your kids.
3. Let them brag in front of you and then steer them in the right direction.
4. If you talk of equality, give them equality.
5. Competition will always be there—stick to your lane and focus on yourself.
6. You cannot be a great parent if you don't have a receptive child.
7. Don't be afraid to be that 'bad parent'.
8. One parent's 'no' should never be followed by a 'yes' from the other.
9. Being a working parent is not an excuse for bad parenting.

2

Sushmita Sen

'Sometimes we need to learn to take a step back and trust them.'

Instagram: @sushmitasen47

Sushmita Sen created history as the first-ever Indian to win the Miss Universe title in Manila, Philippines, and was the youngest Miss India in 1994. She is a Bollywood actor, who has received awards and accolades for her work as well as an entrepreneur, a philanthropist and a single mother to her daughters, twenty-four-year-old Renee and fourteen-year-old Alisah.

Her father, Shubeer Sen, is a former Indian Air Force Wing Commander, and her mother, Subhra Sen, is a jewellery designer and owner of a Dubai-based store.

If you were a girl growing up in the 1980s, you probably remember the moment when Sushmita Sen was crowned Miss Universe for India. All of us wanted to be her after seeing her, especially at Miss Universe. Susmita Sen was so much more to me than just Miss Universe—she was a woman who was comfortable in her own skin, someone who spoke her mind, made her choices, and most importantly, was so articulate in her thoughts. She stood tall through everything the world had to say about her.

When I reached out to her office, the interaction was just as I thought it would be. I got an email back within 24 hours from her team in a style I haven't read in the last fifteen years.

From the response time to the style and respect, it almost felt like Ms Sen was writing it herself. When I complimented them on it, they were very sweet and responded that 'we are an extension of the brand that Ms. Sen has built for herself.'

Also, as a woman who has admired her over the last three decades, to finally know the child behind the woman was a dream come true.

At her office in Bandra, I was introduced to Sushmita's father, Mr Shubeer Sen. Her office was exactly as I had imagined it to be—a clean desk, a minimalist space and respect for all.

Sushmita's father, who otherwise lives in Kolkata, was visiting his daughter's family in Diwali 2022 and we set up this interview in the summer of 2022.

'Good evening, young lady,' greeted Mr Sen, 'tell me about your book. It sounds so interesting.'

I narrated the thought behind it and he said, 'How do you guys come up with such cool ideas?' While we were discussing our thoughts and questions, my team was busy arranging a few cushions for me to sit on so the video frame didn't look weird with the height difference between the two of us. It wasn't an easy one to fix.

The camera kept rolling and soon the height gap between us didn't matter at all, and everything else faded into the background except for what he was saying.

'When Sushmita was a child, did you ever imagine that she would become Miss Universe and a cultural icon?'

'To be honest, Mansi, as parents, we didn't see this coming. *We wanted them to grow the way they felt like and we saw that they have talents.* You know, in certain areas, they are stronger than other kids. Sushmita was good at drama and all kinds of things that attract the attention of other people. So, that's what she was an absolute expert at. And she was very rigorous. She had lots of friends. We kept moving bases since I was in the Indian Air Force and whenever we went to a new place, she would make friends in no time. And she wanted to kind of, initially, if I can recall properly, be a journalist at thirteen or fourteen, and she was good in studies, so we thought that her potential was quite enough to explore on her own, and then as she grew up, she became attracted to this. By the age of fifteen or sixteen, she had turned around.'

He continued, 'Initially, she said no. No fashion show and all that. Even though she was very interested in it, there were a lot of people looking at her and the attention she got became overwhelming. My wife and I disagreed on the freedom that the kids got. I was a man in uniform, in the armed forces, and extremely regimented. I told her this is not the time to give them so much freedom. For instance, in those days there was a popular TV programme called *The Bold and the Beautiful* that she used to watch when she was in the tenth grade, even when her board exams were around the corner. So, I told my wife, "Don't encourage them to see this." My son was even younger and both of them used to sit in front of the TV and watch. I got it disconnected. Then we went to a party the next day, expecting that they would be studying. When we came back around 10–10.30 p.m, from the window, I could hear those dialogues of *The Bold and the Beautiful*, I said, "How come?" I had disconnected the line. Then, stealthily, we opened the door and saw that it was on in full swing. Those days, you had that antenna on the roof, so not only did I cut the line, but I turned that antenna so there was no scope at all. Later on, I came to know that she had called that cable fellow within half an hour, paid him some money and then got it fixed. She always knew how to fix her problems and work towards what she wanted.'

I asked him about his experience of the pageant world and he honestly replied, 'As parents from a service class background, these were uncharted waters for us, and we are a bit conservative too. So, initially, in the first few rounds, when she went for her rehearsals for her fashion show and all that, including finals, I used to go along with her, just to find out what this place was like, how the atmosphere was, what the ecosystem there was and whether she was in the right company or not. Sitting there for hours, I realized that this is just like any other profession, so I knew it wasn't as flimsy as one might assume if they didn't work in the fashion industry.'

He added, '*We may initially disagree with the choices our kids make, but it's important to be in that moment with them and see it through their eyes. As parents, we naturally believe that our ability to make decisions about the unknown is superior to that of our children.*'

Mr Sen related an anecdote to me, 'I remember on one particular occasion she was being photographed for some advertisement, I don't know which one, it was in Nehru Place in Delhi, and the photographer was a veteran, a very old man, and very good at that time. Still, I accompanied her because I figured we'd be free after no more than an hour of him clicking away at his camera, and since I had some work on the ride back, I thought I might as well finish it and then accompany her home. She was placed in a number of different locations to take advantage of the many angles and lighting set-ups (including the umbrella and diffused lights). As more and more time passed, I was getting more and more impatient. So, I told her, I call her Titu. I said, 'Titu, let's go home, the remaining things you can do tomorrow,' but she remained there. And when we were done, the photographer pulled me aside and said, 'I've got a lot of experience in this line and this girl is special. She will succeed greatly if you encourage her to continue developing her skills in this area.' So, after that, I realized that maybe I was wrong in my perception or understanding and that I couldn't sabotage her efforts or stand in the way of her progress.'

'Since you spent so much time away from home as a parent due to your duties in the Indian Air Force, I have to wonder if you ever felt guilty about neglecting your children?'

He answered, 'Mansi, it's important to realize that *all parents connect with their kids in very different ways.* You can't avoid working, so guilt is out of the question. It's important for kids to see their parents working hard, both because they want to and because they have to.' I was prompt to ask, 'How do you inculcate the right values?' and he swiftly replied, 'We were conventional, and to an extent, we sort of never went outside our boundary. *It was freedom within discipline,* but they didn't overstep that. Then, they would have been asking for trouble. They adhered to that for quite some time, after which they grew up and now have their own lives, their own personalities and understanding of life.'

I wondered, 'How do you decide rights and wrongs and draw boundaries when your kids are venturing into uncharted territories?' Mr Sen replied, 'Mansi, for all parents, our kids will take on uncharted territories that we don't understand, and *we can't train for specific values*. Whatever you do works across the board. She had already shown streaks of her strong personality and I was very proud of that, and I knew that she would not do anything to hurt her parents. And that feeling is important.'

He added, 'Sushmita was very mature for her age. She was strong-willed and strong-headed—she had very strong likes and dislikes, and she was never apologetic about them. She was never a 'yes-man' to someone, never tagged along with somebody for their status. She's got her own ideas of things and she goes by that.'

We spoke a little about academics. 'Sushmita was a very good student but I was a little concerned about what she was going to do. Those days, she used to study with a blaring transistor. One day, I said, "Beta, how are you studying like this? Your performance in the upcoming exams will suffer if you continue to procrastinate like this." She handed me the book and said, "Ask me anything from this book, I'll answer it." I asked her some questions in jest, but soon realized that she was giving me the correct responses. She said, "Dad, I need the music to focus." These small instances made me sure of her decisions every single day. This was just one of them. *So, she was always a little bit out of the ordinary.*'

Mr Sen then told me, 'I was on duty overseas when she decided to enter the Miss India pageant and while we were supportive, I ultimately told her to go experience the competition for herself. There were never any doubts in our minds. When she was crowned Miss India, I was living abroad at the time, but I remember being absolutely ecstatic when I heard the news. She had already started getting ready for Miss Universe when I returned. She relocated from Delhi to Mumbai. The *Times of India* also played a role in facilitating her preparation. I had no idea what kind of programme they have, so I flew down to Bombay and stayed with her.'

He continued, 'After that, she was completely at ease, without stress or anxiety. When I said "Beta you have to go for all these sessions," she replied, "Let them wait a little and I'll go." I said "It's for the best that you commit to attending all of their training sessions, you might be missing out on important information that they'll provide." She said, "Yes, yes," but the whole time she was thinking about it and preparing in her own way. That's why I said she wasn't that run-of-the-mill, follow-the-book type, she had her own ideas. *Sometimes we need to learn to take a step back and trust them.*'

He then told me about an incident that took place before she flew out for Miss Universe. 'With maybe three or four days to go, she misplaced her passport. I began to sprint to the *Times of India* office in Delhi, and I said, "Well, this is what has happened," and there was this gentleman, who said, "We can't help it if she can't make it. If the passport is not found, then Aishwarya Rai goes, because she was second."'

He narrated this incident with so much zest, it was like it happened yesterday. 'Desperate, I used my position in the government to arrange a visit from my wife and me to the home of the home minister, where I broke the news to him.

He reassured me that everything would be fine and after a day of running around (and a few phone calls made by his secretary), her passport was ready. I heaved a sigh of relief. *Sometimes our kids will make huge blunders, but rather than yelling at them, we should try to help them figure out how to fix the problem. While appealing, the former option will not help you resolve the issue at hand.*'

He continued, 'Her mother and brother had already travelled to Manila in preparation for the Miss Universe pageant when I arrived in Bombay to bid her farewell. I stayed behind to take care of business and two parents are unnecessary anyway. It was a very busy moment with so many dresses, shoes and ornaments. It felt like my daughter was getting married. I saw her in deep thought and asked her if there was something bothering her and she said, '"Dad, I had seen this one gown in Dubai and I really liked it but, of course, I couldn't buy it then because I couldn't afford it but I had told him if I do become Miss Universe, I will." At the same time, our home phone rang, and it was a gentleman from Dubai who called and said, "Sushmita must be busy with all the preps, I have sent the gown for her and it's lying in customs. Could you please collect and give it to her?" Concerned about the high cost of customs, I said, "Ok, let me speak to the customs officer." I explained to the customs officer that she was competing in Miss Universe and we would appreciate a reduction in duties if possible. For our benefit, he waived all obligations and let us get the gown early. And that wasn't the worst of it—we also had to deal with airport baggage fees when we had neither extra bags nor the Rs 7000 to pay for them. At midnight, she packed as much as she could into an airport bag we bought, gave me a quick hug and took off. As she was walking away, the ornament package burst and scattered its contents across the floor.' I gasped in horror. He continued, 'A man in first class noticed that she was crying and became concerned, so he asked what was wrong and offered to take her luggage. He said "I'm flying to Manila as well." My blood pressure went up and I ran to hand the bag off to the security guards so they could deliver it to Sushmita. When I saw him run up and hand it to her, I finally understood all the sacrifices parents make. We scramble, think on our feet and beg for favours in order to obtain passports at the last minute. *All of this is done with no questions asked, zero qualifications and no conditions attached, simply because we love this person.*'

Then we spoke about the D-day and I couldn't help but feel goosebumps as Mr Sen narrated, 'Just as I was beginning to feel human again, the big day arrived. Although I haven't told many people about it, I'll never forget the day Ranjan Bakshi from the *Times of India*, said, "Let's watch the ceremony together." We had other friends as well. After that, when Sushmita was in the final five, the phone calls started coming in. That's why I spent those last seconds anticipating her victory. Then, a woman from Canada called me and I didn't recognize her. She asked, "Is this Mr Sen speaking, with his American accent?" When I confirmed that it was, she congratulated me on the recent crowning of my daughter as Miss Universe.'

What?! Even Mr Sen had a shocked expression as he continued, 'So, I thought to myself, *abhi toh khatam hi nahi hua hai* [It's not even over yet], this is the last five or something. So, I said "Thank you, thank you," but I thought someone was pulling my leg. Then, after some time, my brother from Miami called and he was so excited, he said, "Dada, she has made history, she won Miss Universe." So I said, '*Yeh kya hogaya* [How did this happen]? She's still in the last five, they are still showing.' So, when she was in the last three, I was absolutely sure, because my brother would not pull my leg. So, when the guy from the *Times of India* said "Miss Sen has done wonderfully well so far," I said cheekily, "Don't worry, she'll become Miss Universe also," because I knew. So, of course, the rest is history.' History indeed! How privileged I feel to know the exclusive behind the scenes and the things Mr Sen contributed to, to get Sushmita on that stage.

With pride, he said, 'All those people who said, "How can you send your daughter for all this?" were silenced. *You see, success silences all criticism and doubt.*'

Sushmita's father responded to all her fan mail and distinctly remembers one from Japan, where a father named his daughter Sushmita. He said, 'That moment is so well-etched in my memory. I didn't need to respond to every mail, but I wanted people to know Sushmita as someone who cares for them and values the love they shower on her. She saw how much I valued the love she received and I think she imbibed it from there to value what she has received.'

Mr Sen continued to say, '*We fully believed that our daughter would always act responsibly and within the limits we set for her. Due to the difficulty of modern life, today's youth don't need an adult to teach them anything—they learn everything they need to know from experience. All you can do is warn them about potential pitfalls and where they could go wrong.*'

He then told me about her college admission process, 'As parents, we definitely felt like, "Okay, she must have a degree," especially because she was a good student. In economics, she got 95 or something. I took her report card and went to St Stephen's College while she was preparing for Miss Universe. So, I said this is the time I should get her admitted and then let her go. St Stephen's explained that they couldn't take her because their overall cut-off was "95 or more" but they would add her name to a waiting list nonetheless. It was a bit of a toss-up so I left. After that, I visited a variety of universities, filled out applications and sometimes even paid fees. After that, she went away and eventually won the title of Miss Universe. My phone rang and it was the vice chancellor of Delhi University, who said, "We understand you wanted to put her in St Stephen's College, she is most welcome to come." As a result, I felt an intense emotional response. I said, "Really, it's a good thing, you know, for our family." After that, of course, everything else was irrelevant. When she told Mahesh Bhatt, "I'm not a good or trained actor," he responded, "Well, don't worry, I am a good director."'

'Furthermore, their paths are so unpredictable that, as a parent, you must be there for them, especially during the low points. I encouraged her to hold out for a positive outcome. Be confident in your future and let hope be the only constant light in your heart. God will never fail you. And if you look at anyone's life, you'll see that it has its share of highs and lows. It's unrealistic to believe that life will always move upward without ever levelling off. Therefore, that outlook on life must be maintained at all times.'

He went on to say, '*You know, as parents, we want everything from our children, we want them to listen to us, speak to the world in front of them and voice their opinions. We should be open to the idea that if they are allowed to speak, they will make mistakes.*'

He then spoke a bit more on 'mistakes.' 'If she's open to ideas, then she will make mistakes. We are not unduly apprehensive about that. We knew that mistakes would be made and it was best to correct those mistakes and then move on. So, in the real world, everyone makes mistakes and eventually improves from them. Unless he has an inflated sense of self-importance and a skewed view of reality, he should not assume that because bad things have happened to him, life is unfair. So, life is always like this.'

He added, 'As parents, we have this habit of telling our kids "I told you so" but honestly, I wanted to see that she's on the right path. Even after she became Miss India, she would ask me, "Can I go to a nightclub?" Once, I said, "I haven't seen even one in my life, you know, so a nightclub is not a good thing. Who's your company?" and then a car full of ladies came out, and they said, "Uncle, we are taking her out." I don't know if they had boyfriends with them or not.'

'Anyway, so long as they came and told me, I let her go. I told her to be back by 10 p.m. and she said that it started at 10. She came back at 11 p.m., when I was pacing up and down the house, a bit upset. She came with those friends only and they said together, "Sorry, uncle, we are late," so she cushioned the impact like that.'

'*Every parent has to go through that tussle of deadlines, pacing up and down. Whether your child is six, sixteen, twenty-six or forty-six, you will still do it. Your child will break rules and deadlines, and let me tell you, there will be nothing else you can do but trust them.*'

Mr Sen spoke about his views on Sushmita's decision to adopt: 'We knew Sushmita was different, like I said earlier, she was raised to make her choices and speak about them out loud. She was fearless. So, when she decided to adopt at twenty-four, I was really nervous but she was very confident and had a strong desire. I told you earlier that she always had a strong desire for anything that she did and she did everything to see to it that it was fulfilled.

'So, when she told me that she wanted to adopt, I said, "Beta, you are still young, you'll be a single mother, you'll be busy with your profession, most of the time you will be outdoors, who will take care of the child?" She said, "Dad, don't worry, I'll take care of the child, and when necessary, I'll take her along with me."'

He continued, '*It wasn't an idea that we agreed with or were inclined toward, but Sushmita followed her heart.* She went and picked up Renee, who was very sweet but not so well. The people in the orphanage said to her that "She's not well, and we don't advise you to take her." Nevertheless, she was brought with much happiness, fanfare and all that. The second day, she fell sick and was badly dehydrated. We rushed her to the hospital where she was put on drips and then she recovered. This continued for a while, but Sushmita was determined, and she said, "If she cannot be alright under my care, she will never be alright under somebody else's care." So, she had that kind of confidence.'

We then talked about disagreements. '*As parents, it's okay to disagree with your children,*' he said. 'We have disagreed a number of times. You know, you have a different background, you have different days that you have seen and you are conventional by nature, but the world has opened up in the meanwhile and the perception of these kids has grown far and wide. They are not conditioned to your ideas, so give them the space to think in a new way. *A parent must accept that "I am growing old, my ideas are conventional and I am resisting departing from them."*'

Protecting our children and supporting them, whether it's our decision or not, comes naturally to us as parents if we believe that times are changing and are more accepting of their ideas.

'As parents, you share the possibilities within the boundaries and bring to their attention the possible scenarios that your child is likely to encounter. Just remember that as things start falling into place, the friction will ease out.'

When I asked him about all the awards and laurels Sushmita has won, he shared, 'All that is great, Mansi, they are milestones. But we have to always see that 'whole man' concept. How is she growing as a human being? I am very satisfied that she is unconventional. She's got a line she chose and she is sticking to it and most importantly, she's making a difference to others too. That is much more important to me than anything else.' This I found simply beautiful.

I always wondered, 'How is it for a child to see success and global dominance at eighteen? What goes on inside that family knowing that from here you could soar higher or fall so deep to never be found? What happens to their siblings, their parents and their own mental health? How do you, as parents, not let comparison creep in? How do you not tell your child, "Look at your sibling, they are doing so well?"'

As Mr Sen put it, 'As parents, we have to let each child take his or her own path., find their own rhythm and navigate their way through life. Pressuring them is not going to help them.'

In the same way that you wouldn't dare compare your kid to anyone else's, it holds true for sibling comparisons as well. For the simple reason that they inhabit entirely separate universes. *They'll need to forge their own protections against the world's inevitable comparisons.*

He continued, 'Still, we pushed Rajeev (her younger brother) forward, telling him to follow his passion if he developed an interest in fashion. We said "Your time right now is better spent learning and planning. All these things will eventually materialize and it won't be because of anything we did wrong." He understood that the circumstances were such that she could not proceed further academically.'

He continued, '*But at the end of the day, she is self-taught and self-educated.* That also opened up a space of understanding for the younger one that maybe she is destined to do something good for herself, and for us. So, he was never affected by her fame in that way. And we never pressured him. She too was unsure at some point and we also reassured her that it was possible to become Miss India despite the presence of other well-known women in the country. You are unique because you are you. "You don't have courage?" her mother asked her. "The race is yours to run. You must participate."'

Mr Sen then shared another instance, 'When she was getting ready to compete in Miss Universe, the same thing happened. She told me, "Daddy, I don't know what I'm doing here. All the girls are so beautiful—they're all six feet tall and I'm totally lost." I said, "Never ever think about that." *Sometimes our kids are just saying all these negative things to prepare themselves and us for worst case scenarios and disappointments.*'

Coming from a modest family, a service background, I asked him how he instilled the fire and desire to achieve in her?

He answered poignantly, 'See, you can encourage them, you can tell them a lot of things, but finally the fire has to be in their belly. We were very clear—we wanted our kids to reflect and they were given the time to do that. They must be allowed to see the grass, a flower, nature in its grandeur and beauty, and life properly, otherwise, it becomes a rat race. And in a rat race, no one is a winner. At the end of the day, you fall sick, you struggle to do things that you are no longer able to do and you get disheartened. So, what's the point?'

Mr Sen then told me about the toughest phase in parenting. 'I think the toughest phase for a parent is the teenage years, because their kids undergo hormonal changes and become a little obstinate, and then it becomes all the more difficult because they are open to so much of information. Perhaps they have more up-to-date information than we do. So, that's the point at which you can no longer impart gyan. It's crucial to keep your cool as a parent at any age. First, I thought, "Okay, she's a mother of two and my job is done," *but then I remembered that once a parent, always a parent.*'

We then discussed the phase of her disease and he said, 'When Sushmita was diagnosed with an autoimmune condition called Addison's disease in 2014, I had a lot of faith in God. I sent out prayers and I said "If he desires for this to be okay, then it should be ok." Combined with her confidence and her knowledge about things, as the days passed, I became less and less apprehensive. I knew she would overcome it and she did. I shared my ideas on the line of treatment with her. *Parenting is laying out the options for them, fully aware that they are going to ultimately do what they want to do and you need to be okay about that. At the end, what matters is not what you said or what they said. It's always about the end result.*'

According to Mr Sen, five qualities that shaped Sushmita are her zidd in a positive sense, her determination. The second is that she is very sharp, you know, she was quick on the uptake; whatever she read, she talked about. The third thing is memory. Fourth, she is very generous. Very generous. Fifth, she's got a lot of love in her heart, though she does not openly display it, and I know it as a father. She has a lot of love in her heart.'

I asked him, 'If you were to give one piece of advice to parents today on how to raise successful, humble change-makers, what would that piece of advice be?'

'Success, I don't know. But as a good human being, you must give them our background, our ancient Indian wisdom, our literature. You must acquaint them with these instead of going overboard with western terminology and western teachings and things. They must be proud of their own culture, their own heritage and their own legacy. So, that is one thing I find missing these days, sadly. It must be instilled in them and it must come not only from parents but also from teachers and the school curriculum. Otherwise, you'll find you know, in our time also, we only read about the Mughal dynasty and the English operation and the freedom struggle and all. We have a 5000-year-old civilization with a strong heritage and a treasure trove of wisdom. So, children must be acquainted with all that. Then their perception will be better.'

I was curious to know if there were any mistakes that Mr Sen thought he made in parenting, and he replied humorously, 'Mistakes were made for sure. I told her not to wear short dresses a zillion times. You know, that was in the initial days, now she doesn't anyway. In those days, we lived in a clustered society and there it doesn't go over well so, we as conventional parents, said it openly. Then, I kept on telling her to study as I told you. She also had boyfriends which would keep the telephones ringing all the time. You know, before that incident happened, I always felt that "She's not studying, she's always on the phone, always distracted." She was good at studies, which her results showed me, but I kept telling her to study anyway. Now that I think about it, it all sounds so silly.'

It was time for the rapid-fire. Sushmita's favourite colour is black, her favourite food is sushi and her favourite holiday destination is Switzerland. She is a night person and the most magical moment in her life according to Mr Sen is when she was crowned Miss Universe. He also, with a cherry-sweet smile said, 'She loves me the most.'

We concluded with a sweet message to Sushmita from him: 'Take care of your health. Crucial in every way. Moreover, I have been reminding her of this fact ever since she was a student—having good health allows you to take pleasure in life, while ill health causes that pleasure to evaporate. And health encompasses all aspects—physical, mental, spiritual, social etc. In other words, maintain equilibrium.'

Mr Sen assured me that this book is essential as we wrapped up our conversation. 'What you're doing is fantastic and will have a positive impact.'

If you had a huge billboard on parenting, what message would it read?

Give your children freedom, but always within discipline. Freedom within discipline.

We asked parents on Instagram about their opinion on the following:

Learnings and Observations

1. Success silences all criticism and doubt.
2. Your child will break rules and deadlines, and there will be nothing else you can do but trust them.
3. As parents, we shouldn't force our kids to conform to our ideas.
4. A parent must accept that 'I am growing old, my ideas are conventional and I am resisting departing from them.'
5. As things start falling into place, the friction does and must ease out.
6. Of the many things your child will achieve, the most important one is the whole man concept. How is she growing as a human being and how is it impacting others around her?
7. Kids should be given time to introspect—to see grass, a flower, see nature in its grandeur and beauty and to understand life properly and not as a rat race. Because in a rat race, no one is a winner.
8. Parenting at every stage is challenging and you must not lose your cool.
9. Parenting is laying out the options for them fully aware that they are going to ultimately do what they want to do and you need to be okay about that.

3

P.V. Sindhu

'My job as a parent is to tell her that even if you did not win today, you are still capable of winning. Maybe it wasn't your your day, maybe the opponent played better, but always remember, "I am capable of doing it."'

Instagram: @pvsindhu1

Pusarla Venkata Sindhu, commonly known as P.V. Sindhu, is an Indian badminton player who has won medals at numerous tournaments, including the BWF circuit, the 2019 World Championships, where she won gold, and the Olympics, where she remains the only Indian woman to win two Olympic medals.

Both her parents, P.V. Ramana (father) and P. Vijaya (mother), have been national-level volleyball players. Her father was a member of the Indian volleyball team that won the bronze medal at the 1986 Asian Games in Seoul, South Korea. In 2000, he received the Arjuna Award for his contributions to the sport.

I knew this book would be lacking without a sports figure, especially one who has provided us with so many nail-biting moments. I had given up all hope of reaching P.V. Sindhu. I had followed every friend and agent, asked for connections and finally hit a brick wall. I attended an event to understand what it takes to nurture an Olympian, with a minuscule chance of landing this interview, knowing that there was clear no path to it. However, four months after the event and through consistent follow-ups, I managed to contact Mr P.V. Ramana, P.V Sindhu's father and who manages P.V.'s time. He impressed me with his openness, simplicity and crystal clear communication since I first contacted him.

I immediately flew to Pune to meet him and, of course, P.V. What I found was a sports-loving family with two parents who had sacrificed everything for their daughters' athletic careers. At the age of eight, P.V. Sindhu began to play badminton. Her father would get up at 3 a.m. daily to drop her off at the train station, from where she would then travel a distance of 120 km.

Her sister, Divya, is a gynaecologist. Sindhu was born to two volleyball players who worked for the railways. Mr Ramana recalls the moment he lost his football-player father at the age of three. 'This sport will not give you any food or pay your bills,' his older brother, who raised him, would frequently say. 'Even though he said that, if you really love the sport, you can't give it up. To all the children who want to play sports but feel unsupported, it's only a matter of time till they see your performance and the results. It was in my genes,' he exclaimed, 'Just imagine being a state-level player in the 1960s. With a tough situation at home, I started my sporting career in the twelfth grade. I played all kinds of sports until then but focused on volleyball only after. I played twenty nationals for the Indian Railways, with six national gold medals, four silver medals and five bronze medals. I rarely sat on the bench as a substitute in my sporting career. My wife played for the South Central Railway.'

He thought it was important for the kids to play sports because he himself did. 'It gives them a certain cushion with a guaranteed job in railways, banks etc. I think being a sportsperson's child is a big advantage for Sindhu. I knew the ropes early on and I enrolled her to train at the age of eight,' Mr Ramana confessed.

'For someone like me who has played team sports, I was very clear that she should play an individual sport and I could see the commitment it took to be a sportsperson in Sindhu's eyes at the age of eight. Not once did she complain about waking up at 4:00 a.m. I would wake both my girls and Sindhu would say, 'Dad, it's okay if didi isn't waking up, let's go. We will be late.' I never had to wake her up,' he said with pride. So I asked him the crucial question—why badminton? 'Choosing badminton happened by chance,' he said, 'because I would pick the girls up from school and they would come with me straight after for my volleyball practice to the grounds. We were both working parents, so my kids have spent their childhood entertaining themselves as we practised our sport. Next to my volleyball court was a badminton hall. That was her first brush with badminton.'

Mr Ramana opened up about the struggles, '*There were days when I wanted to take a break, but being a sportsperson and having a partner who played sports professionally too, we knew champions are built on consistency. Parents of sportspeople cannot have any laziness or lack of commitment in them.* With limited resources like no car or driver, we had to juggle sports, our careers, practice and school.'

As parents, we all keep asking ourselves, 'How is my child ever going to make it to the nationals or internationals or play competitive sports?' Trust me, you are not alone when you think of that. It's difficult to be one in a billion. I questioned him, 'What really motivates you? Or how can we, as parents, alter the belief that "it's not okay if they don't succeed"?'

Mr Ramana was prompt to respond. 'You see, Mansi, it's a really good question. As parents, if your child is weak in studies, you get additional help, right? You have to have patience and make a road map for it. Then why not in sports? Why are we expecting immediate results? The truth is, we want to outsource the work but do not make the effort to do it. This job is to not only be a coach, but also seeing popular videos, strokes and repeats of games. See, it's not a big job—in those days, we had to see, observe and learn. Today, parents don't even have the time to go and spend 2–3 sessions with their kids. Check recordings. Explain to them their mistakes. Let them observe. As parents, you want results as well as your child's motivation and interest. Some students may drop out, but the lessons will stay with them forever.' He was also quick to add that any child can always pursue a degree online and through distance education, through which Sindhu also completed her MBA.

The question still lingered in my head: if studies and that extra nudge are essential tools for survival, what if your child doesn't make it to that Olympic gold, coupled with injuries and short fitness spans?

'As parents, we find it hard to balance our duties as parents with our work and home, but we still do it with planning. Just like that, the child can also do it. In fact, he becomes very efficient in managing studies and sports if you don't allow him excuses. I would wake up at 3 a.m., prepare everything, then get ready. I used to wake her up at 4. For half an hour, she used to get ready, get into the car and sleep. I used to then take her to the ground that was around 29 km away and she used to play there, then we would travel 29 km again to get back. I requested the school authorities, worked with them to manage her studies and even made her miss the first period. I would come home in my two-wheeler and rush to work and life was tough, but no one complained. We knew this was what it would take. Mornings were not enough. The same routine took place after school as well. I would excuse myself from work, pick her up and drop her home to finish her homework before I came after work to take her for practice. I asked for permission to make things happen and support her wherever I could.'

When I asked him about teenage distractions, he talked about a fruit that we should make all our children taste and that is success. 'Sindhu started winning at the age of ten and she now had this drive to constantly win. To motivate and encourage her, we made separate cupboards for her medals, just like mine. We cut every small news clipping about her and pasted it in a scrapbook. Her grandma made 5–6 such books, and I would cut out every paper clipping about her and make her read and say "See what they are writing about you." Every day, when she came back from school, she asked, "Daddy, are there any paper clippings today?" *Success, as a product of hard work, was now becoming a habit,*' Mr Ramana quoted.

When our child gets used to success, as parents, we also need to get them used to losses. 'There's only one way you can do it and it has to be done differently from how the world does it,' he explained, 'which is to bring them down and make it unpredictable, volatile and sometimes not desirable. As parents, we are the only ones who can communicate constructively. Be very clear and talk to the teacher to know just what to do, how to do it, or any special cases that are required in addition. Don't be afraid of course corrections. When you take a chance in every area of life, why not in sports too?'

My next query naturally arose from the fact that every sportsperson experiences failure in public, and in my opinion, it is the hardest kind of failure. How does one prepare their child for it, then inspire them to pick up the same sport and instil in them the confidence that they can do it?

Mr Ramana's effortless responses to the most difficult questions almost convinced me that nothing teaches you more about life than sports. He revealed what he says to Sindhu on a bad day. The answer is likely something you and I have always been curious about. 'I know that no one will spare her when she loses. I advise her to prepare not for failure, but the hundred tough questions people ask her. *My job as a parent is to tell her that even if you did not win today, you are still capable of winning*. Maybe it wasn't your day, maybe the opponent played better, but always remember, "I am capable of doing it." Remind yourself that you will work hard again; their expectations are their love and it's normal to expect.'

He added, 'So, you tell me it was not your day. You did not perform well, but you are capable of doing it and you will do it. So, I'll work hard. I have toughened her enough to just listen in one ear and remove it from the other.'

For anyone who is starving for success, know your lapses, work on them and work so hard that you will inevitably bounce back as high as your goals.

'I always tell her that stress will do you more harm than good. Case in point: her stress fracture in 2015 in the ankle when she lost many matches. They realize that and nobody knows the value of time more than a sportsperson. For a sportsperson, their body is their temple, and every passing year is one important year of their life gone,' he explained with dread.

As parents, while we are looking to strike balance in all forms, sometimes it has to be at home between our two kids. It's a fine line to walk between praising one and making the other feel appreciated. As a parent, how does one handle it? This answer was presented to me in the course of this discussion.

'For us,' said Mr Ramana, 'our kids were six years apart and my elder one almost mothered Sindhu. On days when Sindhu couldn't perform, she would weep. She was invested in Sindhu's success. She made her study, read, write, do her homework and go to class, and used to check on the first and last periods that Sindhu missed, make notes and understand so her sister could perform. She would often teach Sindhu, "This is how you smash," because she had great wrist work. *Each person has different skill sets, and knowing and acknowledging that is so important as a parent.*' Build a bond as a family and make everyone invest in each other's results—a wise lesson.

I then asked, 'As modern parents, we all want to carve out a niche for ourselves and make our own way in the world. Even though I doubt its significance quite often, I know it is crucial. I've always wondered how the parents of highly successful people do it. What would the steps be like?' Mr Ramana responded in a jiffy. 'There was no family life—it was all duty. Our duty was sports. I didn't even spare her on Sundays. I would take her to the railway grounds and ask those officers to make her play. I asked all my friends—athletic coaches, badminton players or weightlifting coaches—to give my child invaluable training. There was no fear of asking them or being refused.' I realized what a huge aspect sports was in all of their lives. 'Sindhu never asked for anything, like no dresses or anything like that. She used to ask, "Daddy, we'll have biryani today or we'll go to a movie?" No family functions, no relatives. Life was sports and sports was life. We are used to giving up so many things for sports that now there is no feeling bad for anything.'

When I quizzed him on the volatility of success, he said, 'Sindhu is aware that the ads, shows and guest speeches are all products of her game. That's the only place where her performance matters. If you score there, you score everywhere. I remind her time and again that if she does not perform, she will be forgotten.'

It made me wonder if we are telling our kids that they need to play and perform each time for that external validation. He expressed that being number one at the national level is of utmost importance and everything else is secondary. 'Be number one in India,' he said, 'and at the same time, you will be sent from India as a representative to the next level. So, these are all the things you know. As sportspeople, we need to accept the responsibility that when we go and represent our country, we have to do something for the country.'

There were no toys that Sindu gravitated toward as a kid. Life was in between school and playgrounds. As parents, we get so invested in our children's results that, at times, it's hard to detach ourselves. But he believes in three things:

1. A sportsperson has to experience both success and failure.
2. If it goes to your head, you are finished.
3. When you are representing your country, take that responsibility very seriously.

A sportsperson's parent has no off time. Whether or not the coach shows up, parents always do.

I asked him if he had a long-term plan, and he said there was no plan. 'I would have been satisfied even if she made it to the national level. *Ek do* (one, two) medals and she could have then settled well, but when she won nationals at thirteen, I thought she was different. She was then supported by Bharat Petroleum and that gave us a cushion as a sportsperson that she had a secure future. Being a sportsperson, I know that a secure job is what makes a huge impact and I wanted that for Sindhu. You have to, as parents, show your child the blue sky. That blue sky was the Olympics for us. I hadn't reached there, but I wanted her to dream about it.'

With a breeding ground like India, what really separates success from talent? I quizzed myself. Mr Ramana believes a large part of it depends on coaches and they should seize the talent. They need to be present in the remote villages to hunt down this talent. He is a strong proponent of the idea that a parent is an equal coach for the child and believes that it is a group effort. 'They have to be on the same page,' he emphasized. '*The parent has to invest 200 per cent. Coaches can come and go, but parents are always there.*'

Mr Ramana also believes that parents who come from a sporting background like him find it easier to keep the pace with this long journey. 'We want our kids to have freedom because we know this space is not permanent.'

He shared, 'As parents, we have struggled, but it was our duty. Support your child. Don't give up on them. There are times when you want to cry as a parent. I also felt that when she injured herself. We've reached this level and now we are stuck, but take it in your stride, and you will come out of that injury too.'

He explained, 'In those moments of anxiety, you may even scold them and they may scream back at you. Like once, she said, "Dad, why don't you fly and come and play?" But the very next moment, she realized that what her dad has said is right. She had that faith because I watch so many matches that I don't think any coach will also watch. I sat her down for weight training. I sit with her for on-court practices; I help her on the court with food, water and everything else that she requires. Sometimes she forgets her shoes, so I go and bring them back. You will not believe me, whether she's on the ground for six hours or eight hours, and though I have a driver now, I drive myself and take her to the ground. So, I am just like a shadow,' he shared with dignity.

'Her friends also used to tempt her to come chill, but I reinforced in those moments that "They were playing better than you at first, but now where are they and where are you? Don't forget your roots." Even in her peak teen years, she knew she could call me and say, "Dad, I am done chilling with my friends, come and get me." That trust, that bonding, is a long process,' he expressed.

He went on to advise, 'As parents, we've always reassured them that we are there, but we never took hasty decisions. *That unconditional support is most important. Have a discussion, not a one-sided conversation.* As parents, we also make mistakes. I do feel I was quite harsh on her. Whenever she would make any mistakes, I would never speak to her. Instead, I would just go away from there. The next day, I would call her and we would discuss it. We also fought a lot. The biggest reason being her nails. With the right hand, your grip will change and the second reason was her hair,' he said with a grin.

Mr Ramana's passion to keep his daughter at the top of everything is infectious and he is unapologetic about it. This focus leads him to even watch her walk when she is wearing heels or check her path to ensure the road ahead is even and she doesn't hurt herself. 'As a parent, I will blame myself for not protecting my child. I am constantly battling for her to be on time. Fifteen minutes early everywhere.' Yet truly, this battle with children doesn't ever end. Whether they are kids or Olympic winners.

Now it was time for the rapid-fire. Sindhu's favourite food is the infamous biryani, she hates when she is told to cut her nails and is a 'mommy's girl.' When asked about one quality he admires about her, he replied, 'Her commitment, her hunger.'

We end with a short message for P.V. Sindhu:

'As parents, we are constantly guiding our kids, whether it's in sports or life. I always ask her to reciprocate the love and blessings she gets.'

If you had a huge billboard on parenting, what message would it read?

I just say that if you encourage your child, be with them and motivate them, that will definitely help the child grow.

We asked parents on Instagram about their opinion on the following:

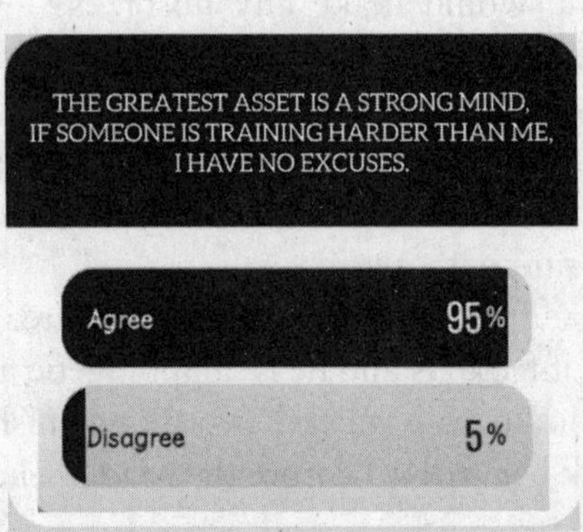

Learnings and Observations

1. If a parent wants their child to take the first step toward success, they need to take the wheel.
2. Catch on to the hints.
3. When your child shows dedication, you can't afford to slack off even for a day.
4. When bringing up a sports star, you have to devote so much time and energy that you can't do anything else.
5. It's not the child who is performing or who is a sportsperson. The entire family is performing.
6. Every member of the family is an integral cog in the well-oiled machine of success.
7. Today's parents should change their mindset and accept both success and failure and be okay if their kids get either.
8. Consistency and perseverance are the road maps to success.
9. The bond between a parent and child should be very strong so that the children can confide in their parents.
10. Our job as a parent is to tell our kids that even if they are not successful today, they are still capable of being successful.

4

Sushant Divgikr

'I don't even want to know the sexual orientation—whether your child is this, that, or the other, the least you owe them is unconditional love. I think that there's no way we can actually run away from that responsibility.'

Instagram: @sushantdivgikr
LinkedIn: Sushant Divgikr

Sushant Divgikr is an Indian model, actor, singer, columnist, psychologist, motivational speaker, drag queen, pageant director and video jockey. Sushant has participated in the television reality show *Bigg Boss 8*. Rani KoHEnur, his drag queen avatar, created history by becoming the first contestant from the LGBTQ+ community to participate in the show *Sa Re Ga Ma Pa* in 2018.

His father, Pradeep, is a retired assistant commissioner of Indian Customs and Central Excise and former president of the Greater Mumbai Amateur Aquatics Association (GMAAA), and his mother, Bharati Divgikr, is a retired manager of a Japanese bank and runs an NGO.

It was clear that the experience I was about to have was going to be lovely and humbling after I spent half an hour with this lovely duo. While Mr Divgikr was teaching me the proper way to pronounce his surname, we started with our conversation. While he has many professions, Sushant is best known for his advocacy on behalf of the LGBTQ+ community in India. His work is phenomenal and has helped many individuals who are struggling with opening up about their true identity. In order to fully appreciate the amount of self-assurance and bravery he exudes, I had to meet his parents and learn first-hand *what it takes to raise a child with such a strong sense of self*. I knew that having Sushant's story in the book was an absolute must. When we were growing up, there were no conversations about LGBTQ, sexual orientation or preferences. It is still a topic many parents think is best addressed in school, by sex ed councillors. I remember this one wedding I went to where someone mentioned, 'Our kids won't ever take our consent on whom they marry,' and another parent laughed saying, 'Just be happy if they marry the opposite gender.' I know this conversation isn't an anomaly and you guys have all come across it. *I know children today find it easier to end their lives than to share and explain to their parents about their sexual preferences*. The feeling of having your people on your side just helps you battle the rest of the world more easily. *It has a very calming effect on the opinions and judgements that are passed on to you every single day.*

To begin, we discussed Sushant's upbringing and the Divgikr family history.

With both parents working in the sports field—Mr Divgikr from the world of swimming and Mrs Divgikr from the world of basketball—both Sushant and Karan, his elder brother, were naturally drawn to sports. This led their parents to sign them up for swimming lessons, which Sushant quickly mastered. 'Sushant was extremely good and used to top his age category till he was about ten years old,' said his father with pride.

The two youngsters were also members of the Khar gym's swimming team. Mr Divgikr remarked that 'participating in a swimming programme teaches discipline because of the early morning commitment required of swimmers and their families.' He went on to say that '*There are numerous lessons that can be learned from participating in sports, including how to accept failure and success with equal grace and not let it affect your mindset.*' He added that he would be disappointed when either of them lost a game but would not hold them accountable or chastise them for it. While Karan was away attending boarding school in Panchgani, Sushant continued his studies at Arya Vidya Mandir (AVM) and was a very popular young man. His grades were excellent. He was particularly well-liked because of his singing ability.' He continued, 'Both of them had normal childhoods—Karan did commerce from Hassaram Rijhumal (HR) College and Sushant did arts from Mithibai.'

Even though *Sushant appeared to be a gifted child from the start, he put in a lot of effort*. In the same way, he put his all into everything he did. Being a parent on the sports field can make you feel a strong desire for your child to achieve success. Yet Mr and Mrs Divgikr have seemed to master this detachment well. '*Even if there was some dream that was unfulfilled, I did not believe in fulfilling that dream through them,*' stated Mr Divgikr.

But how does one become so detached? The success of our children in the activities we choose for them occupies the forefront of our minds as parents, especially in the modern era. In our eagerness to see them succeed, we often neglect to inquire as to whether or not they actually enjoy participating in the activity in question. Mr Divgikr answered by saying, 'So, Sushant, like I said, was a damn good swimmer, till he was about nine or ten, and suddenly he took his foot off the pedal. In the sense that he just lost interest. *As our kids grow older and slowly start speaking their mind, you will have that moment where you have invested as much as your child, but you will feel helpless because you can no longer force them or get them to listen to what you want.* He would not respond when Bharti and I would wake him up in the morning. I realized it was getting to him.' He added, *'I mean, the most important thing is that we let them be and do what they have to do. That's been my policy.'*

The conversation revealed that the youngsters enjoyed close relationships with their grandparents and that Sushant's grandmother loved and accepted him just as much after he came out as she had before. Sushant's interests have always veered away from what society considers 'boys' to be interested in. Like the time he wanted to dress up as a Barbie doll for a fancy dress event. *And there wasn't even a hint of awkwardness as his mom told me about the incident and how she ran around getting the dress and the wings and stuff.* This fascinated me. Because she was talking about Barbies and dresses for a boy, like it was normal, and besides, Sushant hadn't come out of the closet yet. When I inquired about it, she simply said, 'If you can't just guess who someone is, then why does it matter? As long as the person is very sweet and good-natured and everyone loves him.' I know so many parents would just squirm if their boy ever said, 'I want to dress like Barbie.'

It made me think. Why are we so attached to defining things, people and places instead of just letting them exist?

The conversation then turned to Sushant's much-acclaimed singing talent. I was told that it was actually Sushant's grandmother who started it for him by sending him to learn ragas at the age of five. His love for singing only grew through college, as he won a number of competitions and also started taking part in pageants. Seeing his singing prowess and sharing the same love for music, they started taking him to karaoke bars. This did wonders for Sushant. 'And the great thing that happened to Sushant is that even after he was seventeen or something, his falsetto came to the fore. He was able to sing in the female falsetto very effortlessly,' Mr Divgikr exclaimed. 'This was his USP as a singer,' he stated. One of Sushant's many glories was when he performed at a contest and left everyone flabbergasted as he sang in a 'female' key while doing acrobatics. Well, that's a showstopper!

I also learned that Sushant was trained in dance under Terence Lewis. 'So dancing was also something he was learning with Terence Lewis. He was one of those students who was given a free scholarship. He was not charged money, so he was doing cartwheels and stuff while singing, and people were completely zapped,' he exclaimed.

From all these anecdotes, one thing was clear: Sushant is highly diligent in whatever he takes up. Our conversation then steered to the most important part. *'He's pretty much an influential voice for the LGBTQ+ community and he has a voice that has a responsibility that comes with it.'* But what role does a parent play in such a journey? Mr Divgikr answered, 'I think where we come in is that we have never hampered his progress or his thoughts because he's, I mean, an adult, right? Now people call him by his pronouns, which I'm still not getting used to because we are used to seeing him. He now identifies himself as transgender and performs in his drag of Sahar most of the time. But for us at home, he is still Sushant. So, he's transforming, he's evolving and we've let him be,' explained Mr Divgikr.

But how do you accept this evolution? 'We have only seen the talents and as parents, we have honed those talents. We are not bothered about his personal life,' Mrs Divgikr simply answered. And what about the world? *She told me that when the world sees that the parents have accepted him, everyone falls in line.* So simple and so true, and yet, as parents, we often fail to realize this and wait for the world to accept our kids first.

Their easy-going demeanour got me curious to know how they must've reacted when he did tell them about his whole gender epiphany. Mr Divgikr said, 'Oh, that's interesting. When he was in college, being in an arts college, there were many girls, and he had a lot of them come over home for sleepovers. He participated in all these competitions and he was the sports captain too. Till this time, it never occurred to me that he could be gay.' 'Now, we were not ignorant about there being gay, lesbian or trans people. I did not know much about trans people. We would see them at the signals and all that, but I wasn't so well-informed of bisexuals and all that. Our knowledge was very perfunctory. And I never bothered reading. I still don't read too much *because that's why I think my mind is very clear, and I'm very accepting of anyone and everybody.*' He further revealed how some of *Sushant's friends come home when they feel caged in their own place.*

He then began the story: 'Bharti goes often into Kolkata because usually she is remote-controlling the NGO virtually from here. So on one of our visits to Kolkata, Sushant and I shared a bed. Karan was also around. Karan had told me a couple of days earlier that, you know, Sushant attends gay parties. These were exactly his words. So, I just said,

"So what? He attends gay parties, so what are you trying to say?" He had stopped short of saying that Sushant is gay and therefore he attends because who else would attend a gay party?' Mr Divgikr continued, 'Sushant was furiously typing on the phone that night and I guessed that Karan must have told him. I finished reading my paper and before I hit the sack, like they say, I called him, "Sushant." I did not confront him. I just very casually asked him, "I'm told you attend gay parties, are you gay?" Without batting an eyelid, he said, "Yes, dad, I'm gay and I attend gay parties. In fact, I want to talk to you." But since you asked me so, in a manner of speaking, *I raised him out of the closet.*' He then admitted that it wasn't as simple as he had explained.

After Sushant confirmed it, he was taken aback for a second. And just to be sure, he asked again, as some kids see this as some kind of trend. But after Sushant reaffirmed the fact that he was, in fact, gay, the first thing Mr Divgikr did, which brought a huge smile to my face, was give him a big, warm hug. 'So, I immediately gave him a big hug and told him, "*Sushant, it doesn't really matter whether you're gay or straight or anything. You're my son and my love for you is unconditional.*"' It was amazing and heart-warming to hear that. Mr Divgikr went on to explain how he became more protective of him as this occurred before the Delhi High Court decriminalized Article 377 (which happened in 2009). He stated, '*Both of us started accompanying him for all his shows. And also to let people know that we are perfectly okay with his orientation, his sexuality, call it whatever.*' When I asked Mrs Divgikr about her reaction, she said, 'I think he just mentioned that "I'm gay." I said, "Okay, fine."'

It might sound absurd that they accepted it so easily. But at the same time, why should it be absurd? It's their kid, why should it be complicated? As the conversation flowed, I learned that his coming out to the public was very natural. *'I've only told him to be a little careful when you make certain statements because today, it's a world of trolls who are just waiting for a slip of the tongue,'* said Mr Divgikr. *'I used to go with him everywhere. Everywhere.* And it was good that I had given up my job, so I could go with him,' said Mrs Divgikr. *The two most important people in Sushant's life provided him with genuine protection and support, which is why I believe he was able to accomplish whatever he did.* And because of the immense support, love and acceptance he got from his loved ones.

But it wasn't only Sushant who was receiving this support. Mr and Mrs Divgikr even guided and comforted his friends who were struggling to tell their truth to their own loved ones. This piqued my interest and when I learned about the challenges these children faced, I was deeply saddened by them. *'See, most of them have left home and are living by themselves in Mumbai.* So they come when they need a little help. Sushant has also given them a lot of help to earn a good livelihood. But yeah, still, there are a lot of people who are scared,' said Mrs Divgikr.

What is so heart-wrenching for me as I write this, is the privilege I see Sushant has extended to those around him that he received from his parents, acceptance. But there are many things that are changing. I learned about organizations called Gay Bombay and Sweekar: The Rainbow Parents Support Group. 'Now, I'm happy to inform you that Sweekar has grown all across the globe. There was so much activism among the parents and now we have more than 100 branches. In fact, someone like me has taken a step back because there are so many young parents or even older parents who are doing their bit. There are parents of transgender kids who are doing everything for transgender rights. Getting their passports, their educational certificates and getting them organized in a manner that they don't have problems when they have to go overseas. Then there are parents of gay, lesbian and bisexual children too,' Mr Divgikr explained. This made me really glad. He further clarified that *this community is not asking for favours; they are asking for equal opportunities*. Their constant struggle is for equal rights. They are not asking for a percentage (like being a minority). And the one thing that these kids desperately need from their parents is acceptance.

Mr Divgikr said that whenever he talks to the parents of these kids, he says, '*That child is your child. I don't even want to know the sexual orientation—whether your child is this, that, or the other, the least you owe them is unconditional love*. I think that there's no way we can actually run away from that responsibility. *If you leave that child in the lurch, you're actually shirking your own responsibility*. This is very simple, and I really keep it simple. That's why it works well.' Mrs Divgikr added, 'It's all about instilling confidence.'

Mr Divgikr also pointed out very sternly that, '*There could be a discussion, there could be a debate or there could be an argument, like there is everywhere across the globe. Not once do we cross the line of calling him names in terms of his sexual orientation*.'

This was something that I'm so glad he addressed. There are so many times we, as parents, take advantage of this title and hurt our kids using their insecurities, knowingly or unknowingly. We must be aware, no matter how angry or heated the situation gets. We further discussed Sushant's qualities, and his mother, without missing a beat, said, 'He's a very sweet child. He has never fought with anyone, or at least he's never been that boisterous type. He's very calm and especially at home, he's a very simple person.' Mr Divgikr added, 'Another two very important qualities that he possesses are abundance and self-confidence, and he's not someone who takes shit very easily. He's capable of giving back as well.'

Being in the public eye is never a calm or predictable space. Sushant succeeds spectacularly, though, with their assistance. Mr Divgikr also encourages him to do more than sing and Sushant is now also taking up roles as an actor. When asked to define success, he said, 'I think . . . *Enjoy every moment. Success is so momentary and when you achieve it, it becomes an ongoing thing; it's not over. Maybe then you move on to something else.*'

They also explained how it is a task to get all spruced up when he gets invited to events as Rani KoHEnur. The amount of effort and time it takes is shocking. Sushant has really come a long way, and so have his parents.

Now it was time for the rapid-fire, and I learned that his room is always a mess because of the dress changes and that he is a slow eater. These two things still annoy his mom, who said, 'He takes forever to finish his food.' But she does find his smile the most endearing part of him, so I guess that balances it out. One skill that they wish they had from Sushant is his gift of singing.

Their favourite anecdote was when Mr Divgikr accidentally left him in a park and rushed back only to find little Sushant playing by himself. His favourite food is the classic: dal and rice with aloo (potato).

When asked if he is a 'Mama's boy' or a 'Dada's boy,' Mr Divgikr immediately replied, 'Mama's boy!' Even though he respects him a lot, he is still closer to his mom. Mrs Divgikr addressed the fact that the LGBTQ+ community's kids are so loving. She said, 'So many call me and they're all so loving. If they can be so loving to me, why not to their own mothers? Mothers should understand that it's their child. So naturally that attachment is there.'

If you had a huge billboard on parenting, what message would it read?

Acceptance is the way to go. Acceptance is everything.

We asked parents on Instagram about their opinion on the following:

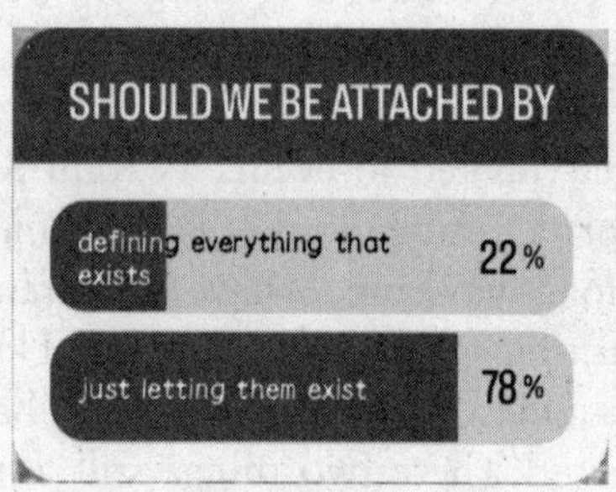

Learnings and Observations

1. Acceptance and a lot of unconditional love.
2. Let your kids be comfortable in their own skin. Don't push them to be something they are not.
3. Don't wait for the world to acknowledge them; they just need your support.
4. As parents we have a very strong desire for our kids to be successful but we have to master detachment.
5. Your unfulfilled dreams do not need to be met by your children.
6. When you accept your child the way he or she is—the world will follow.
7. Success is not one moment, success is ongoing.
8. Share your privileges.
9. Make your home a safe haven for your children. Home is where they come to when they are tired and don't know where else to go.

5

Harteerath Singh

'What sets your child apart is not which school he goes to but what he does after school in those four hours. That will make or break him.'

'You are Shah Rukh Khan to your child, he doesn't need another role model.'

Instagram: @harteeratsingh
LinkedIn: Harteerath Singh
Website: https://hemkuntfoundation.com/

Harteerath Singh, a social worker, grew up in Gurgaon. His family established the Hemkunt Foundation in 2010 to carry out the Sikh principle of *sewa* (service to society). Harteerath oversees the disaster management department as the organization's community development director.

His father, Mr Irinder Singh Ahluwalia, is the founder and CEO of Hemkunt Foundation, and his mother is a homemaker.

For me, the story of Harteerath was like a seed planted during the COVID-19 pandemic. It made me ponder if I could ever give freely and without reservation. My idea of success was reframed as a result. Before this, as per popular belief, I thought only the wealthy and famous could achieve what the rest of the world considered to be success. By 2020, I had already conceived of the book's premise and had begun jotting down names, Harteerath being one of them. But I was curious as to whether or not this was merely a COVID phenomenon and if it would eventually peter out.

We exchanged a few voice notes and I'll never forget his response when I told him about the book and my vision: 'I'm happy to be in the book, but I'm happier that people believe doing good can also be a profession and a respectable one.'

My conversation with Mr Irinder Singh Ahluwalia happened over Zoom. When he first switched on the camera, he was wearing a turban. To me, the turban is a symbol of respect and honesty that the Sikh community has earned over the years. The volatility in Mr Ahluwalia's life, his relationship with money, his ability to think and dream big, and his ability to give or do sewa have been instrumental in shaping Harteerath as a child.

Mr Ahluwalia's grandfather was a very famous person, a contractor who built hospitals, airports and other buildings. He grew up in abundance, with over twenty-five of the most luxurious cars and a big house, only to see it all go away in front of his eyes. He has memories of his grandfather going to London and buying six luxury cars at once. 'I've seen so many ups and downs with money that when I was blessed with a son, Harteerath, I wanted to give him all that I couldn't get. I was also deprived of time with my father and grandfather and while I couldn't give him as much time as I would have wanted to, I gave him the liberty and comfort to do whatever he wanted to do, personally and professionally.'

Mr Ahluwalia had a strained relationship with money—his father was unable to pay his school fees and his mother was forced to sell her bangle, and years later, he was unable to pay Harteerath's school fees, which was 17 lakh back then, and had to sell everything to pay for it. I asked him why he would pay so much and sell everything he owned rather than simply switching schools. Trying to not shed a tear, he responded.

'Beta, I had so many dents and scars from my childhood, and I saw that my father didn't uproot me and gave me the best education. Somewhere, that was in the back of my head and I wanted to follow the same path. I think, as a child, I realized what my father was doing, and so does Harteerath. The school bus fee was 1 lakh, and instead of that, I bought him a scooter that he would drive through mud roads and farms.'

He continued, 'The other kids came in big cars and the scooter was not allowed inside the school, so his principal, who was very understanding, allowed him to park outside the school or on another farm. We used to pay Rs 50 to the guard to park the scooter close by. Harteerath never said anything, but he sensed and understood everything. *Kids have such sharp intuition. They know everything, even if they don't say anything. I did all this jugaad, but I didn't remove him from the school.*'

Coming to Harteerath's academic performance, he commented, 'Harteerath was very intelligent. He didn't study, but his grasping power is very good and sharp, and he used to pick up things very quickly and intelligently. Until the seventh grade, he was spoiled because we had money and he grew up in a lot of luxury with cars, big homes and club memberships, but when we had a downfall again, he would paint a picture that was a reality in the past. It wasn't our time.'

'Our downfall really impacted him,' Mr Ahluwalia expressed. 'He would tell all his friends, "We have these cars; I can do this; my father is a big businessman." But the day we sold off our house, I knew he went through the same thing that I went through. He was deeply impacted. From a brat, he turned into a quiet and mellow kid. I saw him turn to religion. Harteerath's inclination towards religion was always there, but I think it emerged strongly after our losses. They shook him up. His mother used to pray a lot when she was pregnant with Harteerath and somewhere, I do believe those seeds of prayer and God were sown in the womb.'

Mr Ahluwalia then began to tell me, 'In his teenage years, when most kids turned into rebels, Harteerath had already turned to religion. He started going to the gurdwara every day, driving his scooter the 5 km distance. He would only wear his school uniform, and thereafter, our religious attire. He wore that to all big functions, like weddings and religious festivals. He didn't care. I think COVID was probably the first time he wore T-shirts and pants.' This was something that surprised me.

'When COVID hit, Harteerath was eighteen,' Mr Ahluwalia explained, 'Life had thrown so much at him at such a young age that he was fearless. Probably, so am I. We believe we have nothing more to lose. During COVID, essentially, people were scared; there was fear looming everywhere. People would not open their doors and windows, thinking COVID would enter their homes, but we spent 16–18 hours on the streets and nothing happened. *We truly believe that sewa [service] is what will help us in all walks of life.*'

The Hemkunt Foundation was set up thirteen years ago by Mr Irinder Singh with the sentence that he strongly believes in—'*10 per cent of your time and 10 per cent of your money belong to the poor.*' 'Harteerath saw me do this at a very young age, whether we had money or not. In Sikh culture, we believe sewa, or service, is done with your own hands.' He was quick to confess that neither of them has any love for money today. It is just a basic need and there is nothing beyond that. 'With an eight-year-old car that we use, the need to show off is no longer dominant. *My outlook and my values have had a lasting impact on Harteerath. He emulates me and talks like me. Honestly, every child's first role model is in their house and nowhere else*' he stated with confidence.

Was Harteerath the exception in a society where children are taught that their parents can only be successful if they are financially resourceful?

Mr Ahluwalia affirms it by saying, 'You are 100 per cent right! In today's world, being successful in money, cars, clothes, which restaurant you eat at and where you stay, are all metrics. However, for us, that metric is impact.' Stories of impact have left a lasting impression on Harteerath. He has seen auto drivers who have survived after receiving sewa come back and donate generously to save others. Mr Ahluwalia expands on this idea, 'For us, the measurement scale is when we see *sukh* or happiness in other people's eyes. So, we have a different measuring scale altogether—the one that measures the impact of success.'

'Harteerath joined the foundation at the age of eighteen and there was this looming fear that he wasn't studying or had compromised his education, but there was also this strange satisfaction that he was doing something sensible. He continues to study online, but I know his real learning ground is the foundation, and these degrees are perhaps for just getting married,' Mr Ahluwalia said casually.

Humans always have this fear of the unknown that stops us from doing a lot of things.

The COVID outbreak caught me, as a parent, off guard. I asked him, 'Your first reaction as a parent is to protect your children; how did you permit him to enter sewa?' His answer was that 'the sewa's effects on people's lives are so deeply ingrained in the Singh family that it might be challenging to ever change that.' That, in my opinion, is their main source of strength.

He reminisced about the COVID times when Harteerath fed COVID patients with his own hands and even cremated them. 'We survived all this despite Harteerath's grandmother and mother suffering from COVID. I think the biggest reason Harteerath can do all that he does is because he is fearless. The fear is not, "Oh, my god, we will die" but that we will not create an impact or be able to serve others and then die. Life is too precious and we can't waste it. I have always taught Harteerath, "*Don't create a legacy, but create a dynasty. It's not about what and how much you leave behind. It is about creating an impression and impact on the lives of people and teaching them how to do it. That's the only way you will see a ripple effect*,"' he said fiercely.

This made me recall a video I saw that showed the pure and strong relationship Mr Ahluwalia has with his son. In the video, Harteerath said, 'During the second wave of Covid, when I was reading the newspaper, it was written that the nation is burning. I looked at my father. My father and I have a unique bond and without me saying a word to him, he understood that I was going to step out again. He said, "*Peeth mat dikhaio mereko, agar kaam karne jaa raha hain toh* complete it till the last breath. (Don't turn your back on me, if you are going for a job, complete it till the last breath.).''’

At the start of this chapter, I wrote about my doubts, about whether this boy would keep up the good work even after the pandemic. This is my answer.

Back to the conversation, ‘If there is one skill set I want Harteerath to learn, it is empathy—feeling others’ pain,’ Mr Ahluwalia said. ‘We are so miserly in our ways of working that we can’t even share one piece of bread out of the four in our lunchbox. This is the skill set we need to teach our kids, to be able to be grateful for what they have so they can share their privileges with others, but we are so focused on collecting more that nothing else matters.’

As parents, we all have dreams for our children; s/he should be this or that when s/he grows up. What were their dreams for their son? Mr Ahluwalia replied, ‘Maybe I did think of Harteerath joining our family business, but after COVID, I just want him to give, and the only thing I want for him as a father and not as part of the Hemkunt Foundation is perhaps the Nobel Peace Prize. I want Harteerath to always look beyond himself and think big.’ This made my heart feel so warm. Every parent has the standard ‘I want my kid to have a secure life, have a well-paying job and have a good house’ wish, but it’s rare to hear from a parent whose only wish is for their child to make the world a better place.

Mr Ahluwalia also revealed that, ‘Between my wife and I, we disagreed on many things and do so even today, whether it’s his education, his sewa or probably everything else. As parents, we both want the best for our children, but we can’t agree on it for some reason. During COVID, she didn’t want to send Harteerath out of the house, but he was destined to do bigger things and that is why he is where he is today.’

He is very clear in sharing the five qualities that will take Harteerath to his one singular goal at the moment, the Nobel Peace Prize:

1. Turban on his head. It signifies the trust people have in each other and in us as the Sikh community.
2. Respect for all: When you serve a langar (food served at the gurdwara, you do not discriminate between rich or poor, black or white—you serve someone who is hungry. We all need to start believing that the food that we are serving doesn't belong to us.
3. Speech: simple words to communicate small messages to bring about a change.
4. Presentation
5. Humanity

People in positions of authority always make me wonder how they decide what issues to take a stand on. Harteerath and his father were very clear about his impact and how it touched more lives. I always wonder about these New Age role models and how their parents keep them grounded, and Mr Irinder is prompt to reply. '*You are their Shah Rukh Khan. You have your head on your shoulder; they have their head on their shoulder. You are a show-off; they will be show-offs. You do sewa; they will do sewa.*'

Something that will stick with me forever is when Mr Irinder said, '*What sets your child apart is not which school he goes to but what he does after school in those 4 hours. That will make or break him.*'

The question of whether sewa is still considered a profession continues to loom in my head, and I wonder how he will break this mindset. He believes that the only way to make it respectable is by measuring impact.

Harteerath truly is the reflection of his father's values. This chapter has made me more aware of the fact that 90 per cent of what your kids become in life comes from you.

When quizzed on the biggest parenting mistake, he says with confidence, 'Nothing really. I have given it my best.'

If you had a huge billboard on parenting, what message would it read?

Trust your children—they were and are very intelligent. You are the best school and Shah Rukh Khan (role model) for your child.

We asked parents on Instagram about their opinion on the following:

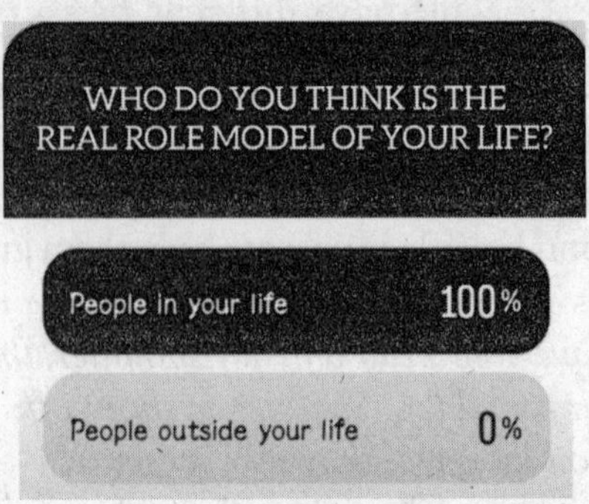

Learnings and Observations

1. The rope of parenting can never be too tight or too loose.
2. You are the best role model for your child.
3. What a child does and sees at home will shape him in a bigger way than any other experience.
4. Humility and the ability to give are what will drive change.
5. Kids have such sharp intuition. They know everything, even if they don't say anything.
6. What sets your child apart is not which school he goes to but what he does after school in those four hours. That will make or break him.
7. It is our responsibility to help our kids think big.
8. Different people have different measuring scales altogether for success.
9. Your experiences as a child will shape you as a parent.
10. Don't create a legacy, but create a dynasty.

6

Karan Bhagat

'You are a generation that didn't get things easily, so you want to give. But don't overcompensate. Give because there's a need. Parents who say "no" are also good parents.'

LinkedIn: Karan Bhagat
Website: www.iiflwealth.com

Karan Bhagat is the founder, MD and CEO of 360 ONE. Karan set up the company, formerly known as IIFL Wealth & Asset Management, in 2008. It has grown from its humble beginnings and is on its way to becoming the leading wealth management company in India with a market cap of nearly $2 billion on the Indian stock exchange.

He holds an MBA in finance from the Indian Institute of Management, Bangalore and acquired his bachelor's degree in commerce from St. Xavier's College, Kolkata.

Karan's father was the late Om Prakash Bhagat and his mother is Madhu Bhagat.

Over the past twelve years, I've gotten to know Karan because our children attended the same school. We have occasionally caught up on Sundays and have been friends the whole time. Karan's mom was very eager to tell me more about her son's childhood when we spoke during the second wave (of Covid-19) over Zoom, despite the fact that she had hurt her hand earlier.

'Karan was one of the most peaceful children at birth—he never cried, was very peaceful and took in whatever we gave him as he grew up. He loved spending time on his own. I was very keen that my kids learn the Montessori way and I remember this one instance where he sat alone in the sandpit and kept filling and emptying buckets of sand again and again. I was a little paranoid, thinking, "Why is he not a social child? Will he turn out to be a loner? Why is he not interacting with other kids?"'

Although it may sound absurd, I am always surprised by the persistence of my own and other parents' doubts and fears whenever our children engage in any form of aberrant behaviour.

'I did the Montessori course back in the day only so I could raise my children better and give them that time and that nurturing that children need in the foundational years. While his teachers asked me to be patient, we realized that children this age need to dive deep into the whys and build patience, resilience and all of it through repetition.

'Karan was an extremely diligent child. Before a test, he would wake me up and ask me to help him revise, unlike kids today, where the mother is chasing the child for days and hours.'

'As a parent, my role was to support my child. After not making it into one of the top schools in the city, he was really upset. He wanted to go back and understand every reason why he didn't and it took him a while to get over it. Unlike today, discipline was not imposed but practised.'

She went on to explain, 'Karan's father was from Calcutta and I was from the South, so we reached an understanding of "let's give our children the space to grow and be." We were very encouraged by scouts and camps. We knew these experiences would shape our kids.'

Mrs Bhagat adds, 'I knew he was a mathematical wizard. If I look back on what I did for him to be a wizard, honestly, all I can recollect is seeing the number plates of cars when we went for drives and giving the kids a few challenging questions looking at them. As a family, you will see one anchoring theme—for us, it was sports. Sports played a very integral part in Karan's growing-up years.'

When it comes to his schooling, she states, 'Karan was among the top-ranking students in school and it continued through his twelfth grade, when he was offered admission with a scholarship from the Shri Ram College of Commerce in Delhi.'

'The times were really tough then and it wasn't the best time for us as a family financially. *As a close-knit family, the one thing we did in the good times and the bad ones was share our problems.* We stuck together and continued to be a close-knit family.

'He declined the admission and refused to leave the family during those tough times. *The difference between then and now is that I think we had time for each other, something that is lacking today. With profound competition, you are compelled to push your child. We were not like that. We traded our social obligations for their extra work and projects because we knew that was the only luxury we had—our time,*' Mrs Bhagat explained.

Like all mothers, she admits that, 'their entrance exams would mean life would come to a standstill for us and we wouldn't stop for 3–4 months. Today, time is the only luxury your generation can't afford.' This really struck me to the core.

'I did feel Karan should have grabbed the opportunity back then, but his resilience to bounce back and come back stronger made me believe this one admission would not make or break him.' Her confession was sincere.

'He had the sincerity to bounce back when he didn't get something that he wanted,' Mrs Bhagat continued, 'there was no sense of competition. But I think what we kept emphasizing, coming from our modest background, was that everybody doesn't get everything in life. You have to move on. *It's not what you have that sets you apart, but what you make of it. It's "you" that matters.*'

'As a mother of children growing up in a culture of abundance, I believe we struggle to instil values in them. We were raised in a time and place where material abundance was scarce, so the desire for more was inconceivable. We are afraid to refuse. It's unfair that we always assume that having nothing means being deprived. We would rather stretch ourselves to make everything a reality for our children. And we struggle with saying "no" to them.'

'That is a transition. I think the big difference is that your kids today have a choice—you give them a choice and then you figure out a way to fulfil that choice. They were taught to "accept" what they were given because they grew up in larger joint families with more children and scarce resources,' she says matter-of-factly.

'*Kids today have things a day or two after they demand them and I see that too. You are a generation that didn't get things easily, so you want to give, but don't give to overcompensate. Give because there's a need. Parents who say "no" are also good parents,'* stated Mrs Bhagat with urgency.

She confessed, 'Karan had a few demands, but he was a child. His one tantrum upset me so much—that was his first and last. We didn't stretch the situation. We picked him up and got him home. As a mother, I did question, "What was I doing wrong when he threw a tantrum?" I did question my parenting.' Something we all do.

'The value of things was earned. I distinctly remember once, when we went shopping together, we bought something and then moved on, and I couldn't see Karan. I turned around and he was still at the same shop, taking back the ten-rupee change that I'd forgotten. Value is best instilled by demonstration. I still remember when we had some really tough times. The only possible reason we could probably sail through them was because of our closeness—we knew everything about each other. So, that made them understand and also made them less demanding. Just the very fact that they had the biggest luxury—our time—no matter what our situation was, made them feel enough.' She spoke with an assurance that suggested she was relieved to have raised him properly.

'Karan decided not to leave the family at those times and declined the admission. Instead, he chose to support me in his spare time while he was preparing for his CA by helping start my travel agency. I distinctly remember that day when the admissions officer from Shri Ram College called us and said, "Why aren't you sending your son? He is such a bright student," and Karan refused because he wanted to stay with the family and support us in those times,' she relayed with a hint of pride.

Mrs Bhagat revealed that they were able to get through the rough patches, including his teenage years, because they talked a lot.

Every single primary parent today wonders, 'Will I lose the race if I put my career on hold to raise my child?' Mrs Bhagat was very prompt to reply, 'The difference between my time and yours is that my children were my priority. It's a role I chose and decided to play seriously.'

'The tide hadn't yet turned in our favour financially when he decided to quit a steady-paying job and start on his own. We disagreed as parents with him, but we left the decision to him and made it clear that we were there for him no matter what the consequences. The key here is that we told him we don't agree, but we also reassured him that we were unconditionally right behind him. It should never be the parents' style to say yes or no, where yes also means no and no also means no,' she warned.

As a follow-up, Mrs Bhagat stated, *'Parents can't be authoritative about decision-making.'*

She added, 'Children look at parents to share their thoughts. Sometimes we get their ideas and sometimes we don't, but trying to make that decision because it suits us is not okay. Parents should not and must not manipulate any situation to suit us.'

She continued to describe Karan's character by saying, 'Karan can bounce back very quickly, whether he falls sick or in any situation. He was clumsy as a little boy. From when he was in Montessori, where he couldn't tie his shoelaces, to a dirty room at IIM, or me being paranoid about him driving because he is just clumsy,' she whined like any typical worried mother would. Then she said something that we parents have a hard time processing but should also learn.

'The fundamentals of parenting are that you need to know that they can survive without you. The day you start accepting that, there will be mistakes, but accept them and move on.'

She added, 'When he was starting out, we knew that success and failure were two sides of the same coin. We have to teach our children to take them both with a pinch of salt.

'I think one of the best pieces of advice I've given him would probably be, "Be honest. Even when you have to do something that is not right, face it and rectify it."'

'Raising a successful child is not a formula; it's like nurturing a plant. You know the plant needs air, water, soil and sunlight. But how much, what quality—all of that plays a huge role. For us, that nurturing was communication, closeness and togetherness, no matter where we were. This is something the world doesn't have right now. The opportunity to sit together for meals and talk about your day.'

'I've always told my children,' she continued, 'do your best. Be sincere and don't compare. There is only one Karan Bhagat. *As parents, for the rest of the world to stop comparing our kids, it is important that we look at them as individuals first too.* We need to remind ourselves constantly that they cannot be alike because they are meant to be different.

'Having two children is always tough, but it is one of the best decisions. I told myself as a parent that they are different and will always be.' She recalled an incident from her son's school years: 'I remember at a PTM for my younger son, I got into an argument with his teacher, who was going on with, "He is not like Karan in almost everything."' She told her to look at him as an individual instead of Karan's brother. And told her to stop comparing.

Mrs Bhagat admitted that, as a parent, she was keenly aware of the tendency to favour the less talented child. 'We should try to push that one first. You let him feel he is something too. While Karan was winning laurels, he used to feel like the odd one out. It is very normal. I made it a point to push him too. My younger one did question me on why he was not like Karan. My immediate response was that "You have other talents that are special too,"' she shared. 'Children need that validation to build confidence and parents need to help them with it in the early years.'

Her eyes lit up as she said, 'For me, the most rewarding part is seeing Karan with his kids. It's almost a reflection of his father and me being with him. No matter who you are, you are a father first, and he takes that role seriously. He still spends time with his kids, teaching them math or watching sports with them.'

After that, we started talking about how the husband and wife's parenting dynamics affected their relationship. To that, Mrs Bhagat said, 'As parents, we may disagree with each other, but what is very important is to believe in each other. One parent needs to be in the driver's seat and the other parent needs to trust that parent. Never voice your differences in front of your kids. The one parent who takes the driver's seat may feel a temporary setback in their professional and personal growth, but don't stop. I continued to work and do something. I took my role as the primary parent very seriously. That time that you spend is important and it never comes back.'

She admitted, 'As parents, you may feel that you failed on many occasions, but those are fleeting moments. I miss the old times. *We had fun. How your life shapes up is really driven by how much your parents trust you and that will decide how liberal you will be.*' This idea astounds me now that I'm writing this chapter.

'As a mother, it's very common to feel like I'm not doing much, but I would just say two things, you are doing something that no one else can do. You are bringing up a human being and it's an important job.' She continued, 'I did a Montessori course, a textile design course, my travel agency and my NGO. I did all this while raising my kids. *I probably could manage to raise them well because my temperament was always that of a fulfilled person.*'

How significant was this final point? It reminds me of the proverb, 'How can you learn to love others without first learning to love yourself?'

I asked her at the conclusion of the interview if she had any advice for Karan and she said, 'Make time for the things you love.'

If you had a huge billboard on parenting, what message would it read?

Communicate, spend time with your children and don't push them into a comparison trap.

We asked parents on Instagram about their opinion on the following:

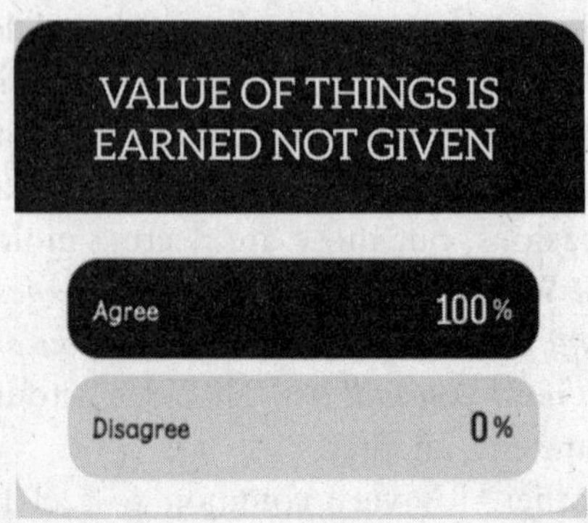

Learnings and Observations

1. We build a story in our heads so easily and always create a worst-case scenario for every situation. Why?
2. We are always expecting our children to confine themselves to a type based on what we see around us or to act like how it is in our heads versus how it actually is. That differentiated picture is what causes unhappiness in most parents.
3. Making good decisions is one of the characteristics of an outlier.
4. The difference between our generation and the generation before is that, children were the main priority, way over profession.
5. Parents can't be authoritative about decision-making.
6. No matter who you are, you are a parent, and one must take that role seriously.
7. As parents, we may disagree with each other, but what is very important is to believe in each other.
8. One of the fundamentals of parenting is that we need to know that our kids can survive without us. The day you start accepting that, there will be mistakes, but we will accept them and move on.
9. How much your parents trust you really determines how your life turns out. And that will decide how liberal they will be.

10. As a mother, it's very normal to feel like you are not doing much. Two important things to remember—you are doing something that no one else can do—you are bringing up a human being and it's an important job.

7

Sandeep Nailwal

'Distractions are there for every child, but you know once you fall in love with your goals, even five minutes seem too precious to waste.'

Instagram: @sandeepnailwal1
LinkedIn: Sandeep Nailwal
Website: https://polygon.technology/home

Sandeep Nailwal is the co-founder of Polygon, formerly known as Matic Network. His family migrated to Delhi after leaving their hometown of Ramnagar, Nainital.

In February 2021, the project was rebranded as Polygon Technology and described as a Web 3.0 and metaverse company. In order to get its Web3 products to the masses, the company has partnered with big names like Meta (Instagram), Starbucks, Reddit, Flipkart and many more.

Sandeep's father and mother were from a small village in Uttarakhand. His father had a small business and his mother was a homemaker.

From a family with limited resources to a family that now provides, Sandeep has changed the meaning of what it is to be truly successful. I could see the pride shining in his parents' eyes as they began, 'Sandeep was a very easy-going kid—no tantrums, no demands—and a favourite with the grandparents because he ate whatever you gave him. When we look back at a five-year-old Sandeep, we wouldn't think he would grow up to be such a big man. We believed he would succeed and might be in a better position than me. Sandeep got a baby sister when he was three. He adores her and is most respectful towards her even today.'

'Even as the children grew, the financial situation remained the same. A small rented house in Delhi, bare minimum needs, no greed and we managed everything for our kids. Sandeep aspired to have a landline in those days and whenever we went to take a call at our neighbours' house, Sandeep would tell them, "My grandfather has two landlines."'

Sandeep's grandfather was then the house help for S.P. Jain. Today, S.P. Jain is one of the most prestigious MBA colleges in India. Perhaps, Sandeep had the urge to thrive. *Perhaps this urge is created when one is in adversity*. As I recall something he often told his parents, 'It's not like, *bada banne ka hain* [want to do something big], but more like, *chhota nahi khelna hain* [don't want to play small]. He was always destined to do something great.'

'*At a very early age, Sandeep had a habit of winning*,' confirmed his parents. 'Even if it was a simple game of carrom, he played it with his father until he won. He played all night until the result was in his favour.' *Sometimes, as parents, we term this as zidd or stubbornness, but this habit shaped him in a significant way for success*. There are so many times, as parents, that we take this zidd in a very negative light. How many times have we really understood their zidd for something?

'Whether it was cricket or coming first, he was competitive. *He didn't like being second.* He loved school and would cry if we didn't send him to school!' exclaimed Mrs Nailwal.

She continued, 'In the first week of school, I distinctly remember that he could not even hold a pencil and his father worried and said, "*Iska kya hoga* [what would this guy do]?." The bond Sandeep and I built made him come home and tell me everything, even the smallest of things.' This is one thing that we, as parents, need to teach our kids. However, it has to be natural, and it will take time. It can't be forced, which makes it even more beautiful. Building such a bond with your kids, especially in this generation, is essential.

Some lessons don't come easily in life. '*We taught them honesty and self-worth.* Once he mistakenly brought someone else's pencil home, and I slapped him twice and asked him why he did not return it. That one incident and those two slaps had a very long-lasting impact. Since that day, he hasn't taken anyone else's things. We know the approach may have been wrong or right but the message was conveyed, "*You don't take what is not yours. Be happy with what belongs to you.*"'

His parents related to me an incident that happened in school: 'Sandeep was such a sincere and dedicated child. He just surrendered himself to whatever he did and once, his Sanskrit teacher called us to school to ask where she should cut his marks because she struggled to. He got 100/100 in Sanskrit in the tenth grade.' Sandeep's curiosity and maturity helped him succeed at school and otherwise. 'We never compromised on their education, their friends or their presentation. We knew the importance of these. We chose not to buy a house and rent in a slightly more expensive society so he would have a sense of worth and make the right friends.'

Sadly, today, the cars you own or the following you have on Instagram have become the standard for selecting friends or judging someone's personality. Are we teaching our kids how to select good friends regardless of their social background? Are we teaching our kids what really matters in life and how to build a relationship with someone?

They expressed, '*He knew the value of money and what it could do for us.* From not celebrating Diwali to giving his glass of milk to his siblings or buying a football for them. He became a parent to our kids instead of a brother. He would request me, "Maa, sister is not studying; just turn off the TV. We will only turn it on it after exams." He understood our conditions and studied on his own and if he did need help, he would take late-night classes because they were cheaper. He scored 98 per cent in tenth grade. Somewhere, I fear our circumstances and upbringing made Sandeep mature before his age. *Uspe ek zimedari aa gayi aur woh bhi jaldi* [A responsibility fell on him and that too, early].'

Sandeep's analytical and visionary skills set him apart. He modelled his actions after those of eminent figures, for whom he had great respect, and explained the reasoning behind his own choices as he made them.

Because of his upbringing in a time of scarcity, Sandeep is especially admirable for his generosity and ability to provide for everyone. Today, when kids study, they need a desk, chair and AC. Sandeep had one *rajai* [blanket]. He would learn by himself, teach his siblings and go buy second-hand books from a street called Nai Sarak in Delhi. In order to read as many books as he could, he kept buying and returning them. For guidance, other children had tutors. Sandeep had his own will. He studied for 16–18 hours at a time.'

Such laser-focus is rarely seen in kids today, considering the million different distractions they have around them. This makes me wonder, is it our situations that are the real makers of our personalities?

'Both textbooks and phones were non-existent back then. It was hard for a student to survive. He didn't spend money and had few friends. In that regard, he was very kind, but as you say, success comes to those who seek it.'

Sandeep was very close to his mother; his father barely made it home by 9 p.m. in those days. 'The two slaps and my constant nagging of him for holding the pencil wrong left a deep impact on him, and he would never speak to me directly. It was always via his mother, never directly. He has seen his family and loved ones struggle so much that he makes time for them, whether it's staying back in the hospital for his mom or dreaming with eyes wide open and twirling a pencil in his hand. He used to say "Maa, when I have money, we will start with buying a house" and to date, he has helped our family with their homes and setting up their businesses,' his dad expressed with pride.

His mom continued, '*Our limited means did not stop Sandeep from dreaming big.* He would always say, "Mummy, *sapne unche dekho, ya toh aise hi reh jayenge, rent ke makan mai* [Dream big, mom or else, we will always stay in this rented apartment]."'

'He often also would say, "*Ya toh sab kuch chahiye, ya toh kuch nahi chahiye* [Either I want it all or nothing]." As parents, we were scared. His risk-taking ability would scare me,' Sandeep's mom admitted. 'All his friends supported him because they knew he would clear IIT, but he missed it by 1–2 marks. That left such a lasting impression on him that, from that day of missing IIT to today, when we have everything, nothing makes Sandeep happy. He would just ask me, "Mom, are you happy?" and I would say yes. He would then say, "That's it; don't worry about me. I don't feel happiness anymore."'

His mom continued, 'After he finished his BTech, I said, "This is enough for us and you will get a comfortable job," but Sandeep wasn't satisfied. He was sure he wanted to do his MBA, so he left everything and went to pursue it. With no alternate source of income, he had to pay three lakh for an MBA. He said, "Don't worry; I will manage my fees." *Taking care of the family and taking responsibility of his siblings early on taught him leadership skills that no other college could*,' his dad stated. He did his MBA at NITIE Mumbai, which is now known as IIM Mumbai.

'For Sandeep, distractions like smoking, drinking and drugs didn't exist because we were very close,' Mrs Nailwal said to me. 'I was with my kids twenty-four hours, day and night. I knew what they were doing, where they were going, who was with them and what time they would come back. I may look back and feel that perhaps so much rigidity was not good, but Sandeep being Sandeep, never argued. Our bond was such that they never found a reason to lie to me.' And then she said something that will stay with me for a long time, '*Distractions are there for every child, but you know once you fall in love with your goals, even five minutes seem too precious to waste.*'

'As parents, we constantly gave him examples of people who went to IIT or became engineers. He saw that all these educated people changed the trajectory of their families, and somewhere, all these conversations became part of his narrative. Also, living in an extended family where we would take care of our siblings, our parents, and press their legs and heads is what our kids have seen. Whether you have Rs 5 or 50, you have to help others. So maybe that has also become his style,' his parents explained.

'Soon after getting his MBA, he got a job at Deloitte. Sandeep has this strange habit of calling me after everything, especially after something good,' his mom said with a twinkle in her eye. 'His first sentence to me was, "Mummy, *aapko pata hai, mai dedh lakh ka admi ban chuka hu* [Mom, you know, I am now worth Rs 1.5 lakh rupees]."'

She continued, 'In the last so many years, Sandeep hasn't paused even for a moment. After Deloitte, he took up another job, and they made it so difficult for him that his mental and physical health suffered. It was the darkest phase of our lives. He had to take a forced break to recover.' While talking about his childhood, his mom listed a few things he always said and it almost felt like second skin to him. Maybe these things have really helped him.

Chota nahi karna kuch bada karna hain [I don't want to do something small, I want to do something big].

Kam ke liye phat se haan mat bol do [When you want to make a decision, don't settle for something mediocre in a hurry].

Har din aise shuru karo mano, yeh tumhara pehla din hai. Phir woh padhai mein ho ya kaam pe [Start every day like it is your first—be it in studies or work].

'When he started with his start-up, he worked for twenty hours at a stretch, but what drove him was his dream: "*Maa, kuch bada karke dikhana hai* [I want to do something big, mom]." Those were tough years. There was a bad crisis and he lost all his funding. For the first time, I saw Sandeep hold a pillow close to his chest and get anxious. He said it was all over. I respect him,' she said in awe, 'but founders and entrepreneurs are made with some other blood. He quickly gathered himself and said "I will start all over again."'

They continued, 'As parents, while all of this monetary and professional growth is great, we want our kids to settle down. He did marry and luckily, found a supportive life partner.'

'Today, when we have so much, money has lost its worth. We have seen so many different phases of life that we don't care much for it. For us, when we see Sandeep and his son now, that is far more precious,' his parents expressed honestly.

When his parents think back on his success, they see three key characteristics: his leadership ability, his capacity to inspire others and his perseverance. 'He is just constantly working to get somewhere,' said his mom.

She continued, 'Whatever you do, focus on it, like Sandeep does, and be honest. If you want to prosper in life, take everyone along with you, including family. What good are you alone? And lastly, if you can, bring up the people who are below you too.'

'It's easy to say a parent is biased towards one particular child, but a child also comes with his or her own nature and temperament, so yes, for me, Sandeep and I had a connection that was way beyond a mother and son. Today, we barely talk because he is busy, but a parent doesn't get biased by the fame of the child but by the temperament of that child,' expressed Mrs Nailwal when I asked her about maintaining the balance between multiple kids.

Today, Sandeep's measure of success is not how much money he has, but rather how he can maintain it and use it to benefit his family. This comes from his parents. Are we teaching our kids the right sense of success? Is success just money or is it what we can do with the money to impact lives?

They left a small message for Sandeep as we concluded: 'We would love for Sandeep to continue doing charity with whatever little or more he has.'

If you had a huge billboard on parenting, what message would it read?

Give your kids space to do what they want, support them and listen to them.

We asked parents on Instagram about their opinion on the following:

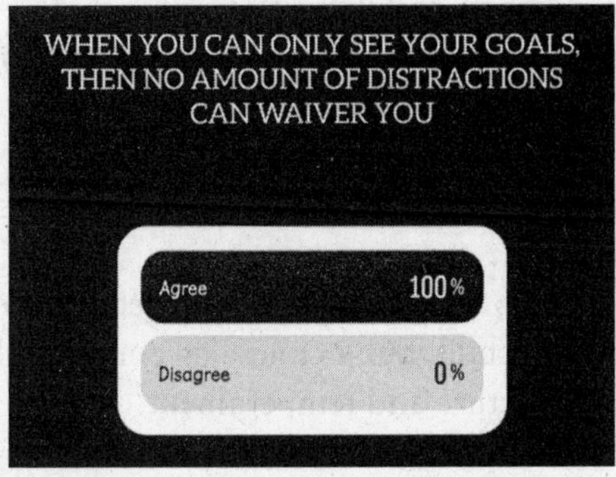

Learnings and Observations

1. Allow your kids to dream big. If you dream beyond you will go beyond.
2. The ambition to do something should be strong and well-supported by the family. Sometimes, as parents, we term this 'zidd' or 'stubbornness.' But this is significant for success.
3. The measure of success is not how much money one has, but rather how one can maintain it and how it can benefit the family.
4. Give your kids space to do what they want, support them, and listen to them.
5. If you want to prosper in life, take everyone along with you, else success can feel lonely.
6. The hunger to work hard and be successful, wherever and whatever stage in life you are at, is important.
7. It's easy to say a parent is biased towards one particular child, but a child also comes with his or her own nature and temperament.
8. Parents always think that their kids should do better than them. Our measure of success is whether they surpass us, whether in height or success. We need to change this mindset.
9. Each and every person should have the ability to analyse and think big to be successful. The hunger to work hard and be successful, wherever and whatever stage in life you are at, is important.

8

Mithun Sacheti

'I was their friend, and they could come and tell me anything. I also believe that nagging at your kids doesn't help. Guiding them and letting them know that you are on their side makes all the difference.'

Instagram: @mickystu
Website: https://www.caratlane.com/

Mithun Sacheti, the co-founder of CaratLane, is a certified gemologist by the Gemological Institute of America, California (GIA). He started CaratLane with Srinivasa Gopalan in 2008. One of the first companies to sell jewellery online, it has been a subsidiary of Titan Jewellery since July 2016 and is marketed as a partnership with Tanishq. Starting with its first physical store in Chennai, CaratLane now has over 165 retail stores across more than sixty-six Indian cities.

Mithun's family has been in the solitaire business for five generations. His mother, Manju Sacheti and his father, Padam Sacheti, started the niche jewellery store, Jaipur Gems, in Mumbai in 1947.

The decision to interview Mithun came from seeing so many people around me complain that their kids did not have that drive to do something. Today's children are surrounded by abundance, making it difficult to teach them to value anything, be it a new pencil case, a pair of shoes or their education. I often wondered how someone who had enough would have the hunger to create more, build more and still have his head on his shoulders.

Mithun spent the majority of his formative years in Mumbai, where he attended IES Elementary and subsequently, Sydenham College. When his parents moved to Mumbai, they didn't know much about the elite schools and on a neighbour's recommendation, got him admitted to IES. Jaipur Gems was founded in 1974 by Mr Sacheti, who is less risk-averse than the rest of his family. Most of Mithun's summer vacations were spent at his paternal grandparents' home in Ajmer—an old house with over 100 rooms—with lots of cousins, waking up at 4 a.m. to fill buckets of water since it was scarce back then, and sitting in a line with all the cousins to eat mangoes.

'Growing up as a kid, he was an average student—not very sincere,' said Mr Sacheti. But he thinks the one thing that struck the most about him was that he was a people's person. 'He would be friends with everyone—someone who was well-to-do and someone who was not. It was very hard to not be friends with Mithun. He was most loved by his cousins, grandfather and uncles. He was very sure he would do business. The mindset was there since early on.'

Unlike in most business families, he didn't spend his childhood at the showroom, despite his mom working full-time and being ambitious. His mom made sure she was back home from work by the time the kids were back. 'I made sure they had a very well-rounded upbringing,' she said,

'Studies are okay, but sports were equally important in this household.'

'Once they were back from school, I would play badminton with him,' said Mrs Sacheti. He would play cricket in the building. When he was not doing anything, Mithun would be playing badminton, sometimes for hours on end. 'I never had to worry about studies because they were good kids and sports taught discipline. Also, as a mother, I always stood by my children and they were always focused. *They knew they had my unconditional support. I was their friend, and they could literally come and tell me anything. I also believe that nagging your kids doesn't help. Guiding them and letting them know that you are on their side makes all the difference.*'

'I think parents should not lose the respect their children have for them by repeating the same thing again and again. Let them figure it out and act on their own accord.' She continues, 'As a mother, I knew that if their father was at the shop the whole day and I had to be the one taking care of them, I would do a good job with it. I would play carrom, badminton, hop around or just about anything.' I think parents also forget to have a mutual admiration for each other, which makes sure their kids don't take either parent for granted. Mr Sacheti said, 'As a father, I really respected my wife's ability to manage the house and the business, and also have big dreams to expand. We really valued our parents by just observing them and I think our kids possibly did the same.'

Without Siddharth, his brother, Mithun's childhood likely wouldn't have been the same. Together, they did so many things that their parents had no idea about. They attended a very modest school, which, according to Mithun, made them very curious and inquisitive. They spent so much time playing together that nothing else mattered.

'Mithun hated to lose as a kid. When he played cricket, he would throw such a big tantrum if he got out that all of us as friends just gave him an extra chance, thinking he's just a kid,' Sidhharth sweetly said.

When Mithun left India to attend the GIA, it marked a significant turning point in his life. He took that very seriously, and given that he was anyway a people's person, could immensely benefit from it. He actually thrived at GIA, according to his parents. At GIA, where he developed his skills, Mithun became a leader of society—of all Indians, the college, the institute—and everyone there would look up to him. I asked his mother if she thought he might get sidetracked and take the wrong route. But with a very reassuring smile on her face, she said, '*We knew our kids, we had faith in our upbringing and we were very sure about our values.*'

According to her, allowing your children to breathe and be themselves will help them develop all the traits that will lead to their eventual success. '*Parents must have faith in themselves. When you have guided them and spent enough time with them, then it doesn't matter.* We understand the perils of that age, but because they also had trust in me, it worked,' she expressed. They spent so much time together, which is a rare commodity today, and shared a strong value system. She also advised me to be aware of the friends our children have. That the friends they keep really define who they will become. 'I also believe that because of his strong sports background, he would get everyone together and instead of doing anything else, play sports with them. He would always be in the driver's seat. Sports played a very critical role in steering his leadership, his mindset and managing distractions,' she said confidently.

When Mithun wanted to start CaratLane, Mr Sacheti was a little reluctant, but he was convinced after a two-hour meeting with Mithun. Just two hours! 'I was always going to support them and stand by them. I had so much confidence that they would not go wrong. *I wasn't sure if they would find success, but I am always positive they will do the right thing*. I still remember Mithun was in Bangkok, and he called us and shared the name he had in mind; he was just ready to take the next leap,' his father said with a sense of pride.

The one characteristic that, in his father's opinion, defines Mithun is his capacity for persuasion. Every VC who funded him believed this boy would succeed just as much as his father did.

As we discussed the next leg of the interview, his parents were trying to get the timeline right of whether he was married before or after CaratLane.

Straight after GIA, Mithun was asked to move to Chennai, as it was seen as a huge market for the business. There were no questions asked about whether he wanted to move or not. But he knew he wanted to go beyond. He planned another store, his online business and everything else while running that shop in Chennai.

Business was his main focus. He had the idea to open another store there. He found the place and set up the shop all on his own. When I inquired about CaratLane's early years, his parents acknowledged that they were extremely difficult, but he never gave up. His father explained, 'We were positive that we would do well, but we knew that online businesses to start off with would need money with no window to success. Profit never occurs online, sometimes for years. Everybody knows. There is so much capital required and till you become stable, *paise manage karna, yeh karna vo karna, difficult tha hi* [Managing money, doing this and that, it was difficult for sure].' Still, he succeeded. Later on, he continued to receive assistance from his business, his employees and one of the partners who had a wealth of experience. Even though that partner has left now, they maintain the same relationship.

In contrast to the majority of the parents in this book, Mithun's family had a prosperous lifestyle and a very stable career. When asked how they kept Mithun's enthusiasm for hard work alive, they simply said that GIA was a huge opportunity for him. He was influenced by the wealthy and accomplished peers he met there to pursue his own ambitious goals. '*Mai pura toh nahi keh sakta lekin vo wahan se shuru hua* [I can't say GIA was the complete reason, but it all started from there],' said Mr Sacheti. Perhaps he learned to appreciate hard work and success after witnessing the success of his parents and Jaipur Gems. After talking with them, I came to the conclusion that their children's modesty, diligence and sense of grounding stemmed from the fact that their parents maintained a middle-class mentality despite their vast wealth. Mithun isn't the type to feel compelled to fritter away his wealth simply because he can. 'Keep your head high but live grounded' is what he lives by.

When asked about where he gets this drive from, his mother explained, 'He was a sportsperson, so for him it was always like, tomorrow is my match and I have to prepare for it.' During the course of the conversation, I realized how significantly sports can affect a person's outlook on life.

His Nana (mom's father) too, was one of his greatest sources of inspiration, his mom shared. I also got to know that Mithun was, in fact, his mother's favourite. He even confided all of his secrets to his mother rather than his father, who said, '*Muje toh malum hi nahi hai kuch*, [I didn't know a thing].' Knowing all of this, I tried to figure out the secret to being such good friends with your children. His mom proudly told me how she still knows everything about her kids. It was because she was always playing with them. '*I was a child with the children*,' she stated. While Mr Sacheti was a little reserved, the moment he would go out of the house, they would dance, sing and watch television. 'And by the time he would come back, everything would be back in its place,' she confessed with a grin. Mrs Sacheti was both a parent and a friend to her kids. She shared with me that 'you are not supposed to question them—they come and tell you; they yell at you sometimes—you're supposed to be quiet, and they will come back and apologize. Mr Sacheti humourously added, '*Gussa hona mere upar hi tha* [Getting angry was my role].'

What surprises me is how commonly we believe the myth that vacations equal quality time with our children. This interview opened my eyes to a profound realization—quality time with your children can be forged in any setting. Money, time and other resources are merely icing on the cake. Only two or three times a year did the Sachetis take actual vacations—the summers were spent with their grandparents. However, Mrs Sacheti then confessed that the three of them went out a lot more. This led me to wonder how much Mr Sacheti is unaware of.

Here's where Siddharth jumped in and spontaneously exclaimed, 'I'll tell you honestly, in our upbringing, you know, we kind of just grew up.' He went on to say that their sense of competition was fostered by the contrast between their posh South Bombay environment and their Dadar school. He said they were 'just brought up as random kids' despite coming from a wealthy family.

Mithun is a good human being first and then a successful person. And the family is very proud of that. When asked about his qualities, they said, 'He is a good human being. He is a very simple person.'

How ironic that the most common values are those that matter the most. Mrs Sacheti went on to say that our generation is so enmeshed in the rat race that we frequently lose sight of the fact that they are just kids. We set high standards for them from an early age, expecting them to be the best at everything and to be skilled in a wide range of areas. She said, 'I really believe, *ki yeh baat sabko bolni, likhni chahiye ke, bacchon ko itna push nahi karna chahiye* [Every parent should know and write it down that we mustn't push our kids). The child gets up in the morning, goes to school, then comes back, then again goes to classes—what is this?'

This interview taught me a lot, but one of the most comforting things I took away was that parenting isn't something we have to be perfect at. There are no precise formulas or ideal lines for it. You just need to be present and have fun. As simple as that. Mithun Sacheti is a grounded individual who is very social and well-connected but who also thinks he still has a long way to go. He may be a 'not-so-good' diver, however, he is a true 'gem' of a person. And after this interview, I know exactly where that comes from.

If you had a huge billboard on parenting, what message would it read?

Stand behind your children. Be with them. Support them.

We asked parents on Instagram about their opinion on the following:

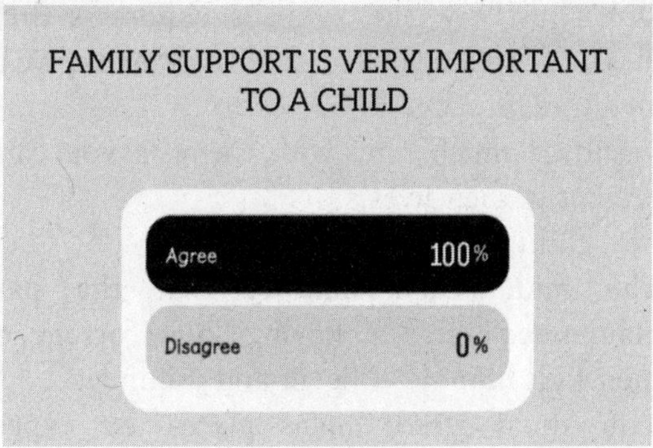

Learnings and Observations

1. Don't just say 'no' to your children's dreams. Instead, explain your reasons to them or give them an alternate suggestion.
2. Spend as much time with them as you can. Be present in their lives.
3. Be a child with your children.
4. The middle-class mindset that the parents maintained even after having a huge fortune, made their kids humble, diligent and grounded.
5. You don't need fancy places or expensive experiences to build that bond with your kids, all you need is you and them.
6. The most ordinary values are in fact the most important.
7. You should be a people's person.
8. Parents should stand by their children and give them unconditional support and should be there for them always so the bond between parents and children gets stronger.
9. A strong value system should be inculcated in kids right from the beginning.
10. We can't be sure if our kids will find success. But what's in our hands, is to make them good humans.

9

Jemimah Rodrigues

'It's never easy. Every day you are not going to see results, so you need a lot of patience. It's like a seed you are sowing, you can't expect to get fruit the very next day.'

Instagram: @jemimahrodrigues

Jemimah Jessica Rodrigues is an Indian cricketer—an all-rounder who plays for the Indian national women's team as well as the Mumbai women's team. She started playing cricket at the age of four and was selected for the Maharashtra under-17 and under-19 hockey teams. At the age of thirteen, she was selected for the under-19 state cricket team and made an impressive debut in her WPL 2023 (Women Premier League) match, scoring twenty-two runs off just fifteen balls against Royal Challengers Bangalore.

Her father, Ivan Rodrigues, was a junior coach who started the girls' cricket team at her school. Her mother's name is Lavita Rodrigues. Both her parents now run a successful academics coaching class in Bandra.

This was one of my very last interviews, but I knew I had to get it. Cricket is a national religion in our country and in a sense, unites the nation, but for a very long time, it was difficult to recognise the contributions of women on the field. The women's IPL had just concluded and the nation couldn't stop talking about it.

The male cricketers are praised, acknowledged and idolized. Is there any interest in female cricket players? Meeting Jemimah's parents and learning about the lack of knowledge, communication and opportunities for all the girls who love cricket out there was a truly eye-opening experience. Even though circumstances have improved, this male-dominated game still needs to take these amazing women into account!

Jemimah, born the youngest to two elder brothers, is called a true blessing from God by her mom, who, by the way, always wanted a daughter. It wasn't ideal to have three children in those days and her mother received a lot of flak for it but she didn't give a damn. Jemimah was more than just a child—she was a miracle. 'I always tell her that she is a restoration that God gave me and my family,' cooed her mother. Her parents had a modest life in Bhandup, where she was born, but they gave it all up to pursue their love of sports, which led them to the thriving, opportunity-filled Bandra. But before stepping into this sunny area, the three kids stepped into the bus and travelled from Bhandup to Bandra every day for almost a year—without their parents. And Jemimah was just in the first grade! 'This was done to make them strong,' Mr Rodrigues reasoned. But after an incident where they came home two hours later than usual, Mrs Rodrigues's heart couldn't bear it and asked for an alternate solution, which was to shift.

I heard this in horror. In today's urban dwellings, where we are afraid to send our kids alone even down the elevator, they were sending their kids to a whole different place all alone, not to mention, that none of the three were even preteens. This makes me wonder, was it safer in those days?

If my daughter is even half an hour late, my mind starts running in all the possible directions. I can only imagine the anxiety and worry that Mrs Rodrigues went through when her kids were two hours late.

Coming back to the conversation, I was told that growing up, Jemimah watched more IPL games than Disney movies and had played the sport ever since she was four.

Jemimah's family are strictly religious and believe in surrendering everything to the Almighty. Maybe that's why He blessed Jemimah with talents that I'd never heard of before. During the interview, I got to know how it wasn't just cricket that Jemimah had aced but basketball, football and hockey as well. Her first-ever trophy was for being the best upcoming basketball player—the astonishing part is that she wasn't even trained for it. Being told that she should play state-level football and highly praised by her hockey coaches and even Joaquim Carvalho, an ex-Olympian, Jemimah excelled in any sport she touched, confessed Mrs Rodrigues. All this was phenomenal but confusing nonetheless. Her parents had to narrow it down for her so she could fulfil Mr Rodrigues's dream of seeing his kid play for the country. It was four to one. After kicking out football and basketball, the tough decision lay between hockey and cricket. Before getting selected for Mumbai's under-19 cricket team at the age of twelve-and-a-half, Jemimah played four hockey nationals. Now, I call *that* impressive. Later, cricket started getting attention, and hockey was left behind.

What intrigues me the most is how her parents allowed her to play everything, get her hands dirty and then see where her interests lie. All the while, they did not place any pressure on her to perform better in any sport. They appreciated her skill and let it take her where she wanted to be.

I discovered during the interview that Mr Rodrigues's one and only dream, and something he was extremely passionate about, was playing cricket. This stemmed from the 1983 World Cup, where India had lifted the trophy up high. Jemimah's grandfather was a peon, and her grandmother was a housekeeper then. Even though her grandfather wasn't very educated, he made Jemimah's father study and made notes for him too.

Despite coming from a poor family, Mr Rodrigues began tutoring students in order to raise the necessary funds for his cricket coaching. In the end, he had to give up on his desire to please his parents and chose to become an engineer instead. He was an all-India topper. Aside from learning that Mrs Rodrigues was a top student at her university, what really caught my attention was the fact that they had grown up together and had even competed for the top spot in their school. Mrs Rodrigues was a talented athlete while Mr Rodrigues was a devoted cricket fan. To excel in both sports and academics? It's unfair, isn't it? I guess that's why Jemimah has the sports DNA within her while being academically great too.

Her parents still run their classes in Bandra called Scholars Coaching Classes, which are quite well-known. Talking about academics, I asked how she managed it with her matches and her mother said, 'When we shifted to Bandra, we put her in St Joseph's Convent. Ivan now coaches the girls there. The principal and the teachers, who also recognized her talent, gave us a lot of support. Studies were the only thing that worried them. I assured them that I would prepare her for those, but they had to allow her to miss school. She used to take half days off school and we used to sit with her during our coaching sessions whenever we had free time.' They weren't as worried about academics because, as Mr Rodrigues said with a smile, 'they knew that would come from their genes.' *For them, prayers came first, sports second and studies third.* Her brother was good at cricket too, attending camps with her and going for selections. However, he never made it due to 'over-aging' which, as explained by Mrs Rodrigues, was when parents gave false documents of their kids to make them appear younger than they were just so they would not miss an opportunity. 'This was a huge problem back in the day,' Mr Rodrigues informed me. 'Kids used to have false documents about their age. But now I think strict action is taken and it is seen that this doesn't happen much. My boys, both of them, were very good at cricket. But because of all this, we didn't want to do the same. *We stuck to our values.*' said Mrs Rodrigues. But later, the boys found their own paths, with their elder son going into cinematography and the younger, a musician, working in the Indian film music industry.

'That must be disappointing,' I asked Mr Rodrigues, knowing his dream was to see his kids play for the country. '*No, it wasn't. Because my daughter was fulfilling that for me,*' he said, without missing a beat.

When describing Jemimah's early sporting accomplishments, her parents recalled a number of instances that demonstrated that she was not just any girl but, in fact, born to play cricket. This all started in her starting years, 'Ivan and me, we both loved sports. We also made it a priority to play with the kids whenever we could. Each day we played and since our hall was long, we played cricket inside the house only. We wanted to spend time together so we started playing cricket, and they got used to it,' Mrs Rodrigues said. Perhaps this period of time spent with her parents and brothers became a core memory for her, and sparked her passion for cricket. Reminiscing about another incident, Mr Rodrigues told me how the St Anne's coach called him to send Jemimah for a match against Podar International, who had won against 250 schools to reach the semi-finals of the Mumbai School Sports Association (MSSA): 'They were around sixty-three for six, when Jemimah went to bat, they had to still chase 157 or something. This was against Podar, who were in the finals, having defeated about 250 schools. To my surprise, when I reached there, I saw Jemimah still batting. She was in the third grade at that time, which means she was eight or nine, while the boys were all under sixteen. The opposite team had the fastest bowler, yet Jemimah was standing and facing him. All these boys were bribing her, "*Ek* chocolate *dunga*, catch *de na* [I will give you a chocolate, just give me a catch]," but where was she listening? She had an amazing defence and sometimes she hit one-two runs and gave the strike to the other batsman. St Anne's ended up winning the game against Podar International because of Jemimah. The next day they went to play the finals, and they won that too!'

Another instance that was dictated to me was from one of her selections. At that time, women's cricket was not known to Mr and Mrs Rodrigues. So, for one particular selection, Mr Rodrigues took his sons and later was informed to get Jemimah too. He recounted the tale with a fervour as though it had just occurred. He said, 'Now, she was very small, very thin. When we got there, all the other girls were college students. When they saw her, they started giggling and laughing. Then the selector asked me for her department. At that time, her department was bowling, not batting. So she went on the pitch, the first ball was good and the second ball—bowled. She immediately took down Jemimah's name and made sure that Jemimah played every game, and that she never sat on the bench. And it was she who discovered Jemimah's talent in batting.' In the next phase of the interview, they made me aware of the difficulties they faced in getting Jemimah an appropriate platform to showcase and hone her skills. Just because she was a girl, *Mr Rodrigues had to fold his hands in front of coaches to let her play matches and got rejected by many popular names in the industry too*. He explained further, 'When she made it to the under-19 Mumbai team, her coach there supported her like anything. He sent her for as many matches as he could and that's why her level of play advanced significantly. Within one year, she came to Mumbai's senior team as a junior. She was only twelve when she was in the under-19 team and thirteen when she was in the senior team, and would open matches along with 33–34-year-olds.'

As I listened to these stories, *I noticed two parents who were both incredibly proud of their child and equally astounded by her talent and abilities*. To ensure that their daughter received what she deserved, they battled and gave it their all. When it comes to developing their own personalities, children learn the most from their parents. *Jemimah's parents undoubtedly contributed to her perseverance, hard work, dedication and consistency*.

The other children often feel a little left out when one is so successful. When I asked about this, Mrs Rodrigues sweetly said, 'In the house, no one is a good hockey player or cricketer or who's earning more and who's earning less. Everyone's the same. Even now, all three of them have their own chores to complete, which they do. And my boys are the best boys; they completely support Jemimah.' She related how, at first, when Jemimah began to receive attention, she advised her not to let pride creep into her thoughts. '*You play well because you love the game, don't play for fame.*' I think most of the time, we forget that *just because they are kids does not mean they aren't capable of having complex conversations.*

It's crucial to communicate. When Jemimah was dropped from the world cup team, she was devastated. She told her parents she needed a break from playing, and they gave her the time and space she needed. It was when she broke down and wanted to talk that they spoke about the situation, and the very next day she was charged up and could practise diligently for two months. When she appeared for the domestic season, her performance made the coaches regret their decision to drop her. *When your child asks you for something, whether it is a gap year, a month off from practice, give it to them. Trust them. They also know the pressures of the world, and what this means for them and for you.*

In this very situation, I thought to myself, 'What would I have done? Would I show my child compassion? Would I get frustrated and tell her to hold herself together? Would I get mad at her decision to take a break?' I was amazed at how Jemimah's parents handled the circumstances. And the advice that they gave for parents whose kids are interested in sports and want to pursue a career, was as simple as always backing up your kids and encouraging them. Let the kids make the decision about which sport they want to go into. Mrs Rodrigues sternly stated that, 'It's never easy. *Every day you are not going to see results, so you need a lot of patience. It's like a seed you are sowing, you can't expect to get fruit the very next day. So don't pressure your kids even more.*'

When I asked them about the qualities they thought made Jemimah who she is today, they said it was her hard work, determination, sincerity and 'never-give-up' attitude. It made complete sense to me where these qualities had come from now that I had met her parents. These qualities clearly showcase her ability to continue to perform astoundingly well.

As I end this chapter, all I can ask is, as parents, are we comfortable letting our kids follow their own path, even if it is completely different from our plans?

I didn't even notice how much time had passed because talking to Jemimah's parents was so enjoyable and delightful. For young girls who want to pursue their passion for cricket, Jemimah is unquestionably an icon. It was such a lovely chat and there is so much I'm going to take away from this meeting.

If you had a huge billboard on parenting, what message would it read?

There are two lasting things that we can give our children: roots and wings.

We asked parents on Instagram about their opinion on the following:

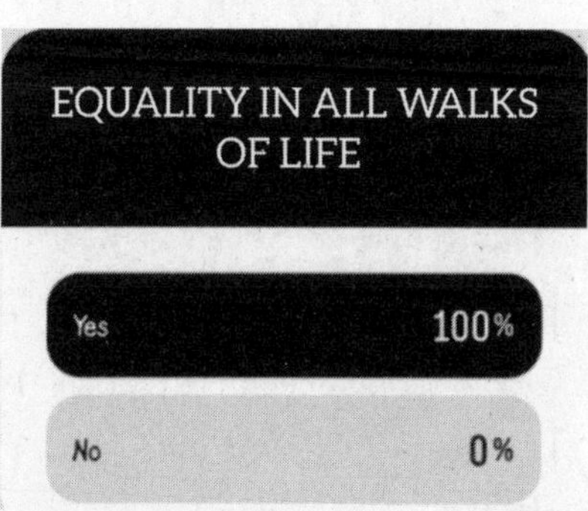

Learnings and Observations

1. Communication is key.
2. Give your kids their space to realize their emotions when they encounter disappointment.
3. There are two lasting things that we can give our children: roots and wings.
4. Parents are like shadows to kids so most of their learning comes from parents.
5. Do something for the love of doing it, not for the fame.
6. You are not going to see results every day, so you need a lot of patience.
7. Expose your kids to different things.

10

Vilas Nayak

'Toh aadmi kitna bhi bada ho jaaye, rehna same hi chahiye [No matter how big one becomes, they should still stay the same].'

Instagram: @vilas_nayak
LinkedIn: Vilas Nayak

Vilas Nayak is a self-taught artist from India who started painting at the age of three. He specializes in speed painting, wherein he completes a painting within three minutes. Vilas grew up in the small town of Ujire, Dakshina Kannada district, India. He secured the seventh rank at Mangalore University for his bachelor's degree and the second rank at Mysore University for his postgraduate degree.

His father, Vasudeva Nayak, owns a shop in Ujire, and his mother's, Jayashree Nayak, is a homemaker.

As children, we have all had the desire to become artists at one time or another. However, in the hour we took to perfect our standard scenery drawing, Vilas completed several portraits, each within 3–5 minutes. I had to include him in my book because I was curious about the magic brew his parents must have prepared for him in the mornings that enable him to display such talent. He has painted portraits of the Joker (Joaquin Phoenix), Atal Bihari Vajpai and many more in less than three minutes and with both hands! That laser-sharp focus, grit and speed—how does he do it?

Even though Vilas hailed from a financially challenged background, he never used it as a sob story to get to where he is. It was pure hard work. When his family's paan/bidi shop couldn't make enough to fund a five-year course at his dream college, JJ Institute of Art, he was forced to complete his Master of Social Work (MSW) from Mysore University instead. But this did not weaken his spirit and he did his best.

For me, Vilas' story is one that stands for someone who didn't challenge the tide but rode with it. It is about people who walk with others and don't leave the path that is sometimes imposed on them. It's about how it's never too late to follow what you want to do.

When I first decided to interview his parents, I knew he was talented and that he does what we can only dream of doing. I had no idea he came from such humble beginnings.

Indian families and art haven't been a match made in heaven. We are people who believe art is extracurricular—it's that period the math teacher can always take away and no one will bat an eye. Artists are often admired but rarely respected or considered successful. It can always be a hobby and never a profession. Vilas's parents thought just that.

What was quite astonishing to me is that one can be self-taught and still be so well versed without any formal help. Mr Nayak said with pride, '*Yeh sab uska hard work hai. Khud se sikha hai usne* [This is all his hard work. He has learned everything on his own].'

Vilas told me that at home, he used chalk and made his art on the slate, or he used coloured pencils and painted on paper. He had been very keen on art since childhood. While talking about his childhood and the boy that Vilas had grown up to be, his parents were proud to say that he was the most obedient, hard-working and helpful child. He spent his childhood in school and the shop. *Whenever he got time in between, he would study or paint.* He pursued any and all painting-related activities as a youngster. Like painting the signboard or *Ganpati* idols, or wherever he was called. *He never assumed that any job was small. His father reminisced about how the other kids would get scared to participate in art competitions because Vilas always won first place.*

When he entered Mysore University to do his masters in social work, he bought a bicycle with the money he had collected, to go all over Mysore as he was required to do. Mr Nayak also told me about the two scholarships that Vilas got because he was good in his studies—one scholarship was from the government and the other was from a gentleman from America, M.P. Jayaram. Once it so happened, this gentleman came to visit Vilas and gave him a check for the next three months. However, the following month, he sent money again. Vilas informed his dad, and that man was so delighted and touched by this boy's honesty. When I inquired how they instilled these values of honesty and humility in Vilas, his mom whispered in Mr Nayak's ears, '*Hum maa-baap bhi aise hai, toh hume dekh ke sikh gaya hoga* [We, as parents, are the same, so he must've learned from watching us].' *What they see, they learn—this will never go out of the parenting rulebook.*

Vilas's honesty and humility definitely came from his parents and from the time he spent in his shop, seeing his father being an honest shopkeeper. This was not a one-day result—these values were built over time and now so strongly reflect in his personality.

His father informed us that when Vilas stood second in Mysore University, he immediately got a job at IBM in an HR role. The reason he agreed to do something other than art was because of his father's simple philosophy: *'Tum thoda padho aur naukri dhundo pehle, aur yeh side mai karte jao* [First, you study and find a decent job, and you can do this as a side hustle].' Vilas continued to do his full-time job and pursue his passion on the side so as to make sure his family was financially in a better position.

What's important to note here is that *his parents didn't put a 'no' sign on his passion but gave him a different approach to keep pursuing it*. His life started to change after *India's Got Talent* came to Mumbai in 2011. He thrived and reached the semi-finals but didn't win. However, when life shuts a door, you find an open window. And such a window of opportunity came in the form of commissions from around the world. But the more calls there were, the more difficult it got to manage his passion and his job. 'As the shows started increasing, he found it difficult to handle both. So, he approached us and told us he was planning to quit and concentrate on his art. We just told him, "*Agar tumko uska guarantee hai, kar sakta hai, toh tum karo* [If you're sure about it, you can manage, then go ahead]." So he left his job and gave his time to this,' Mr Nayak explained.

Pursuing a career in art was then considered taboo in India, and in many places it still is today. Art is largely seen as more of a side gig than a stable career path. When asked about Vilas's idea of pursuing art instead of a stable job as an HR manager, his father shared that they were really scared at first. Painting and selling a few paintings once a year was not the most stable source of income according to them.

Vilas would also help paint billboards, as printing in those days wasn't as popular. Going up tall buildings and sites to paint was highly risky. Vilas's zeal, however, was what persuaded his parents to give in to his wishes. Mr Nayak sweetly said, '*Wo bahut khush tha jab vo painting karna chalu kiya* [He was very happy when he started painting].'

Vilas is entirely self-taught and acquired all of his knowledge of art without any kind of formal instruction, but according to his father, he occasionally sought the advice of B.K.S. Varma when he had some doubts or questions.

Vilas is the youngest of three kids, having two elder sisters. I asked Mr Nayak how he maintains the balance between all three kids, knowing that one is doing extremely well, better than the others and with a smile, he said, '*Humlog ke liye vo teeno same hi hai. Hum unko bolte hai, jo humare taqdeer mein likha hai, hume vo hi milega* [For us, the three of them are equal. We keep telling them, whatever's written in our destiny, that's what we get].' The three siblings also keep helping and supporting each other.

Continuing the conversation, I asked them about some of the qualities they felt make Vilas who he is today. To this, they said it was a mix of their support, his will to do something great, the support from his professors, and his hard work and consistency. '*Jab bhi log hume uske naam se pehchante hai, toh bahut khushi hoti hai* [Whenever people recognize us by his name, it makes us happy],' his parents confessed with a twinkle in their eyes. I think the one thing that makes a parent the proudest of their kid is when people recognize them because of their children. '*Hume puchte hai ki aap itne bade artist ke parents ho, aap itne simple lagte ho. Toh aadmi kitna bhi bada ho jaaye, rehena same hi chahiye* [People ask us that why, even though we are the parents of a great artist, we look simple. No matter how great a person becomes, they must stay the same].' Maybe this is what makes Vilas the humble lad he is too.

Mr Nayak's advice for parents whose kids are interested in art is to let your kids complete higher education too. They can always get into art, but education is equally important. Vilas has had the honour of meeting countless celebrities, both national and international, and many important political figures too. When asked to pick the person they were most excited or happy about, his father said that when he met A.P.J. Abdul Kalam and PM Modi, they were very proud.

Surprisingly, Vilas's parents had no idea how he got into speed painting or how it all began. I had to ask Vilas himself and he revealed that a few events led him to realize his talent. The very first realization was when he was in the 4–5th grade and he took part in a Ganesh Utsav art competition but the judges arrived late. So, within 10 minutes, the kids had to do whatever they could manage, and Vilas was the only one who completed a proper and complete Ganesh sketch. This made him realize how he was not dependent on using the eraser much and could sketch accurately on the first try. Vilas also revealed that he was an extremely introverted kid. When he topped his first year of BA, he couldn't even go on stage to collect his award. But with the help of his friends and professors, he slowly came out of his shell.

He was in his second year when he performed his first-ever speed painting. Vilas had heard about B.K.S. Varma and that he performed such art but had never seen it. Another person who inspired him was Denny Dent from the US. His friends pushed him on stage and encouraged him to perform his art, and that was a big turning point in his life. And it was when he worked at IBM as an HR manager that he realized he wasn't an artist but a speed artist. He further explained that his one dream ever since he was a kid had been to be an artist, and he thought coming to big cities like Mumbai or Bangalore, where he was currently residing, would expose him to better prospects. But when he came to these big cities and worked for five years, he was away from art and it suffocated him. *Every night. Vilas was introspective and one night, he applied the SWOT analysis to himself and realized that speed painting was his strength and that this is what he wanted to do.* After participating in the reality show *India's Got Talent*, this idea strengthened.

I recalled an interview where he stated, 'I used to spend a lot of time with myself. These days, the problem is that we don't have time to spend with ourselves. Because of technology, we can connect with anyone sitting in any part of the world in a matter of few seconds. But we do not have the time to connect with ourselves and the moment you start doing that, is when you know what you really want to become.'

Today, we are pushing our children to attend different classes and want them to expand their skill set. But do we leave them any time to introspect where their interests lie?

Vilas confessed that even though he was disheartened that he couldn't pursue art and had to study something else, his parents' concerns made sense. The gentleman from America also told him that 'When your stomach is empty, how can one pursue their passion?' As a rank-holder, he was awarded two certificates for advanced study in Mysore and Mangalore. Mysore was picked because it is the cultural and economic centre of Karnataka, giving him the chance to perform his art there as well, which he did during Dussehra. Vilas finally said, 'Looking back, I think it all happened for good. Imagine if I were to choose to go to JJ College of Arts or any other college; I wouldn't be happy as an artist because the education system there is such that you are made to think a certain way.' He admitted, 'I believe taking art to the people is more important than sitting in a studio and doing it all alone.'

I completely agree. Art can be such a lonely field, but not anymore. When he was a kid, they didn't have enough money to buy expensive paints and canvases. So, little Vilas used colour pencils and watercolours to make art. This made me realize that you don't need the best of things to give your best; you just use whatever you have and make your masterpiece. Vilas further told me that his inspiration till today is nature.

He left his corporate job eleven years ago and hasn't looked back since. When *India's Got Talent* happened in 2011, he hadn't left his job yet. He didn't take the risk until his artwork generated an annual income equal to it. Vilas has now travelled to thirty-six countries and performed over 1000 shows. It is opportunities like performing for the United Nations and the military in Leh and Ladakh that make him proud that he took this risk. 'My wife's most treasured performance was with Hari Haranji and S.P. Balasubrahmanyam, where we were both honoured by them. But the most memorable was with His Holiness the Dalai Lama in Delhi,' said Vilas.

When asked what he thinks his parents did right in his upbringing, Vilas said, 'They were always honest with me ever since I was a child.' He also said that his father was the best-liked individual in their community, and was well-known for his humility and integrity. It was also he who taught Vilas the value of discipline. This was no surprise to me.

Humility can never be taught, it can only be passed down. Vilas's parents and Vilas are a great example of that.

His parents were shining with pride. This interview taught me so much—it was so inspiring to learn how he built himself up and still continues to stay the same humble and sweet boy whose only wish was to paint.

If you had a huge billboard on parenting, what message would it read?

What they see is what they learn. No other method is more powerful than that.

We asked parents on Instagram about their opinion on the following:

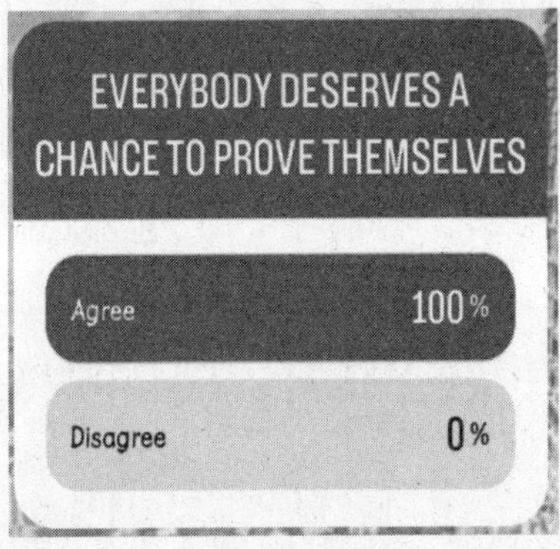

Learnings and Observations

1. Do your best in whatever you do and and wherever you do it.
2. The child needs to be invested in what he wants to pursue.
3. You don't need the best of things to give your best, you just use whatever you have and make that a masterpiece.
4. No matter how rich or successful you are, you have to be grounded and humble.
5. Own your background and your beginnings.
6. Sometimes we put a 'no' sign on our kids' passions as careers, but we should give them a different approach to keep pursuing it.
7. Honesty never goes unnoticed.
8. You can follow your passion on the side until it earns as much as your annual income.
9. Try new fields within your skill set and keep learning.

11

Suhani Shah

'Yes, we have to make them understand, but in such a way that they know you're trying to communicate something. The minute they feel you're telling them to do something according to you, that's when there's friction.'

Instagram: @thesuhanishah
Website: www.suhanishah.com

Suhani Shah is an Indian mentalist, YouTuber, artist, magician, author, counsellor, corporate trainer and therapist. She was born in Udaipur, Rajasthan. She has won several awards and has been conferred the title of *Jadoopari* (magical fairy) by the All India Magic Association. She is the first and only female magician in India, and has been performing magic for twenty-two years now. She also works as a clinical hypnotherapist at her clinic, Suhani Mindcare, in Goa, and has given several TED talks.

Her father, Chandra Kant Shah, is a personal trainer and fitness consultant, and her mother, Snehlata Shah, is a homemaker.

Suhani's childhood was spent in Ahmedabad, Gujarat. She studied only until the first grade and dropped out in the second. Until then, their whole family was in Ahmedabad. 'Honestly, the decision to drop out of school wasn't a big one because, when she was six, she completed her diploma in computer studies. She still holds a place as the youngest person to complete their computer diploma. She was also the state-level swimming champion. *So, she was very different from the start and after observing her, learning the way she thinks, and what she wants to do, I tried to create that atmosphere of understanding. Accordingly, we supported her wherever she went and things fell into place along the way.* As she grew a year older, we saw her suddenly attracted to magic. But she was interested in many things at that time and we thought maybe this is one of the things she is good at,' explained Mr Shah.

When I heard this, the obvious next question in my head was—she dropped out of school at six, was a state swimming champion, the youngest diploma holder in computers and did magic. What did her parents do between the ages of 0–6, that she accomplished so many things?

They both giggled because they have faced this question many times. Mr Shah is quick to trot out a childhood incident where Suhani's brother, who is five years her elder, was learning multiplication tables. Suhani, clearly thinking that she was no different from the other person, also started, and in no time figured out that it was nothing but repeated addition. She then went ahead and wrote it all the way till ten.

Mr Shah went on, '*All we did as parents was provide her with logic and reasoning, and never shun any questions. We explained to her everything that she wanted to know.* The moment she wrote those tables and solved her brother's math homework, we knew as parents that she was different and that we had to nurture her mind. Nurturing did not mean we had to make that our mission. We didn't have those luxuries. We were both working and neither of us could stay home. She did it all on her own. She went to school and we kept the house keys in her bag. She used to come, open the door, warm the food, eat it and head out to her computer classes. She was five at the time. She used to then go to her tuitions, then the club, in a rickshaw.'

I was shocked. Suhani's level of maturity at that age was a magic trick in itself. This gave me a slight sense of déjà vu about Jemimah's parents, who also sent their kids at a very young age all alone, to a different place. This made me question once again, 'Were those times safer?' At least today, we have a constant source of contact with our kids through the phone. But in those days, without any source of contact, these parents truly had some different level of faith in their kids.

Mr Shah continued, 'As parents, the thought of being scared didn't really cross our minds because we had to work. We would see our kids at night. Of course, her mind was really sharp, but it helped her with sports as well. She learned how to swim and drive a car at the age of eight. If you gave her logic and made her understand once, she could learn anything related.'

Everything they said was utterly phenomenal to me. 'I remember how she learned to swim all in a day,' said Mr Shah. 'She was all of four back then. She sat by the poolside, saw how the people moved their hands and legs, and came out comfortably. So, there was no fear. She then told the coach, "I can do this." He took her to the middle of the pool on his back, and when he left her, she did not panic. She started comfortably swimming towards me. Most of the time, people can't learn to swim because of fear. Suhani didn't fear anything,' he stated. 'After two days, she went to the deep end of the pool; she could dive from 20 feet. For her, you move your limbs, you can't drown. So, her brain worked like that and she learned things from the basics,' he explained.

'For us, pulling Suhani out of school was not a very difficult decision,' Mr Shah revealed. 'She had already tasted success with the media's writing about her—it was a lot of publicity. More than that, as parents, we knew where our child's heart was and how awkward she was in school because she was really mature for her age compared to her peers.' Mr Shah added, 'She was so focused that she didn't want to waste any time doing anything other than magic or studying. *For us, the happiness and interests of our child were important*. Suhani loved to study, so she continued to do so and read a lot of books. The only thing missing was a structure called school and a degree.' With pride, he told me, 'Her library consisted of more than 5000 books, and she loved to read and learn.'

As I write this, I wonder if people who are so passionate and work within a niche know this—do they love it from day one or is it talent that is nurtured? How are these kids so sure? I probably don't know what I want to do tomorrow, and at ages six and seven, they are sure they want to be magicians. Are they gifted or is it nurtured talent?

Suhani's first brush with magic was while watching a TV show. She was so enamoured by it. Her parents gushed, 'Each time Suhani took a leap into doing something, she was very sure and she told us the same sentence: "I can do this." When she said that, as parents, we knew she could do it and we just needed to support her. We told her, "Let's do it on a large scale if you are keen. We will make it to the Guiness World Record." We did five shows back-to-back over five days. The chief minister of Gujarat opened her debut performance. And we had many VIPs too. For five days continuously, we showed people her talent and she is now a public figure.'

Now let's get this straight. They did this on a large scale for five days back-to-back with VIPs such as the CM of Gujurat—all because their daughter was good at magic. Ask yourself, if your child comes up to you and tells you they want to showcase their talent at this level—would you have faith in them?

'*When we supported her, we didn't think, "What if she fails?." We knew that whatever she did, she would give it her 100 per cent.* That faith in her was proven right time after time, whether it was swimming, driving or studying. She instilled such confidence in us that we never felt the need to think of a backup plan.' I don't know what Suhani's parents are made of, but they really are a class apart. This explains why Suhani is the way she is.

Somewhere, when I reflect, I wonder if Suhani ever got along with her peers because she was way ahead of them. She was constantly looking up to adults and setting her goals and standards by them. *She never limited herself, thinking she was small or just a kid.*

Managing two children with different abilities and interests can be challenging for parents. Sometimes I wonder how other parents do it. Mr Shah said, 'You need to, as parents, treat both of them equally and appreciate them for their strengths. One may get more fame than the other, but when they are at home, they are just kids to their parents.'

I wouldn't lie when I say this, but I do catch myself now and then wondering if this means that one parent needs to take a step back in their careers. My husband and I have discussed this. I've seen so many mothers take a step back to accommodate their busy schedules. They may continue to work, but they do pay a price with their personal lives, personal time and health. We can't have it all.

Suhani's mother was the creative force behind the costumes, equipment and props for her tricks, while her father managed a lot of admin and marketing since that was his strength. Mr Shah continued, 'Our journey continued with shows all around Gujarat. She practised English, pursued her interest in hypnotism, wrote her book, *Unleash Your Hidden Power*, and then wrote three more books later. The books fostered her career as a speaker and while it seemed exciting early on, it dawned on her that this knowledge transfer was momentary. So, she started hosting seminars and workshops on how the mind works and all this at the age of thirteen. Her age did not play a critical role because people came for her knowledge and what she had to share.' Age was somehow never a factor in Suhani's case.

And this is proven every time I hear her speak. Like in one of her TED talks, she says, 'Our life is a buffet which has all these varieties, but we haven't tried many and we expect to find our favourite dish. We're searching endlessly for that one thing that we are passionate about without trying, how is that possible? It comes by taking and understanding the hints that come our way.'

Coming back to the conversation, Mr Shah said, 'That wasn't enough and Suhani opened a clinic in Goa. We knew our role as parents was to nurture and support Suhani. We moved to Goa as well. Suhani's fame had moved beyond Maharashtra and Gujarat, and Goa seemed like a central stage for southern and western India.'

The time between thirteen and twenty-three was very hectic, and she did very well. As the pandemic hit, offline came to a full stop and so did Suhani's work. She didn't do anything for two months and then she knew she had to survive, so she gave online shows a shot. As parents, you will see so many phases in your child's life and each phase will be challenging, but you just have to be with them.

As Suhani continues to thrive, I can't help but wonder how her parents, who hail from the Marwari culture—where women traditionally marry at twenty-five, have their first child at twenty-seven, and have a second by the age of thirty—managed to resist the cultural norm. It's a path from which few deviate. How did Suhani's parents navigate that? Suhani's father responded, '*I didn't care about society from the start. Why will it bother me now? For us, the only thing that mattered was the happiness of our child.* Feeding society and relatives with excess information is a waste of time. They questioned us when Suhani dropped out of school, fully aware we were going to stick to what we believed in and what our child wanted.'

Witnessing unparalleled success at such a young age did not deviate her from her values. She wondered why older people respected her, and if they did, how could she retain it?

Her confidence and faith in her abilities have made her witness this level of success. 'She doesn't believe that she is gifted. On the contrary, she argues we all have minds, but maybe no one got a chance, or their parents never understood or couldn't support them,' said Mr Shah.

Suhani's parents continue to believe that she has been a really mature child from the very start, 'when she ate on her own and never questioned if we didn't take her anywhere.' Her independence and confidence in herself were tremendous.

It was almost the end of this interview and Mr Shah was quick to sum it up:

'I'll tell you what the problem is: poor communication. I have observed this in today's parents. There is a lack of communication. The parents say their kids don't listen to them and the kids say their parents don't listen to them. Listen to your kids. Whether it was magic, swimming, driving or anything else at all, Suhani knew she could do it, and she knew her parents would support her. *As parents, it is our job to keep feeding that curiousity.* I know my child is different. She has come into this world with a very unique purpose.

As a parent of someone who has been there and done that, I would say:

1. Listen, understand and talk to your children.
2. First, understand them and support them. Don't force your plans on them.

Yes, we have to make them understand, but in such a way that they know we're trying to communicate something; the minute they feel we're telling them to do something according to us, that's when there's friction. Kids understand and are very sharp. They are very open-minded now, compared to before, so talk to them. *They like to listen. What they don't like are orders and then they get stubborn.* Suhani was never stubborn because we never forced her to do anything. So, communicate, understand and support them.'

Communicating, understanding and listening to your kids is what he emphasized time and again. As we started concluding, he was reminded of the 'om' Suhani always carries with her. As parents, we will always feel like 'I want to give my child more,' but when we look back, the child never thinks 'my parents didn't give me enough,' barring time, which is an exception.

We ended with a sweet message for Suhani: 'At thirty-two, all we can wish for her is love and success. Maybe after four years she will take up something else and we are sure she will do well in that as well. Her hard work will take her places.' To me, they said, 'We've always been more friends than parents to her and we would only leave you with the advice to listen to your kids. They are right and even when they sometimes do make a mistake, before getting angry, find out why they are doing what they are doing.'

If you had a huge billboard on parenting, what message would it read?

Don't care about society. Care about your child's happiness.

We asked parents on Instagram about their opinion on the following:

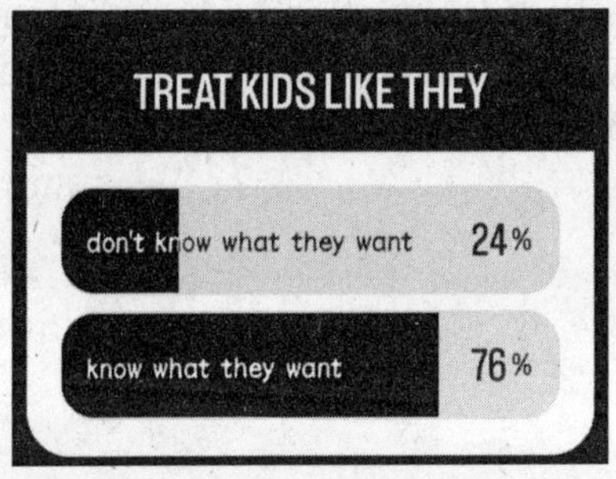

Learnings and Observations

1. Confidence and faith in your abilities will take you to success.
2. Communicating, understanding and listening to your kids at any given time is of utmost priority.
3. Don't chase qualifications, chase knowledge.
4. They like to listen. What they don't like are orders and then they get stubborn.
5. As parents, it is our job to keep feeding that curiosity.
6. Age is just a number for any profession.
7. Allow your kids to try different things and always support them in their decisions.
8. All we did as parents was provide her with logic and reasoning and never shun any questions. We explained to her everything that she wanted.
9. Always keep learning and tapping into new fields.
10. Observe your kid's abilities, strength and weakness and do what is best for them.

12

Captain Anuj Nayyar

'Ghar ke kamre mai baith ke kisiko success nahi milti [No one achieves success sitting in a room of their house].'

Instagram: @meenasatishnayyar

The late Captain Anuj Nayyar, MVC, was born in Delhi on 28 August 1975 and was an Indian army officer of the 17 Jat regiment. He was awarded the Maha Vir Chakra for exemplary valour in combat during operations in the Kargil War in 1999. *LOC Kargil* is a 2003 Indian Hindi-language historical war film based on the Kargil War fought between India and Pakistan, and actor Saif Ali Khan played the role of Captain Anuj Nayyar.

A book titled *Tiger of Drass: Capt. Anuj Nayyar, 23, Kargil Hero,* authored by Meena Nayyar (his mother) and Himmat Singh Shekhawat, and published in 2022, narrates his journey.

His father, Satish Kumar Nayyar, was a visiting professor at the Delhi School of Economics, while his mother, Meena Nayyar, worked as a librarian at the South Campus, Delhi University.

I knew I needed a parent whose child was serving in the military when I made the decision to write this book. Given the risks involved, I have to say that parents have the biggest hearts. I've often pondered how exactly these parents arm their children to face the horrors of battle and the finality of death.

I was looking for some advice and suggestions when I came across videos of Mrs Meena Nayyar. Her positive attitude and desire to live life to the fullest despite the death of her son piqued my interest in her story.

It was a cold November morning when I landed in Delhi to meet Mrs Meena Nayyar. She was one parent who stayed very forthcoming in all our conversations. When my team and I reached her house, it was decorated with the late Captain's medals, trophies and photos, and those photos made me realize what she had lost. She is so brave to give her young son to the country, and really, is there anything more devastating for a parent than to lose their child?

She fed me and my team some home-made pinnis, cutlets and the best adrak *wali* chai on that cold winter morning.

As our conversation began, the room got warmer and the cold stopped bothering me.

'Anuj grew up in a joint family with grandparents, aunts, and uncles, and his childhood was full of freedom. Being a full-time working mother, I barely had time for his brother and him. They would spend most of their days with their grandparents and Anuj was a very determined kid. If he put his mind to something, he had to get it right and learn it. His childhood toys included guns, pistols and tankers, and he would open the smallest of parts to know how they functioned. He was a very inquisitive child and while studying at an army school, he had a lot of friends whose parents were in the army.'

Mrs Nayyar continued, 'While we never thought that he would join the army because he got a form to do his MBA and got it signed by his dad, when he shared that he wanted to give it a shot, we thought, "Why not? It's a great field with great discipline. Let him do it." We didn't think much because kids that age are so volatile—one day a doctor, the next day an engineer and the day after something else. You know, parents ask their kids, "What do you want to be?." We never asked that in our house. *We always thought that what had to happen would happen and the kids would do what they wanted.*' I found this thought genius.

She went on to say, 'So firstly, we never planned anything as such, and secondly, when he brought those Army Public School forms to get them signed by his father, there was no negativity or resistance. Of course, when he was going, I got emotional. He had three places that he could go, but he chose the army.'

I always thought that only people with some army background chose the army because nothing prepares you for the curveballs of this job. The late Capt. Nayyar's grandfather fought in the 1939 war. While his grandfather had shared all those amazing stories with him, I don't think Anuj's decision was based on them. He was just so intrigued by the homes he visited and the parents he met at the army school that it drew him to the profession.

Anuj, being the elder child, was very dutiful and responsible. Even in school, he watched over his younger brother, Karan. 'Karan always thought of him as his shield and Anuj always said to me, "*Meri maa kuch bhi kar sakti* [My mom can do anything]." Even in the last letter, he wrote, "Maa, God listens to you; pray for me." In the letters that came on 22 June, before his death on 7 July, he said, "I'm your kid and without completing my purpose, I won't die. Till my last breath, I will kill every last enemy that killed our Indians." He had a high morale. When he took on a responsibility, like when Major Ritesh (a senior officer) was hurt and he got the responsibility of the platoon, at that moment he didn't see that his mom would be crying or that his fiancé would face problems, he just saw his purpose and his duty. When there are platoons behind you shouting slogans, I don't think a soldier is thinking about his family at that time. He just saw the enemy and knew he had to kill him. Anyhow, soldiers have a lot of love for the nation in them. Their hearts are filled with purpose and responsibility.'

Mrs Nayyar narrated an incident. 'As children, they were all naughty, but that naughtiness wasn't foolish. He always supported his friends. Once, his friend got into a fight and the bus was about to leave. He got off the bus and solved the problem, but when he turned to go back, the bus was gone. There were no phones at that time, and he did not have the guts to call his father from the principal's office and tell him that he missed his bus. So, without even thinking, he started walking home. He and his friend reached home at five in the evening. He knew the bus route and followed it home. He saw the end result first.'

Given that Mrs Nayyar was at the library all day and Mr Nayyar was working, I wondered where their kids really learned all their life skills and, most importantly, the skill set that Anuj needed: bravery. I think his bravery and fearlessness were largely inherited from his father.

'*For me, pursuing my career was important. We needed to. Ours was a struggling generation. We did our own work, we taught our kids on our own, we did it all. And kids observe how their parents are pulling on life. So, I think the kids observed and learned.*' They went on to reveal, 'There were no negative discussions in the house. We lived with his grandparents until Anuj was ten and when we moved into our own house, Anuj and Karan lived alone when we were out. I used to cook food and I used to tell him to always close the door after the maid, because he was only ten and Karan was five. And he used to say, "If we have to see to all this, then why do we need a maid?"' Mrs Nayyar humorously reminisced

She continued telling me, 'Even my neighbours would say, "Nothing will happen to your house because it is always open and they keep roaming about. Their friends come and go. And kids like that house, where the parents are not there, so they have a nice place to hang out." So, they could do *masti* (mischief) and watch however many pictures they wanted—there was a lot of freedom. *But Yet he knew he had freedom, but only within a certain limit.*'

This made me wonder how they made that limit so clear to the kids. 'I think it's the culture of the house itself. Like they never saw their parents fight, argue or nag. Kids observe and they know. He knew what he had to do when he came home from school and just giving them responsibility early on made all the difference. *They knew they had freedom, but they knew if they misused it, it could go away.*' This made so much sense.

She later told me some things about his academics, 'Anuj was a good student. We taught them no matter what. We got late at work, but his father would teach them and only then come out and eat or socialize with friends or family. Out of an income of Rs 800 per month, we spent Rs 50 as tuition fees only for grades nine and ten because we finally couldn't cope.'

Mrs Nayyar continued, 'But we saw the discipline in him—before his teacher would arrive for class, his books were ready, he had changed and he was ready to learn. His things were always in the right place. On the other hand, for Karan, his younger brother, there was no place to even open a book on his table. Along with all the discipline, Anuj was a very warm person and built deep connections with all his friends, whether from school, college or National Defence Academy [NDA]. They still come home and choose to stay connected with me. So he has definitely left a mark on people.'

'As a student, I feel like I have learned so much from him,' Mrs Nayyar said. 'I distinctly remember one incident where he gave out his friend's Parker pen for repair because he wanted to help his friend, but the pen got lost and his mother demanded Rs 200 instead, and we paid. The next day I saw Anuj hanging out with him again, and I said, "You are hanging out with him," and he said, "Maa, his mom is not a nice person, but that doesn't make him a bad person." For a child to have so much clarity in judgement was remarkable.'

As parents today, I think our children's backs seem heavier with every passing day because of the expectations we load onto them.

Mrs Nayyar's response made me realize that, as working parents, we have unrealistic expectations of our children. '*We never burdened our children with exam pressure or marks.* I was also aware that I was a librarian and his father worked for a small Japanese company, so we never had such big dreams or hopes. I never had any problems when it came to the education of my kids. Once, Karan got low marks and Mr Nayyar was called. While the teacher was alarmed that he had only gotten fifty marks, Karan's father told him forty-five was enough to pass. So they must've thought, "If the father is like that, then what can we say?" So we never pressured them as such. And also, one thing about being a working parent is that we had to work and the kids were free the whole day, so it's not their fault. We couldn't just come and start shouting at them.' Now that I pen down this interview, I realize that Mr and Mrs Nayyar had a very simple ideology of life—getting high marks doesn't define your child's success, but the person they grow up to become.

Next, we took the conversation more in the direction of his enlistment in the Army and when he left for his duty. Mrs Nayyar said, 'It was a different time. His first posting was in Sri Ganganagar, Rajasthan, and he'd packed his bag and was all ready. That time I got emotional and he said, "*Maa, agar aap ke jaise sab* mothers emotional *ho jayegi toh* Pakistan *iss desh ko le jayega* [Mom, if all mothers like you get emotional, Pakistan will capture this county]." That one line changed me. I realized that I was the mother of an army officer now and I had no right to bring him down. I had to become strong as I couldn't be his weakness. And I made myself strong—that was his profession. Of course, you feel bad. There are birthdays, Diwalis and other occasions when you miss your child. If I think back, the last birthday that we celebrated for Anuj was when he was in the eleventh grade. And as soon as he passed the twelfth, he went away. So, for as long as he was there after that, until 1999, I don't think we celebrated his birthday or Diwali together. These things are felt by the mothers and the family, and maybe he felt that sadness too. So, when he was posted in Sri Ganganagar, I called him on Diwali. I didn't know how things worked; I thought these officers must be celebrating together but he said, "*Mai toh apne room mai hun maa, mai kya* Diwali *manau* [I am in my room mom, how can I celebrate Diwali]?." So, you know, maybe he was missing us too. All these things are still in my head, but it's okay, things happen. Even when the youth ask me about an army veteran's life or a soldier's life, I say that they are special kids. God creates them in such a way that they go on their mission, accomplish it and leave. *Vo apna karm karke nikal jate hai* [They complete their destiny and leave]. I believe in this. For the parents—you can share your happiness with everyone, but your suffering is yours. You can share it with others for five, seven or ten minutes but not daily. In a recent interview, they asked me, on Facebook, Twitter and everywhere: 'Proud, Jay Hind.' —how do you feel? See, being proud is a different thing but the pain is way more than that. It's not that we aren't proud—we are, but you see, for parents, no one can substitute their child. When your child is gone, your life is almost over. But we learn to move on. It's not like we haven't done anything; we do a lot of things, but a parent's life changes forever. *Baccha khona koi choti cheez nahi hoti* [Losing your child is not a casual thing]. But we feel that if God made him live such a short life, and if he did, then I am proud that at least he did something with his life. Death can come anyhow, by accident or disease, but these kids have done something and gone, for a noble cause. As parents of army officers, we don't sit and grieve forever. *Grief is everywhere, but yes, we move on because work goes on, and we know life is precious and purpose is important. Impact as many lives as you can along the way.*'

I kept this entire answer compact so you, dear reader, could feel the pain and the pride when you read it. I want you to pause for a moment. Read this maybe once more. Maybe twice. I ask you this, not so that you feel sympathy for his parents but so that you understand how ugly and disheartening parenting can be sometimes, and yet you wouldn't have it any other way. They knew from the very first posting that their child might never return to them, yet they sacrificed him for the greater good of the country. I think if Mrs Nayyar said that these children are born with a different purpose, even their parents are created as one of a kind. I salute the parents of all the armed forces, for they possess strength beyond my or your imagination.

This was what inspired my next question. We prepare our kids for exams for all professions, but what do you teach someone who needs to fulfil a purpose and can lose his life too?

To this, she said, 'I think he was very focused on his purpose. When you are enrolled in the army, they train you for life. They train you in such a way that you can face any situation. When I spoke to people in his platoon after learning what Anuj did and what were the conditions in his last few days, they mentioned that Anuj was successful in his mission only because of his strategies. It took me back to his childhood, where Anuj learned the best strategies over games of volleyball. When I went back to Kargil to understand what happened at that time, it was very tough. The soldiers informed me that in the last few days, sometimes for 2–3 days at a stretch, they didn't get food. One day, someone shouted, "*Khana aa gaya!* [Food is here]!" and they threw their old rotis away so they could eat fresh food, but the food never came. So, Anuj said to one of his soldiers, obviously being deprived of food for so many days, "Let's go back and collect those rotis." They picked them up, crumbled them, added some water from the streams and made ladoos out of them. Your purpose takes over your needs and that's what these children are made of. Just be reminded that they are just twenty-two, twenty-three and twenty-four. They are really young. We crib and complain if we have to fast for a day, and here these children are fighting, carrying such heavy guns and missiles.'

As mothers, we all think our kids are exceptions. They are stars. But this level of focus, dedication, purpose and courage is special. The late Captain Anuj was awarded the Maha Vir Chakra on 6 July 1999. 'We never thought that this child, who was a normal kid, naughty as hell, like all other kids, would ever do this. We didn't think of this. I still don't understand. I think their biggest strength is the balance they have in their minds. Anuj never lost his balance in any situation. You could do anything to irritate him, but he would remain unfazed,' Mrs Nayyar said in astonishment.

We talked about some more of his qualities and she said, 'Anuj's ability to make friends and lead people was admirable. He was also very strong-willed and strong-headed. You could see it in his eyes.

'I still remember when he was about to leave. He was engaged, and if he wanted, he could have extended his leave, but he knew he needed to go.'

She then began to tell me about the heroic story, 'The day Anuj left for his mission, there was an India–Pakistan match, and secretly, as a mother, I was like, "If Pakistan wins, it's fine. At least there will be less firing on the borders." We got a call from his senior, who said, "Anuj has left for a very important mission and has said goodbye." Before he left for his mission, he even tried on his sherwani. He was about to get married in September of that year. The house was painted, the venue was booked and all the wedding preparations were done. The next morning, we got another call. I couldn't hear because his father answered the call, but all I heard was, "Did he die fighting?"' She continued, 'To the world, it was Anuj *ki body kab aa rahi hai*, but to me, it was Anuj *kab aa raha hai* [To the world, it was when's Anuj's body coming home, to me it was, when is Anuj coming home]?'

'We didn't let anyone see his body, including us. Only two people had identified that it was Anuj. For us, the last time we saw him was at the airport and that's the last memory I wanted of him.'

Then she stated sternly, 'I don't regret sending my son to the army. The thought has never come. But yes, I did wish that the government could provide them with better equipment, simple things like more bulletproof vests. For the government, it's just an army person, but for us parents, it's our son. I pacify myself today by thinking, "He came for a purpose, he completed it, and he went."'

We concluded our meeting with tears rolling down our faces as Mrs Nayyar showed me his medals and his favourite toys as a kid—guns and pistols. She told me to teach my kids the value of honesty and hard work—it always pays off. As we packed up, I asked her if she has any regrets, and she said, 'None at all, but yes, as parents, we were so time-pressed packing tiffins, filling water and doing household chores that we didn't get any time with our children. We couldn't leave our jobs because it was important for the family. *Our short holidays in Kashmir were memorable. The boys had so much fun. In spite of our limited offerings, I don't remember Anuj ever asking why we didn't have this or that. For him, his father was his hero.*'

To all the parents and kids reading this book, dream. There's no life without dreams. *'Ghar ke kamre mein baith ke kisiko success nahi milti [No one can achieve success whilst sitting in a room at home].'*

If you had a huge billboard on parenting, what message would it read?

'Allow your kids to do whatever they want.'

We asked parents on Instagram about their opinion on the following:

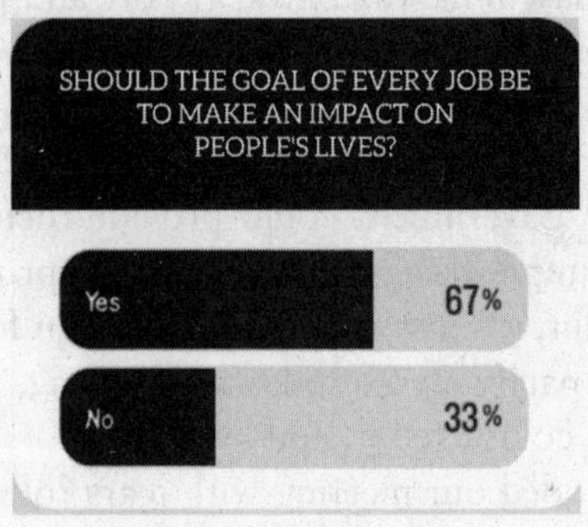

Learnings and Observations

1. Your children's biggest strength is the balance they have in their minds.
2. Your heart should be filled with purpose and responsibility, and you should be focused towards them.
3. No one can achieve success whilst sitting in a room at home.
4. Impact as many lives as you can along the way.
5. Getting high marks doesn't define your child's success, but the person they grow up to become.
6. As parents, we must accept that what has to happen will happen and the kids will do what they want.
7. Give your kids freedom, but to an extent.
8. Let your kids know about the struggles in life. They will learn the value of things.
9. Be there for them all along the way.
10. Life goes on, learn to move with the flow.

13

Shlok Srivastava

'That first brush of disappointment is very important for all kids.'

Instagram: @techburner
LinkedIn: Shlok Srivastava

Shlok Srivastava grew up in Mayur Vihar, Delhi. He has a bachelor's in technology and mechanical engineering. His first YouTube video was released on 29 September 2014. His channel, Tech Burner, focuses on making tech simple, fun and accessible while adding value to people's lives. He does mobile and car reviews, gadget reviews, how-tos and life hacks. With 3.4 million followers on Instagram and 10.5 million subscribers on YouTube, Shlok has been making videos for eight years now.

His father, Jai Srivastava, works as a divisional manager at Voltas, the home appliance company and his mother, Sadhana Srivastava, is a homemaker.

While Shlok grew up in humble surroundings and was extremely reserved as a kid—even getting him to say hello would require urging and pushing—he excelled in his academic pursuits and was a model student.

Growing up, Shlok was largely unfazed by most situations and had a very cool, collected demeanour—perhaps something he inherited from his grandfather. He executed everything with great serenity, without hurry or disarray. In my conversation with both his parents, Mrs Srivastava told me, 'Shlok and his sister once attended school together. He used to take a bath, sit on the bed and painstakingly button up each button without hurrying, while she used to hurry to get dressed so they wouldn't be late. The dissimilarity between their behaviours used to astound us.'

She continued, 'Shlok would do well in his academics and examinations. I used to pressure him to read and would reprimand him if he received even two marks less in exams. But he was quite clear—if he didn't receive those two marks, he would tell me why in detail. He was also highly curious. I used to be terrified of buying him new toys because I knew the next day, they would all be opened up and I was always right. He used to do a "post-mortem" on each of his toys, wanting to see the insides.' Laughing at this, she shared, '*Shlok has always had the quality of living in the present. Even as a child, he would only pay attention to what he was doing at a given time*. For example, if he were in class, all of his attention would be on the lesson; if he were painting, all of his attention would be on the painting; and if he were playing, his thoughts would be focused on playing. We have been aware of this about him from the beginning. His thoughts don't stray. Even when he rarely studied after school, what he had learned in class would stick in his mind. To be honest, he never seemed very interested in academics. He had extraordinary talent as an artist—he drew Pikachu and cartoon characters with such deftness that they seemed to be coming off the page. I was able to tell he wasn't interested in academics because of how well he could draw. I used to be after him for studies as a result and had informed him that I wanted him to score full marks. He also has a great memory. Even though he didn't do much studying, what he did learn was retained in his mind. Simply one revision before the test was enough.'

Mrs Srivastava was very proud when she said, 'His marks were never below ninety. He was intelligent but also creative. I didn't realize it at the time, but his education was far more significant to me than anything else.' Mr Srivastava was quick to share that Shlok always wanted to study science. 'He always said that he wanted to be a scientist. And until the tenth grade, he got good grades and enjoyed studying. But in the eleventh grade, when he took up science and joined IIT preparatory classes, he hated it. He used to tell me that those years were the worst phase of his life. There was so much competition, with kids wanting to outdo each other and being put against each other, that he dreaded that atmosphere. But he still completed his studies and did them well—he didn't leave in the middle. He didn't make it to the JEE exams and while the coaching classes were the worst two years of his life, we were all—including his teachers and Shlok himself—upset that he didn't make it.'

He continued, '*That first brush with disappointment is very important for all kids*. I had to tell him that not making it to IIT was not the end of the world. He took admission at SRM College, Chennai, to pursue a BTech, which I think changed his life. He got to pursue football, join clubs and work on his personality. It worked so well that in a span of three months, the shy kid who would never even go on stage was ready to take the mic and manage the activities at a relative's wedding reception. He pretty much controlled the next three hours of the show, to everyone's surprise.'

Mrs Srivastava explained, 'At college, Shlok made a friend in Ritvik Mishra, who really pushed him a lot. I think joining all the clubs, playing sports and doing what he loved blew the steam off, so he got back to living the life he loved. The pressure on a child between the ages of fifteen and nineteen is too high in our country. They are dealing with their own bodies, hormones and the pressure to constantly perform. He would study rigorously for seven days a week without a whimper, but that is also true for our Indian kids, who just succumb to everything because we've never taught them to say no.'

Mrs Srivastava then reminisced, 'Our kids listen to us out of respect, and we, as parents, use that to our advantage. He loved watching a show, and every afternoon they would all sleep next to me and sneak out when their favourite show, Pikachu, would come on TV. I would be napping and they would have found their way to the nearest TV.'

She continued, 'But when I look back, I feel I pressured him a lot for his studies. He studied well, but later I started realizing I was pressuring him. So, when they used to come from school at 2 p.m., I used to give them food and then forcibly make them sleep with me so that they could be energized again to study in the evenings. That Pikachu show used to play at 5 p.m. and he was very fond of it. So, when I would be fast asleep, they both would get out of bed and watch that programme. It lasted for half an hour. Then, when I would get up and see that both weren't beside me, my younger daughter, who was very smart, would come back to the bed as soon as she saw that I was awake, but

Shlok was very innocent. He was naive and honest. There was no malice at all.'

Shlok must've really loved Pikachu because, as Mrs Srivastava told me, 'Once, when our house was getting renovated, I found a bag filled with those Pikachu collectibles. He had a friend in the neighbourhood who was his age. So, he used to go play cricket with him in his house. They would also trade cards, and because we came from modest backgrounds, he didn't have many, so he would trade his one card for many smaller ones. One day he took some extra cards, intentionally or not, from a child, and that child came back to ask for them. I thought he was stealing or being dishonest, so I got furious and gave him a tight slap. He was just so upset that day—someone as shy as Shlok suddenly screamed, "Why did you hit me?" This was the first time he raised his voice and the first time he talked back. He left the house, saying, "I'm leaving the house." Then I realized that our kids had grown up.'

She then went on to say, '*As parents, when they are small, we think we can control them, but that day I realized they had grown up*. He said it so innocently that I almost felt like laughing, but inside I was filled with regret. When I went to see him through the window, he was standing there in his vest as he had removed his shirt and said, "Take this away as well." *As parents, we must also have the courage to say sorry when we make mistakes*. I did just that. I went out, hugged him, and apologized.'

There are so many times we hurt and upset our kids too. We feel that, as parents, we have the upper hand and can act however we want. But when we do hurt them, do we have the courage to accept it and apologize?

'I think one of the toughest phases of his life was the one where he studied for IIT and didn't clear it. We had all put so much pressure on him and those three years were so tough that the disappointment was even harder. This is the time when the family really needs to chip in. Nobody in our family made him feel even once that he didn't make it. *Also, our kids don't feel bad for all the effort alone—they also carry the baggage of all the money that is spent behind these training sessions. They are so mature and aware of our situations that they feel bad that the investment didn't go as planned. As people growing up in a middle-class joint family, our noes are more than our yeses. Sometimes I feel our kids ask often because they know one out of ten things will be granted.* I now look back and feel that he really wanted a cycle, and that is the least I could have bought him, but I delayed it for a really long time.' This hit me hard. It was like the unsaid things were loud all of a sudden.

She continued, 'In post-graduation, when all the kids were registering for final placements, Shlok had not registered. He didn't tell us, but one of his friends did. We were shocked. We tried to tell him to, but he didn't. When he came back for the holidays, I asked him again. "Why don't you do this? We need you to earn money; your father and grandfather are working such long hours." He heard me, went for an interview and got accepted, but he refused the job immediately. He sat us down and said, "*Maa main job nahin karna chahta, main apna khud ka kuch karna chahta hoon* [Mom, I don't want to do a job; I want to do something on my own]." He explained to us very clearly what he wanted to do and even though we had a limited understanding of YouTube, we wanted to give him that chance. All he asked was for 1000 days. He promised his father that if he was not successful after those 1000 days, he would take up a job. In any middle-class family, every pair of hands is extra help, both physically and financially, and for parents to support that on the premise that they could possibly work for another ten years, why not let the child experiment? For our family, it is a big deal, but we thought everyone deserves that one chance.'

I think parents must also trust their kids when they have so much clarity.

We talked a little more about how he got into this field and how he learned editing and everything else required. 'Shlok's editing skills were shaped when he was in school in grade 8. His *mama* [maternal uncle] had bought him a laptop and he would spend hours editing videos and honing his editing skills. With a Mahanagar Telephone Nigam Limited [MTNL] connection, it would take hours, and I would always wonder if he was watching porn or doing something else entirely. From then on, he would edit all the projects of his seniors in the hostel and that's where he kept sharpening his skills. His mind and focus were extremely sharp. He could have blown the money he got from editing on the wrong things, but he bought a microphone and some software.'

Mrs Srivastava explained, 'Shlok knew that money was never flowing freely at home and he provided for everything that he wanted to do. He didn't borrow a penny from us. College was very tough on him; the ragging was so intense that he told us much later, thinking we would be worried.'

This is something that I couldn't believe at first. Knowing Shlok the way he is today, the thought that this confident kid could have been mentally broken down once, never even crossed my mind. I asked Mrs Srivastava to tell me about this. 'He was made fun of all the time because he was soft-spoken. It hurt him so much that he decided to do something about it. He joined the drama club in college. He would send me videos of him speaking. He was always creative, be it in kathak, drawing or athletics. Sports and art were his strengths and stress-busters that helped him unwind.'

All the ragging could've made this boy lose all hope and confidence. But he made that very fact a rock to build his personality on. 'We think that college shaped him so much. He designed the covers of magazines and made all the posters for all the functions. He even set up a printing and cutting machine for the eunuch community around his college to empower them with employment,' she revealed with pride.

So much of who we are is shaped in our childhood. Whenever Shlok got any certificates in school, they always accidentally gave the prize to another child and apologized later. 'This happened three times. It really upset him. Finally, once in a table competition where he stood third, they called another child for the prize distribution and that upset him so much that he took a pair of scissors and cut the certificate in half,' she exclaimed.

She then added, 'For so long, he felt like "I am shy and can't speak, which is why they aren't calling me on stage," that he knew he had to work on it. He also knew very early on that if he wanted to do all that he is doing now [sports, editing and other work] that he would have no time to study, so he would be very focused in class. His friends would wonder how he got good marks when he used to be doing everything else the whole day and spent time playing football. They would take turns to check if Shlok was studying in the middle of the night, but he would be sleeping soundly so he could focus in class and on his videos.'

Mrs Srivastava told me about one of Shlok's friends' fathers, who was a businessman and upon seeing him once had said, 'Shlok has a business mindset and he will do business.'

As parents, sometimes, even if we want to give our kids that chance, the pressure of society kicks in and we fall into the comparison trap. It's a trap that convinces you that your child should keep chasing till they reach your desired goal. Even though that goalpost isn't fixed, and keeps moving. But Shlok's mother considers herself lucky that neither she nor her family succumbed to those pressures of comparison. What if he failed? Who hasn't failed?

His parents told me, '*Trusting Shlok wasn't a one-day, one-month phenomenon. It was a trust that he developed over such a long period of time.* Whether it was the calm and composure of doing things calmly even if the whole world was screaming, "We are getting late," editing videos during his BTech to learn or spending his money on buying equipment for his editing and furthering his passion. Even when he decided not to apply for placements, there was no screaming or shouting. It was his ability to stay calm and convince us. My biggest fear as a parent was that Shlok is shy and doesn't communicate or speak well, but it was also put to rest when he took that challenge in college. When that was achieved, I knew he would do well in life. We didn't know much about YouTube, but people around us said he spoke well and anyone who speaks well will get a job.'

When you give your child a chance, don't look at them with those eyes that are constantly seeking results every single day. Be patient and support them unconditionally. In those 1000 days, Shlok was uploading some videos and gradually his views were increasing, according to his mother.

I wanted to know more about the beginning years of his channel. 'Initially, when he started, he made videos on things that his friends found difficult. How to download a certain app or do really simple things in the tech space,' said Mrs Srivastava. 'The first two years saw his subscribers grow from 500 to 2000. We saw his hustle and hard work through those years. He gave it his all. He was very confident that it would work. He would tell us, "See, my followers will grow like that and by this date I will have so many subscribers." I never doubted my son, not once. I won't lie—there was fear, for which I prayed every single day, but there was no doubt at all. *I think as parents, we are never scared of our children's feelings. We just don't want them to be hurt, and sometimes these small failures or disappointments cause pain, and we want to shield our children from that.*' This was a hard truth.

Mrs Srivastava went on to tell me about the thoughts she had while she was pregnant. 'As women, mothers and daughters-in law, we also get angry, but unfortunately, we can't express it, and I do believe that when we are pregnant, what we do is contributing to how our child shapes up to be. When I was pregnant with Shlok, I was angry with a lot of things happening around me, but I could never express it publicly, so I would go read and chant the 'Ramcharitmanas' till I fell asleep, and when I woke up, the anger would have vanished. This, I believe, had a huge calming effect, as did the ability to absorb pressure, respond, and not react. It shows in the grit that Shlok has in him today. Nothing at all can shake him.'

She further spoke about Shlok's values, 'I would go shopping with him to Chandni Chowk to get all the props and mics that he needed for his videos on a budget. He never borrowed a penny. I think the breaking point was when Google asked him to do some work. I thought, "Wow, a company like Google is working with him." He sat me down and asked, "Google *ke liye kaam karna ya* Google *ke saath kaam karna, aapko kya zyada acha lagega* [What would you like more? Me working as a Google employee or as a Google partner]?" That's when we also learned a lesson as parents.'

His parents said with pride, 'After that, there was no looking back. He achieved that silver button as he planned. Those 1000 days have now become a few years and it has changed the way our family lives, works and stays.'

Mrs Srivastava then laughed as she complained about how he still keeps his room a mess and would still prefer to be fed by her when he is busy. Here is where I also learned that his favourite food item is the paratha. Mr Srivastava said, 'If we would've forced Shlok to get a job then, we would not have this Shlok today.' Mrs Srivastava added, 'There are some things you need to instil in them from childhood. Like I told him once that moms are gifted by God with one extra eye, so we can see everything, and he said, "*Sachi mummy, aapko sab pata hai* [Really, mom, you know everything]?" And from that day on, he never lied to me.'

She then told me about Shlok's one quality—in whatever he wants, he wants the best and he'll work hard for it. She also revealed one piece of advice she gave Shlok that has really sunk into his subconscious. She said, '*When negativity comes, it hits you from all directions. How you handle yourself in that moment defines how you achieve success.*'

We ended with some messages for Shlok from his parents. Mrs Srivastava hoped that he continues to do good work, which he is doing and of which she is proud, and Mr Srivastava's request is for him to manage time well and give time to the people he loves.'

If you had a huge billboard on parenting, what message would it read?

Give your child a certain amount of time to do what they want. Give them a chance to pursue their passion.

We asked parents on Instagram about their opinion on the following:

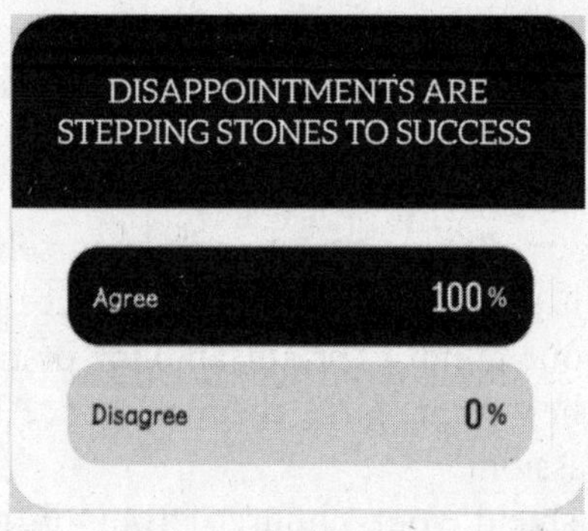

Learnings and Observations

1. Whenever life gets tough, do the things that you like and they will be like stress-busters for you.
2. One should concentrate on what one is doing and never get distracted.
3. One should learn to have a calm and cool demeanour in all situations.
4. When you give your child a chance, don't look at them with eyes that are constantly seeking results every single day.
5. When negativity comes, it hits you from all directions. How you handle yourself in that moment defines how you achieve success.
6. Give your child a certain amount of time to do what they want. Give them a chance to pursue their passion.
7. Don't shield your children from difficulties or pain. Let them experience all types of situations.
8. Trust your child's intuition and passion.
9. Learn to turn your weakest points into your strongest points.
10. Set targets and work hard to achieve them.

14

Ujjwal Chaurasia

'You have to listen to what they want. And you have to take risks—I did. And you must give them a chance to do what they want. Because if you don't, then you will be the reason why they'll regret some things in their lives.'

Instagram: @ujjwalgamer and @techno_gamerz

Ujjwal Chaurasia is one of the most famous gamers in India. He is Delhi-based and has three YouTube channels and they, combined, have a subscriber count of 480 lakh. One of his Instagram handles, Techno Gamerz, has 3.35 crore subscribers. He was announced as the 'Best Gaming Creator' at the Streamy Awards in 2020 and in 2021, was featured in the *Forbes India*'s 30 Under 30 list.

His mother, Usha Chaurasia, is a homemaker, and his father, Vijay Chaurasia, is a shopkeeper.

Ujjwal's inclusion in the book was inspired by the many worried mothers whose children aspire to be gamers like Ujjwal. His name popped into my head when I was researching role models or careers for my book—careers that exist that we, as parents, don't understand the value of.

Ujjwal was one of two sons born into a middle-class family. He grew up in Delhi with his mother, who ran a small boutique, and his father, who ran a small shop.

From a very young age, Ujjwal loved sports. Growing up, he signed up for classes in every conceivable sport and activity, from cricket to football to yoga. Ujjwal's mother, Mrs Chaurasia, recalled how before smartphones were commonplace, the family had a small phone, and her son would steal anyone's phone and start playing games, leaving her out of the loop. 'I still remember, it was maybe 2010. He was probably twelve or thirteen years old and we were in the village when he was playing a game and he uploaded it on YouTube.'

She continued, 'He would go up to the terrace or hide somewhere and play on the phone. He would finish his studies though, because he knew if that wasn't done, I would get angry. Ujjwal was obsessed with cars, especially the remote-controlled ones. He possibly studied until grade 11 only because he was quite sure that if he didn't do well, he wouldn't get a smartphone. I do feel a large part of Ujjwal being an all-rounder was the fact that I spent a lot of time with the kids. I would teach them while running the boutique. Comparing the two kids was not even an option because they were both so good. While my elder son was into graphics and editing, Ujjwal continued to pursue his gaming career.'

Mrs Chaurasia stated, '*As a middle-class family, education was the only way we could improve our lives.* I didn't have the option to study because of family restrictions and the situation at the time, but I knew the importance of education and how it could change our lives. *In spite of not being very educated myself, my kids loved me because I tried and taught them every subject.*' This reminded me of the times when my mom, who had studied in a Hindi-medium school till grade 10, would sit with us every single day and make notes and do everything possible. She even learned English while teaching us every day.

Mrs Chaurasia then told me about her elder son being highly supportive of Ujjwal's career choice. 'When Ujjwal decided to pursue gaming, my elder son was extremely supportive. He saw his brother uploading his gaming videos and getting several views, and would encourage him. Ujjwal's father was busy providing, as is usually the case in most middle-class families, but we were very clear that he still needed to continue his studies on the side. By the time he was sixteen and studying for grade 12, he was getting a good number of views on his videos.' Ujjwal finished grade 11 and requested his parents to give him one year to build a career on YouTube. She added, 'Given that I had seen the number of views he was getting, we agreed.'

In the middle of the interview, my mind races and I wonder how I would have reacted ten years ago if my kids told me they wanted to be gamers. I think of how my parents reacted when I told them I wanted to quit my job as head of marketing for an international fashion brand to start a parenting platform—a concept as alien as can be.

Our conversation continued. 'Ujjwal was a hard-working child and I think it was probably easier that he wasn't starting his journey from scratch after grade 12. He already had the views. I also believe that the younger ones have it easier. I still remember, Ankit, my elder son, told me that there were great prospects in gaming and that I should just let Ujjwal pursue it. Also, people like us don't have too much to lose. *Humare paas jitna hai, utne mein chala sakte hain* [We can make do with whatever we have], for us, success means very linear progress and money.'

Our problem as parents is that we prefer to judge our kids instead of trying to add value to what they are doing or understand the landscape they are a part of.

She confessed, 'Yes, I absolutely felt all this. He would be sitting in front of the computer the whole day. I would ask myself, "What will he do and how will he do it? Is this going to work?" So, even though I had never watched YouTube before, I started to use it to see his gaming videos and then all his interviews. Then I felt relieved and was like, "*Ab theek hai* [It's fine now]." Time went by and that one year became two. He was already successful by then so we didn't bother. *At the end of the day, the kids will always follow their hearts and their passion, and you will not be able to stop them no matter what.* I would tell parents to be happy with what their kids are doing and put their ego aside. We always find happiness when our kids listen to us. *Start finding joy in what they do and where they find joy.* At one point, we tried to get them both to join their dad's small shop and do business, but they were clear that it was not what they wanted to do. They were not enthusiastic about it. *As parents, we wonder why they can't understand and see a longer-term vision, but you see, they aren't thinking through their heads but with their hearts.*' How wonderful and true. I guess, as parents, we worry so much about what our kids will do with their lives that we forget it's their lives, not ours.

'The one quality that I would attribute Ujjwal's success to is his determination to be the best at whatever he does.

Play, study or do sports—he wants to do them all and be the best at them,' Mrs Chaurasia said with pride.

'Today, when people say they want to be like Ujjwal, I tell them "To be Ujjwal, you have to work as hard as Ujjwal." Sometimes it takes him whole nights to finish editing. Sometimes he gets angry because he doesn't sleep or eat on time. But I take it as part of the job. His passion for sports and cricket is still there, but he can't give it as much time. *What also worked well for us was my husband's faith in me and that I wouldn't allow anything that wasn't right for the kids, and my children's ability to trust that their mom wished well for them.*' We need to take this into account. Sometimes, we must trust the parent who has the steering wheel of our child's life completely.

'Also, in our times, children respected their parents; we raised our hands very rarely, but there was this boundary of respect.' She continued, 'As parents, you do wonder what is happening with your own kids when you look at other kids, but you realize that each time you meet someone, self-doubt creeps in. But you have to trust the kids. I would pacify myself by thinking that sometimes you don't get good jobs even after being engineers and management students, so why am I getting so disturbed about this?'

'Maybe my responses would have been different if Ujjwal was the eldest son. Maybe he wouldn't have obtained the permission he did so easily. Not because I didn't trust him, but because our family needed that additional income,' she confessed.

Also, success is such a game changer. People change when they see you as successful. Both your kids see different heights of success, but to you as a parent, they are your kids, and their success is what the world sees. Mrs Chaurasia went on, 'As a parent, you treat them both equally and for the qualities they possess. The kids always think the mother has a favourite. Ujjwal always thought I loved his elder brother more.' Ujjwal was the outlier and as outliers, they may or may not be the favourites because they are always going against the tide. Each time. And so, they might experience a little more friction than the other child.

She added, 'Today, when Ujjwal is twenty and he has seen so much success, I still tell him to behave like he is just starting out. His success is just 5–6 years old, but his hard work through the years is beyond that. *If your head is firmly grounded, success will last much longer.*'

She also stressed how some mothers have complained to her that it's because of Ujjwal that their kids don't study, and she has a befitting answer for them: 'Children and parents need to understand—Ujjwal started with a borrowed mobile phone, a Nokia 5. He started and made what he could with what he had as opposed to all the others who had so much. When you come from scarcity, your hunger is so much greater than when you come from abundance. Also, the will to make it work. Our kids in middle-class families are also responsible. They have seen the struggles, so they know if it doesn't work, they will have to change their path. Therefore, they go above and beyond to make it happen. To the parents who say, "*Apka beta bigad raha hai bacho ko* [Your son is spoiling our kids]." Ujjwal is not spoiling them; you are refusing to accept what your children love doing. If your children want to be gamers, don't go blindly into it. Ask them and keep tracking their progress.'

She then told me more about how his journey to gaming began. 'When Ujjwal started gaming, we had one computer in the house, and we lived in a joint family, so he didn't have one of his own, and because he was the youngest, he would rarely get his turn or often get it last. I don't remember

Ujjwal ever being mean or saying mean things like "I can't do this because we don't have a computer." He built his career with his brother's mobile phone. Even when some videos didn't do well, he never spoke about them, even though I knew everything.'

Mrs Chaurasia told me, 'As parents, we always look back and have regrets or feel like we made mistakes, but I don't have those regrets or thoughts because we did the best we could. We couldn't have afforded or done more than what we did. I had to work, run the boutique and do household work, but nothing came before my kids. They were my first priority. I would look after them when they came from school, review their homework and make sure it was correct. Simple things build lifelong discipline. I remember Ujjwal didn't have great handwriting, and I would erase it and make him rewrite it. This instilled the value of perfection in him.'

This is something I will never stop stressing about—teaching values to kids when they are young. We may think that these concepts are too heavy for them but we may be wrong. Kids are so smart, especially nowadays, that if taught well and taught enough, all these values can be easily nourished within them. Another thing we dismiss in parenting is 'actions speak louder than words.' Mrs Chaurasia proved my point when she said, '*Also, my kids have seen us work really hard. So they know what hard work is. I can't think of one day, one moment or one golden hour where we taught them values and life. It's something they learned through our hustle.* They knew the importance of finishing things because there were rules, and they saw that even though I could barely teach them, I would set their papers and help them with exams.'

I asked her for a piece of advice she had for this generation of parents, and she promptly replied, 'If I had to share that one piece of advice with parents of this generation, I would say, *you can't just keep giving orders and wanting them to do as you please. Listen to their thoughts and what they want. And you have to take risks. I did. You must give them a chance to do what they want. Because if you don't, then you will be the reason why they'll regret some things in their lives.* Now they wanted time, which I gave them, and they became successful. Even if they hadn't been successful, they are kids after all, so it's okay.'

She added, 'Don't keep reminding them of their mistakes in the past. At an age where he could have lost track of his goals, I didn't let him go out much with all the gully boys because I thought he would get spoiled. He would shout and complain, but maybe because he didn't go out much, he would spend that much more time on his games. Give your children what they ask for sometimes, but not always, so they know the value of it.'

The conversation ended with Mrs Chaurasia sharing a few of Ujjwal's favourites, like his favourite food, which is dal makhani and chole bhature; his favourite game, GTA 5; and his best friend Saurabh. I asked her about her favourite travel destinations, and she said, 'Honestly, we haven't travelled in so many years. He loves his family, especially his Nani (maternal grandmother).' She ended by saying, 'He has the ability to attract everyone to him. He needs me around. Even when he comes down and can't see me, he will search for me and come and hug me.'

My obvious concluding question was, 'What are your fears as a parent when your child has seen success at such a young age?' She was honest. 'It is scary. I pray for him, but I do get scared too. I just reassure myself that everything will be fine. That's all I can do.'

If you had a huge billboard on parenting, what message would it read?

Please listen to your kids.

We asked parents on Instagram about their opinion on the following:

Learnings and Observations

1. You should have trust in your kids no matter what.
2. Even if you are a working parent and busy, your first priority should always be your kids.
3. You should value perfection.
4. Don't keep reminding them of their mistakes in the past.
5. If your head is firmly grounded, success will last much longer.
6. You must give them a chance to do what they want.
7. There isn't a day, a moment, or a golden hour where we teach them the values of life. It's something they learn through our hustle.
8. Parents need to trust each other's parenting too.

15

Pooja Dhingra

'Sometimes your kids will lose their path, and you have to hold their hand and help them find it.'

Instagram: @poojadhingra
LinkedIn: Pooja Dhingra
Website: www.le15.com

Pooja Dhingra is an Indian pastry chef and businesswoman. She opened India's first macaron store and is the owner of the bakery chain, Le15 Patisserie. She featured in *Forbes India*'s 30 Under 30 achievers' list for 2014 and the *Forbes* 30 Under 30 Asia list.

The Big Book of Treats was her first book and won second place at the Gourmand World Cookbook Award in 2015. Her other books are *The Wholesome Kitchen*, *Le15 Café Cookbook*, *Bake at Home* and the bestseller, *Can't Believe It's Eggless*.

Pooja's father, Jaikishan Dhingra, is a chef, and her mother, Seema Dhingra, is a therapist and healer.

Pooja has a very affable and approachable personality. She seems to continue to have that girl next door vibe and a humble grounding. She has built a fabulous brand while also sharing her vulnerabilities with her audience.

Having Pooja's parents as part of the book emerged from me knowing her parents, who are humble and have been her grounding force forever.

Their ability to respect and acknowledge people—powerful or regular, young or old, is what draws people to them. We began our interview by acknowledging the fact that they are now known as Pooja's parents everywhere they go. 'How did that feel?'

'*As parents, when people know you for your child, it always feels great and makes you feel proud*,' confessed Mrs Dhingra with a huge smile.

I asked them a little bit about her growing up years, a little bit about their background—'What was life like back when she was a child?' Mr Dhingra started, 'Pooja grew up in a business family, with her grandfather in the freight forwarding business. She saw her father, that is me, as a restaurant owner who opened multiple highway restaurants that, even though they were very successful, saw partner disputes, legal issues, and permissions issues. We also had a plastic goods manufacturing business. So, Pooja grew around business conversations and the volatility of the F&B business.' Her mother chose to stay home up until recently, before she got interested in reiki and tarot reading, and while initially she was doing it only for friends and family, Pooja pushed her to make a brand out of it and open her own Shopify store.

Mrs Dhingra added, 'I never regretted not having a career and watching over my kids because I came from a family where I saw my mom watching her kids and all my aunts were at home; no one really was working, so maybe I didn't see it as something I wanted to do.'

'Choosing to go to a culinary school in Switzerland and pursue this field of F&B is something that the kids did,' they informed. One thing that was clear to me was that their love for food was a result of the environment around them which could've influenced their decision to choose this field. 'There was absolutely no pressure at all,' Mrs Dhingra was quick to add. 'We are a Punjabi family and food is the centre of all conversations.'

She then went on to tell me about Pooja's childhood, 'I think when Pooja was small, there was no career in being a pastry chef, but she loved to play designer. She had all these fabrics kept in a bag, and she would just put them all together on a board and keep creating something. She loved designing. She was good with her studies, maybe not in the top ten in class, but that was good because she was okay with that.'

Mrs Dhingra continued, 'But when she came back from Switzerland and decided she wanted to go to Paris to get her diploma, we weren't surprised. We just knew that no matter what she did, she would give it her best. She was and is a very hard-working and diligent child.'

Even in her school days, Pooja's parents never pressured her on marks or grades but always reaffirmed, '*Do whatever is your best and up to your potential.*'

'Growing up, there were rules about no late nights, being back at 10 p.m. and, of course, no sleepovers. She listened to us. She was never a rebel. Maybe that made it easy for us to give her permission for whatever else she wanted to do,' expressed Mrs Dhingra.

'For us, Pooja is a child who has carved her own path way before it all actually shaped out. She was very clear that she wanted to go to Switzerland. She said, "Please send me to a camp or some school." That's really all she asked us for. Even when she came back, she wrote in a blog that she started, about her Swiss experience and what she wanted to do. She wanted a specialized kitchen: "I want so many outlets." She had written it all out twelve years ago. It's like she thought about it and worked towards it.'

Mrs Dhingra then informed me, 'After twelfth grade, she wanted to go to college, but she did not get through Government Law College (GLC), so she went to another college, and honestly, she wasn't happy there. Seeing her unhappy, we told her, "Take a break and see what you want to do." Around the same time, we saw an ad in the paper about a Swiss representative coming to India, so we went there and spoke to him. Both Pooja and her brother Varun were keen on going and we dropped them off at the Cesar Ritz boarding school.'

She added, 'I distinctly remember when we reached the college and Pooja told me, "Mom, pinch me, pinch me. Am I really here?" She was just eighteen. Maybe sending her at eighteen was slightly easier for us because her brother was there with her, but when she did her internships, she was alone. It was okay. *We had a lot of confidence in her, even as a child.*' From a mom who had rules about a 10 p.m. curfew to sending her daughter all alone to Switzerland, what comforted her was her trust, upbringing and the faith she had in her kids.

I often wonder, as a parent, how it is to send your kids away at eighteen and what really prepares them for the life ahead? To this, Mrs Dhingra said, 'Everything that you've done in the last eighteen years prepares them for the next eighteen, which are just as important. Don't take those years for granted.' She added, '*Parents sometimes think,*

"How will we survive without our kids?" Don't be selfish and scared for yourself. The question to ask is, "Will she be happy? Is this right for her?"

'I remember when she was alone in Paris—I told her to stay connected and, if there was any problem, we said, "*Just remember, we are always there to support you, come what may.*"'

Pooja achieved success at a very young age and I wondered what her parents did to make sure she stayed grounded. They replied, 'Honestly, it's her inherent nature. There's nothing that we can do about it. That's who she is. Her upbringing was very normal, with regular, strict parents, deadlines and restrictions. Of course, they had complete freedom in terms of what they wanted to study. But there was no reason for her to not have her head on her shoulders. We also think that when your children are focused, hard-working and respectful to everyone, they will be just like Pooja is. Simple.'

As we continued our discussion, I wanted them to answer, 'What is it that they want Pooja to work on?' and Mrs Dhingra was quick to respond, 'She needs to find someone for herself. I wouldn't want to wish for anything else. She is such a good child.' I sensed worry in her mother's eyes about Pooja finding a partner now. As parents, what bothers our children becomes our subconscious worry too.'

'As a parent, when your child wins many accolades, like when Pooja was featured in *Forbes* 30 Under 30, do you acknowledge it or be very low-key about it?' They shared, '*Always give your children credit where it's due.*' I wondered, 'How it is for parents who have two kids and one sees public admiration and the other doesn't. Does it bother the other child?' With ease, they replied, 'As parents, you have to appreciate each child for who they are, not how the world sees them.' As parents of two or more kids, this will resonate with you, because somewhere we have all erred in underplaying one child's environment or achievements.

Mrs Dhingra shared, '*Also, as parents, just insulate yourself from what the world is saying, especially in today's times.* Back in the day, people asked us, "Why did you send a girl for higher education abroad?" and we were like, "How can we differentiate something like education between children?"'

When I ask them about the qualities they believe have brought Pooja to where she is today, they both believe it's her compassion, her being grateful for everything she has and her hard work.

Mrs Dhingra told me, 'I still remember when we would go to meet them in Switzerland. When they reached our hotel room in a small village, their legs would be shaking—they had cramps because they had been standing the whole day at school. Even today, giving up all your work, working 24/7 and standing for hours in the kitchen doesn't come easy, but this girl has done it. Also, she is so creative—look at her menus and see how much effort she puts into designing them. It doesn't end with creating it. If it doesn't work, that is also tough to deal with.'

I was curious about what they say to Pooja when she's having a bad day. Mrs Dhingra was happy to share, 'There are moments when your children will tell you, "I am tired and I can't do it." Where the situation tests them so much that it pains you. *In those moments, as parents, you must encourage them but also let them know the real picture. You are your child's mirror. You have to let them make their choices because they are the ones who need to live by those choices.* When she decided to close the cafe, we told her, "It's your baby. You have to decide what you want." As parents, they need to know that you are their shadow, but that shadow cannot make their choices—it's only going to be there for them. Seeing her father as an entrepreneur in the F&B business has, I am sure, helped Pooja make some of those choices wisely. Mr Dhingra added, '*I always tell my kids that losses and businesses are synonymous with each other. Don't cry over them. If you are in business, losses and gains are part of it.* So you have to take it all in and move on. Don't brood over it and don't hold on. If you do that, you will not be able to move ahead.'

I then asked them, 'What is the one piece of parenting advice you would give to other parents?' Their answer came from very confident and content parents. '*Allow your kids to bloom into whatever they have the talent and potential for. Success cannot be guaranteed, but happiness can be.* We cannot taint their vision by saying that this is good, bad, right or wrong. We have to let them fend for themselves.'

Mrs Dhingra added, 'Our definition of success is to be grounded, humble and still grow, and I think that's what she has imbibed.'

'*As parents, we didn't try to be their friends. They knew we were all cool, but we had rules, and we are their parents. There have to be certain boundaries to have a successful parent–child relationship.* Also, as a young mother, I have grown up with them. My whole transformation journey was with them. I was a strict mother. Maybe I was controlling, but I was always there for them and it continued to be that way. I think what we built over those years has made us emotionally very strong and close as a family. She shares everything that she wants with us and we give her that unconditional support. *As parents, your relationship with your children will evolve.* You will be strict and a disciplinarian at first, and you will ease up as they grow older. You realize that it will work and you too are tired of the rules and discipline yourself by then. *You also realize while you are parenting that in some things or situations, your parents had an orthodox mindset,*' explained Mrs Dhingra. Mr Dhingra remarks how his parents used to beat him, but over the years he realized that wasn't right and he didn't like that feeling.

Pooja shares a lot about herself, where she is and her life in her Instagram Stories—I inquired if they ever question why. 'Nope, we never do that,' said Mrs Dhingra, without missing a beat. I always wonder if success and failure are both public, especially today with social media and trolls. How do we really prepare our children for what we have never dealt with? As parents, we want to shield them from it. I asked them about their opinions, and they replied, '*Keep that communication going. When they know you are there unconditionally and without any judgement, they will connect with you.* Even if she had her ups and downs, now she knows. She always calls; she'll talk and we kind of manage it by talking. She is running her business; she is living alone and I cannot hold her hand anymore. Yes, I can give her a hand when she falls, but she needs to learn that it's a part of life, and to know that doesn't mean that's who you are, right? It happens. Life is like that sometimes. There will be highs and lows.'

Mrs Dhingra continued, 'Parents are worriers; whether you are four or forty-one, they will always worry about you. The worries, of course, change. Today, it's about safety, health, finding the right partner and settling down. They are no longer day-to-day worries. There is just trust in the divine, right? When they came back from Switzerland, we realized that they had stayed there alone. What was I worrying about now? Yes, of course, one always worries over their safety, but I just prayed each night and surrendered their safety to the Lord, realizing that was the best for our relationship. I cannot be so hyper and nagging. That is not who I am. That is not what my kids want me to be. They will not like that.'

I asked her about any disagreements they have had and Mrs Dhingra shared, 'As a parent, you will also disagree on many things. I remember this one time when Pooja had to do her internship and Varun, her brother, was coming back with us. Her father was reluctant to leave her behind and she had a bad experience. So, when she had to go to Paris alone, obviously he was reluctant, but we convinced him. *I also think disagreements arise when your value systems or how you have been brought up are different.* For us, our value systems were alike, so it didn't lead to too many disagreements. As a parent, you will also look back and have regrets; maybe mine are that I was strict and hyper, but nothing beyond that.'

Mrs Dhingra told me, 'Pooja has tremendous clarity and she knows what she wants in her life. She reaches out to both of us for different reasons. Him, more for business, like government licences, and me, it's more to deal with emotional issues.'

I got to know that Pooja's favourite food is varan bhat, given that her grandma was from the Konkan region.

'Also, I have stopped calling my kids, at best we text on WhatsApp: "When are you coming home?" I understand that they are busy; they have their lives and I have mine. Also, now they call me. I know she will call me,' Mrs Dhingra said with confidence.

They went on to tell me, 'We know that Pooja will be successful in whatever she is doing, with or without Le15. She is so focused and hard-working. I still remember when she came back at twenty-three and said, "I want to start this." We helped her with kitchen space, people, permissions and outlet space. I still remember when she hired her first set of people and told them, "We have to sweep the floor." All of them were looking at each other. So she took the mop and started, and then everyone was like, "No, ma'am, we'll do it." So she didn't have any thought like "*main yeh nahi karungi* [I won't do this work]" or anything. She used to do everything in the kitchen. She is a very hard-working human. She is creative. She's very good with her people, but where work is concerned, she doesn't want any laid-back attitudes. If you are getting everything, then you have to put in that much effort. She wants everything to be at a certain level. So, if the workers are not doing it, she doesn't bear it. She's a perfectionist, like Aamir Khan.'

There is a price we all pay for our success and maybe Pooja's price has been time. Mrs Dhingra shared, 'There's no time for anything else and she's not had a relationship. But then I keep thinking she motivates so many people—maybe this is her path and this is her journey. And we always felt that she needed to be a fulfilled person and stand on her own two feet. We never had that mindset that she's turned nineteen; let's get her married. We never thought like that.'

She added, '*Sometimes your kids will lose their path and you have to hold their hand to help them find it.* When they want to come home, don't question—understand that it is comfort for them. They will choose paths and make decisions you warn them against, but be by their side, have a conversation with them and understand what their motivation is.'

As we concluded, Mr Dhingra reminded me, '*Mansi, let your kids be who they want to be. You should give them a free hand, whatever happens. Let them follow their passion. Let them do whatever they want.* I wanted to be a pilot, but my father said no. Because, Rs 3 lakh in the 1970s was a big amount. He said, "We could have bought a house for three lakh." I mean, now when I think about it, he was also right, you know, Rs 3 lakh, Peddar Road *mai flat mil sakta tha* [We could've got a flat on Peddar Road]. So that was his thought. "Why should I spend so much money when we have our own business and such a huge set-up? So why does he want to be a pilot?" That way, later, I had that in my mind, "I wanted to be a pilot, but my father didn't want to pay Rs 3 lakh." Yet I didn't overcompensate for that with my kids; but yes, when I could afford it, I did send them to study abroad and provide for it.'

If you had a huge billboard on parenting, what message would it read?

Accept them as they are.

We asked parents on Instagram about their opinion on the following:

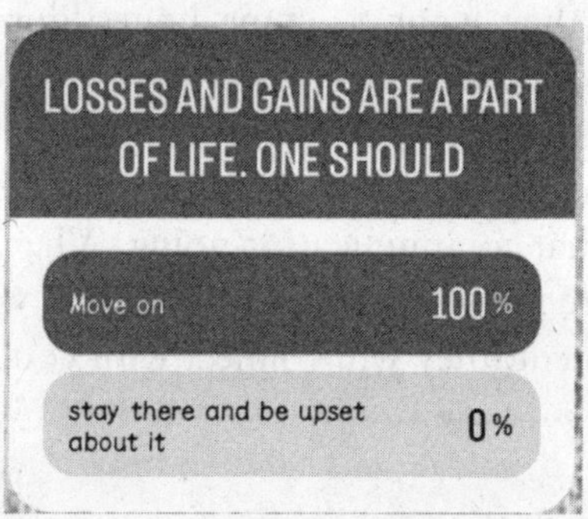

Learnings and Observations

1. You should always have a humble grounding no matter how famous you are.
2. Whatever you want to do, do your best and fulfill your potential.
3. There have to be certain boundaries to have a successful parent–child relationship.
4. As parents, when people know you for your child, it always feels great and makes you feel proud.
5. Losses and businesses are synonymous with each other. Don't cry over them. If you own a business, losses and gains are part of it. So, you have to take it all and move on.
6. Don't brood over things and hold on to regrets. If you do that you will not be able to move ahead.
7. Let your kids be who they want to be. You should give them a free hand, whatever happens. Let them follow their passion. Let them do whatever they want.
8. When they want to come home, don't question it—understand that it is comfort for them.
9. Disagreements stem from when your value systems or how you have been brought up are different.
10. Keep that communication going. When they know you are there unconditionally and without any judgement, they will connect with you.

16

Ameera Shah

'I've always felt that, if you allow a child to grow by thinking for himself or herself, they'll be able to do better in life later.'

Instagram: @ameerashah
LinkedIn: Ameera Shah
Website: www.metropolisindia.com

Ameera Shah is an Indian entrepreneur and the managing director of Metropolis Healthcare, a multinational chain of pathology centres based in Mumbai, with a presence in seven countries. She has been honoured as a 2015 Young Global Leader by the World Economic Forum. Between 2016 and 2017, she starred in and was an investor on the start-up reality television show *The Vault*. In 2017, she founded Empoweress, a not-for-profit initiative for women-led businesses to find advice, mentorship and micro-funding.

Her dad, Dr Sushil Shah, is a pathologist and the founder and chairman of Metropolis Healthcare, and her mom, Dr Duru Shah, is a gynaecologist.

There's something about Ameera Shah that tells you this woman is so comfortable in her skin. I met Ameera four years ago at a talk that she was giving. It's no mean feat that this woman, who has been through so much, is now leading such a big company. She has built each piece brick by brick and I wanted to hear about her journey from her parents.

Dr Duru Shah walked into her clinic at Kemps Corner at 10 a.m. in a gorgeous royal blue sari and her signature red bindi. As we settled in our chairs and got ready to begin this chat, she said, 'While it's been close to forty years since their childhood, I think I can go back to it. *I have always believed that children should be left to themselves in terms of trying to think for themselves.* And therefore, I think initially, when they went to school, I would always encourage them to do things on their own. I know of mothers who sat and did everything for their children so they got an A but I never encouraged that. I would guide them, go to the library, pick up books and then help them finally put it all together. I wanted them to be independent from day one. *Something that I've always felt is that if you allow a child to grow by thinking for himself or herself, they'll be able to do better in life later.* So rather than just nagging them all the time, "Do this; this is how you have to do it; this is not what is to be done," you teach them the dos and don'ts.'

Dr Duru Shah went on to share, 'When it was exam time, my colleagues would take one month's leave. And I asked, "Why do you guys do so?" Their response was quite straightforward. "Oh, we have to sit there to make them study." I said, "Listen, let them study on their own." I have always believed in giving them a lot of independence, right from the time they were children. You may think that, yes, as a mother, you didn't give a child enough attention. I mean, any other colleague of mine would think so. You don't care for them, you only care for your work. But it's not that. That was intentional, because whatever time I spent with them was quality time. Yes, I did feel guilty that I didn't give them enough time and still do today. If I had given them more time, maybe they would have been champions at tennis or excellent in a particular area. But I think they've done well for themselves in whatever they've done. It's okay now. I don't feel so guilty.'

We went a little back in time as Dr Duru Shah shared, 'Growing up, Ameera wasn't the girl she is today. She was very naughty, always playing pranks on people and she loved to travel. Even today, she likes to. She used to go hiking and she made good friends. She was a team leader. And she played volleyball. She seemed to be the only girl who played with the guys and of course, a lot of them had crushes on her, which I was not surprised about.' Smiling, she continued, 'She went to a co-ed school and did sort of stand out, though academically, she would never stand first. I would be called as a parent to hear, "Oh, she's not done well and this is not done well, then this." And, yes, it used to upset me. But in sports and extracurriculars, she always did very well. She excelled in her sport. The one thing about her I feel has changed is that initially, she used to never be sure of anything. You go to a restaurant, "I'm very hungry, I'm very hungry!," and then you get down to order, "What do you want to eat?" "I don't know. I don't know." She was not clear about what she wanted to do, even if it was in the twelfth grade. But as they grow up, the clutter reduces and sometimes what you don't want to do is as important as what you want to do.'

Even though Ameera's initial indecisiveness was pointed out by Dr Duru Shah, there was one thing she was really sure about. 'Ameera was very sure she wanted to study abroad.

Also, given the options here, where barely three students attended class because no one took attendance seriously, I realized that she may be right and that there was merit in her decision. She was also sure that there was no dire need for a private university and a state university would be just fine. That was the moment that gave me enough clarity as a parent that, "Yes, Ameera has a firm blueprint of what she wants."'

She continued, 'She went to see universities abroad and she decided to go to UT Austin, given that it was a state university and known for its business programme. Entrepreneurship was stamped in her head, but she was sure that it was not going to be medicine. Her decision to do her undergrad abroad and do it at a state university may also have come from understanding that, it was expensive and her parents perhaps couldn't support it completely. She knew she needed help and support on her applications, so she drove that whole process all by herself, fully aware that I was very busy and providing for the house too. Her counsellor advised her to apply to her priority universities in any case and then push for scholarships, and that's exactly what she did. Within six months, she got herself a scholarship. She went on the dean's list and was representing the students on it. She worked on campus for four hours a week and made enough money for her regular expenses. At the end of four and a half years, we had hardly spent anything on her. The tuition fees we paid were only one-third of the scholarship.'

'It was just amazing. And she was very determined by then about what she wanted to do. This experience gave her a sense of confidence and she knew she could do anything. Breaking the cliché that doctors' kids should be doctors, Ameera was clear that medicine did not excite her. I don't think I felt upset about that at all. Medicine is something you should have a passion for. Unless you have a passion for it, you cannot move ahead. Unless you are a businessman and a medical person. Then yes, you can create it as a business, healthcare business, which today is expanding very heavily. But the question is, at that point in time, when we were younger and the children were very small, we never thought of what they'll do. But we left it to the girls to decide what they would like to do,' she explained.

She continued, '*I think you can never push anything on your child*. I've seen so many who have become doctors, who were my colleagues, and are no longer walking this path. They have become doctors because of pressure from family or whatever, but they're doing something else today. *So, it's a question of what the child wants to do*. If you look at Ameera today, her own child is two years and nine months old, and still, she's not looking for a school for only academics. She wants an overall development of a child. That's her way of thinking. And that's how we also thought. At some point in time, yes, I have felt that my child should come first in class. I used to come first. I used to cry if I came second, but it's each one to themselves. She's great at sports.'

She went on to express, '*As parents, we assume "I am correct, I am perfect, I am a benchmark, and I am successful." Says who? The truth is, your child may go way beyond*. I don't think her not coming first in class bothered me as much as the guilt that came along with it, that I wasn't giving her much attention. I felt strapped for time.'

Dr Shah told me a little more about Ameera's time abroad: 'Ameera chose to do liberal arts at eighteen and I wasn't really sure what it is. But two years into the programme, she was interning at Goldman Sachs for six weeks. Post her internship, she was handed an offer letter to join them soon after her programme at university was done. She made good use of her time in the US doing so many internships and gathering so much experience. At the end of four years, she had also worked with a start-up and obviously enjoyed it. She called her dad to ask for advice on what she should do next and which offer she should accept and her dad had a very straightforward question:

'"What do you think you want to be? Do you want to be an executive or an entrepreneur?" Pat came the reply, "I want to be an entrepreneur." Or I think she said, "Give me a week to think and I'll come back to you." Around the same time, I was chatting with her, and I said, "Why don't you do your masters and come back? You have done your bachelor's." She wanted to come back home and do an internship at Metropolis for two years, and then go back to do her masters. I said, "If you come back here, you've got the Goldman Sachs offer in your hand. Why don't you do your internship? I mean, you are there two years for your masters." Then she wanted to go to either Harvard or Stanford to do her business programme. I'm of the school of thought—finish your education and then start working. Her thoughts were "No mom. India is changing. Let me come back. Let me do two years at Metropolis. Then I'm going to do my business school." She took the risk.'

She told me a bit more about Ameera's final decision to come back to India: 'There was so much argument about her masters and coming back to India that she finally asked, "Mom, do you not want me to come back? Is that why you're saying this?" I said, "Don't be silly." Then I gave up. I said, "Come," and she came back. And then, for two years, she worked at Metropolis and never went back. She stayed with Metropolis.'

She continued, 'She grew and the company grew by leaps and bounds. *We always believe that we should never influence people around us. When our children get engaged in our business, they should never get that feeling of being entitled.* Because we've seen it happening to our colleagues. When we were younger, their fathers were senior doctors in the hospital and they had an advantage and we never had that advantage.' She went on to tell me about Ameera's first years at Metropolis, 'So, the first day my husband put Ameera at the reception desk but did not tell anyone that she was our daughter. During her summer holidays every year, she would go to the lab at Cumbala Hill Hospital, where my husband first started. She would stop at the entrance of the room and say, "Good morning, sir, can I come in?" She found it very amusing that she's calling him sir, but she maintained the respect deserved by her boss. She grew at Metropolis, starting at the reception. Gradually, she moved up the rungs to become the head of the Bombay division and then the west zone and then all-India, and now she's the managing director [MD]. It's only after ten long years that she is where she is.'

How amazing it was to hear this! They could've easily given her a respectable position at their firm, but they chose to let her climb the ladder from the bottom. I sat in awe while Dr Duru Shah continued, 'She finally went back and got her master's at Harvard Business School. I had a young girl at twenty-one join Metropolis and a Harvard master's programme MD at thirty-one. After a point in your life, degrees don't matter but Ameera wanted to still do it. It was a strenuous three weeks at campus for three semesters and she was the youngest. At the end of those three semesters, why would anyone be surprised that Ameera stood first, unanimously approved as the topmost student? Though there were people who were sixty or sixty-five, flying in their own helicopters and coming to that class, she was the best. For a girl who never stood first in school, whose mom heard about her at every parent–teacher meeting [PTM], to being first at Harvard, she's come a long, long way.' Dr Shah's eyes lit up as she exclaimed, 'She's a brilliant girl who really has her head on her shoulders.'

Both of us continued to discuss the qualities that shaped Ameera and the first one that came about, was that she's a very good human being. Dr Duru Shah added, 'She's very warm and cares for people around her, including her own staff. I mean, she goes out of her way to do things for people whom she cares for. So that humanity is there within her and it percolates down into her business. The fact that she will never think of doing anything wrong, never think of cheating anyone. I think those are your moral values, which you grow up with. So that's number one. Number two is that she's very clear in her head now, she knows what exactly she wants to do and where to go,' Dr Duru Shah revealed. 'None of us have been business people and you need some mentor, somebody whom you can talk to. So, she developed a good rapport on her own with some well-known senior people in the business world. Quite a few of those friends are between sixty and sixty-five but they all get along so well. She took help and support from them to probably make sure that her decisions are correct or to make up her mind. Yes, she talked to me sometimes. She talked more to her dad on these business matters because, to be honest, business is not my cup of tea,' she laughed. 'That I think has helped her. The third is that she speaks very well, communicates very well and is extremely pleasant. Extremely presentable. I think that goes a long way.'

She went on to say, 'Ameera had very strong leadership qualities, whether it was being a monitor in her class, at sports events or hikes, and these have really helped her to be where she is.'

So, I asked Dr Shah, 'How do you foster leadership qualities?' And she said, '*Give them the freedom to think for themselves.* On each of their eighteenth birthdays, I gave my girls (Ameera and her elder sister Aparna) the house keys and said, "Now, you're an adult, you're responsible for yourself. You can walk into that home anytime. You can walk out anytime, I'm your friend. If you are ever in trouble, please talk to me." That's it. And that has been our relationship. As I keep telling mothers, trust your children to call you.'

She told me about the time when Ameera had gone for a summer programme as a ten-year-old accompanied by another senior adult leader and they missed their flight. 'I told the parents. They have an adult with them, they will manage, let's not add more pressure on the leaders and our kids. But I suppose adults have done that when their daughters have gone out. They wait till the daughter comes home. They won't go to sleep till then, right? So I said, "If she's in trouble, she'll call me, that's it." I feel that when you give them a responsibility and that charge, they will take care of it.'

I asked her if she thought her girls misused this freedom and she confidently responded, 'Never.'

She continued to say, 'My logic is very simple, Mansi, she left the house at eighteen. My mother-in-law and Ameera's bedroom were adjacent and she would tell me my daughter had come home at 2 or 3 a.m. I told her "Mom, you're reacting now because you know what time she is coming back. Do we know what time she came back when she was in the US?" Sitting and worrying doesn't help me. On the contrary, just give them good values.'

Dr Shah then talked about her own experiences, 'I'm a gynaecologist. There are so many women who come to see me today with their daughters even though they are eighteen plus. They've got some kind of problem. And nowadays, we are very direct. When I ask the daughters, "Are you sexually active?" they reply with "Yes, I am. But please don't tell my mom." And I respect it because a girl who's eighteen plus has put her faith in me and I cannot talk to her mother about it. So we simply work out a system whereby we don't tell the mother, but can at least educate the girl about what she should do. If people think that their children are not sexually active today starting at eighteen, they are honestly living in a scam of a life. Way back, maybe 10–12 years ago, 25 per cent of the eighteen-year-olds in college, junior college, were already sexually active. Today maybe 50 per cent are. So, what we need to do is educate them. Educate them on how they can keep themselves safe, how to not get pregnant, how to not get sexually transmitted infections etc. And if they are in trouble, we are there for them.'

Dr Shah is so with the times and in acceptance of change. For the kind of relationship she shares with her daughters, it's evident that they have had an open door policy at home, where parents don't need to be present to be available. As working women, we worry if our kids really want us around, or think that we don't spend enough time with them. Dr Shah is very clear about that. She remarked, '*I think every woman should be pursuing her passion if she wishes to and should be self-sufficient. And that's what I used to tell my daughters when they were young*. It's not that you have to study, but why do you have to study? "Why do we want to be educated?" This is the kind of question I would answer. I said, "Listen, if you are educated, you'll be able to stand on your own feet." "Why should we stand on our own feet?" I said, "Because you have to take care of yourself." And that time I gave them an example—"You want to buy a sari, you can buy it yourself." They tease me about it even today, "Who buys your saris, mom?" What I meant was that they should be so independent that they should be able to take care of themselves. But unless you're the type of person who wants to be a good homemaker. Homemakers also do a great job. Their role is as tough as a working mom. But there are some homemakers who say "I'm at home all the time with my children," yet I've seen how they spend their time. They are watching TV, scrolling through social media or on FaceTime. The child is doing something. They are doing something else. *I think if you spend quality time with them and give them the right values in life, you make them independent. I think this is what is needed.*'

Two questions I had were 'How do you manage the attention that fame and titles bring to your children? How you manage it as parents when you know one child has achieved more publicly?' Dr Shah answered them with complete honesty.

She responded, 'I won't lie, Mansi, it does happen. My older daughter is in the US and she's highly educated. She's an American board-certified MD. She has a speciality in genetics and is also certified as a clinical geneticist and lab geneticist. She's highly qualified. But when it comes to the US and you are not in print like in any newspaper or magazine or anywhere else, honestly, you don't get that kind of fame. Today, the lens with which people look at you as successful is mainly how much money you make, which is unfortunate. There are so many successful people out there who are not on the cover page of anything. So the question is about that—two girls, one girl sitting there, one girl here.

I do feel sometimes that the one who is in the US does not get as much prominence as this one. But suppose if she was here, she would have got it because she's a pathologist. She would have joined Metropolis and would have been there as a part of it. Even today, she is the advisor of Metropolis' genetics department and is just starting. She's not running it yet because she is in the US. She guides them on how to take it further. You feel it but it doesn't really move beyond the feeling. *There's nothing you can do as a parent but to give each child their due. Don't undermine any child's work and not give them that credit.*'

Dr Shah then expressed, 'Ameera's ability to add structure and take charge is where I have to give her credit. She brought in the change Metropolis needed. It was the change her father, Dr Sushil Shah, was looking to make.'

'I think her graduation from the business school helped a lot in structuring the place around, though, it was a very well-known lab. But the idea was to understand what the field of medicine is about for her, to get the feel of how to look after customers and provide customer care. So, she started there and then she grew. She didn't say once that she didn't understand medicine. She was willing to learn it to make a difference at every step of the way.'

Life has three folds and the next fold for Ameera was that of her family. She got married to Hemant Sachdev, an Indian retail entrepreneur and then had a baby. But being a businesswoman is different from being a mom who is a businesswoman and leader. 'It was just two weeks after Ameera delivered that we knew COVID was on the rise,' Dr Shah explained, 'She decided that we needed to move out and in spite of all my resistance, she packed all of us up and we left for our farmhouse, where we worked for the next six months. Her ability to make some tough decisions at the right time changes everything for her and the people around her.'

She continued telling me, 'At the farmhouse, as a new mom, she wasn't resting. Instead, she was making all the connections to ensure private labs could start testing to ease the pressure on government labs while also setting up safety frameworks for her employees. She was a mother not only to her baby but also to the employees of Metropolis. She was driving all this while nursing her then-three-month-old.'

When we reflected on any mistakes or guilt that she had, Dr Shah was quick to respond, 'Maybe I should have spent a little more time with her, but I don't regret it. I did what I needed to do at that point.'

I always wonder and I know a lot of us who are self-made ponder over this too: How do we instil that drive in our kids when they are growing in abundance? Dr Shah calmly responded, 'Mansi, in the early years, there wasn't an abundance. When I had my first child, I was still a resident doctor at Wadia Hospital. I was travelling by bus those days. We didn't have an AC in our kids' room for the longest time while we slept in it. I would tell my husband, "Let's put it in for our kids," and he would say, "No, let them get used to it. Because when they grow up, we don't know what kind of lives they will lead. We don't know. *We don't know where they'll go or what will happen. They'll get married. Let them get used to a life that is not easy and not so comfortable that they can't do without it later on. So, we let them get used to life without an air conditioner. Let them get used to walking. Let them get used to taking a bus." I mean, the future was so distant at that time.* My older one used to go to D.Y. Patil University. In those days, children's parents were making a sort of car pool and getting the car and driver to go there. But she used to go by train. We had a car pool to take the children to the railway station but from there, they went on their own. So, the point is, if you get your child too used to comfort in life, it's very difficult for them to give up the luxury or the comfort zone that they have developed. And I give that credit to my husband. I'm the type who will pamper them. But he would say, "No, let them learn."'

I then asked Dr Shah, 'As parents, what is your role when your child sees the lows? And what is it that you tell them when they see failure and when they see success?'

She responded, '*I think when someone sees failure, one should always support them and tell them it's not the end of the world.* I remember once having one of my children not do well in exams and she had to stay back for extra classes. Finally, it doesn't matter; it's okay. If you work harder next time, it will happen. So, when that failure comes, you support them. Don't nag them or hit out at them. Any time any of the girls had done something, they would definitely, if it was related to health, talk to me. If it's related to anything else, they would talk to their dad. But we always made sure that we never hit them. Never. Violence is not my style. Neither of us, as parents, has ever been physically abusive to our children. Never. Not even a slap. So, in short, we have to encourage them when they have failed and support them. And when success comes in, you have to tell them, "Please stay grounded." Ameera is completely my girl. To the extent that she can pour out her heart to me. Her friends are still her school friends who were with her in those days. And they are so very helpful. Any time, anything, each one of them stands up for the other. I mean, there's nothing like success going to her head at all. Dr Sushil, Ameera's father, has played a huge role in keeping the girls grounded and managing that peer pressure. *I grew up in abundance but he came from simplicity, so he made sure that the girls did not define themselves by what they wore or which car came to drop them off.* He's the one who kept saying, "Let them learn the actual facts of life, and then later on in life, they can decide." So today, even if they have to travel by train or bus, it doesn't matter. But I hate it,' she confessed.

She concluded by saying, '*I think it's extremely important. They need to figure things out sometimes. They need to have a process of doing things themselves rather than having everything ready-made.* I mean, honestly, even as a child, when we started giving them some kind of, you know, money to use when they go to college, something they should have, it was a very limited amount. Don't spoil them.'

The last set of questions were a fun, rapid-fire to tell me all of Amira's favourite things. Her favourite food is Italian. The one word she keeps repeating is 'Maa.' And the only thing that Ameera has done to give Dr Duru Shah sleepless nights is by going hiking.

We ended with a sweet message to Ameera from her mom, 'Live happily and have even greater success. That's what I wish for her. Have even greater success. But let success not get to your head. And take care of yourself. She doesn't take care of herself. She is more concerned about others around her.'

My meeting with Dr Shah concluded with my heart full and the confidence that there may not be perfect parents, but there are great parents who raise strong and resilient children. 'Working mother' is a title we give to moms who hold on to what they love doing and do it because they truly believe they can make an impact in the world. I learned that being in denial about your kids is the biggest mistake you make as parents. Freedom with boundaries of values is what we must always give our kids, not boundaries with rules.

If you had a huge billboard on parenting, what message would it read?

Give your child the freedom to think.

We asked parents on Instagram about their opinion on the following:

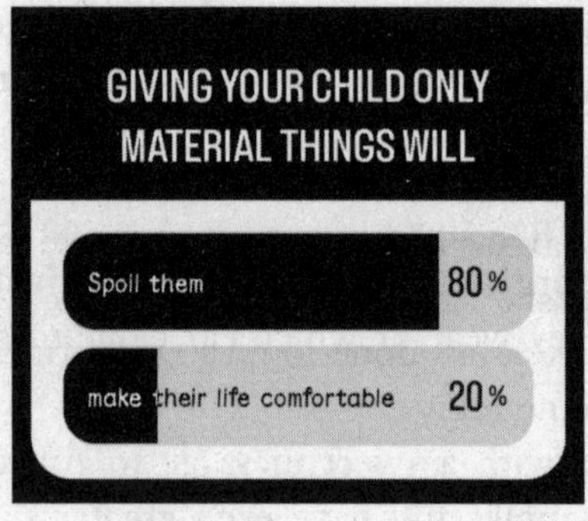

Learnings and Observations

1. After achieving many feats, you should still have your head on your shoulders.
2. Stepping out of your comfort zone is important to achieve your goals.
3. Freedom with boundaries of values is what we must always give our kids and not boundaries with rules.
4. Let your children do things by themselves instead of giving them everything ready-made.
5. You should allow a child to grow by thinking for himself or herself, so that they can do better in life.
6. Every girl/woman should be pursuing her passion if she wishes to and she should be self-sufficient.
7. Make sure your kids do not define themselves by what they wear or which car came to drop them off.
8. There's nothing you can do as a parent but to give each child their due. Don't undermine any child's work and not give them that credit.
9. As parents, we assume 'I am correct, I am perfect, I am a benchmark and I am successful.' Says who? The truth is, your child may go way beyond.

17

Harsh Jain

'You don't have to choose between being a friend and a parent.'

Instagram: @harshjain85
LinkedIn: Harsh Jain
Website: www.dreamsorts.group

Harsh Jain is an Indian entrepreneur and the co-founder and CEO of the Indian fantasy online gaming platform, 'Dream11' and Dream Sports Groups. This platform allows users to play fantasy cricket, hockey, football, kabaddi and basketball. Harsh developed Dream11 in India in 2008. In April 2019, it became the first Indian gaming company to reach a $1 billion valuation.

His father, Anand Kumar Jain, is a businessman, and his mother, Sushma Jain, is a painter.

A mobile game where users can create their own sports teams, compete against others, and win real money. Who would have imagined that? Harsh Jain, the creator of Dream11. I was curious about how he became the man he is today, able to turn his passion into a one-of-a-kind enterprise. So many kids look up to him, and I had Harsh's name written on the first draft of guests to have as part of this book. Something we commonly discuss as millennial parents is how we inculcate drive and ambition in our kids today, who are growing up in such abundance. I'm sure it's a question that has crossed your mind too. We feel that we are overcompensating our absence with materialistic things. Someone once told me that Hamley's will always have their stores at the airport for the guilty parent who is eagerly waiting to get back home and wants to bring a toy home for being away. This exploration of Harsh's upbringing was inspired, in large part, by my curiosity about the motivations of parents whose children enjoyed privileged upbringings. How did they instil that drive and fire in their child's belly? This story could have ended very differently if Harsh's parents had not strongly anchored him in love and values as a child or encouraged him to pursue his passion for sports and business together.

Harsh's mom, Sushma, is a brilliant artist and above all, a great human being. She is extremely warm, welcoming, upbeat and positive. We started the interview by going back in time to when Harsh was just a kid.

'He was basically a very loving, caring and fun-loving child,' Mrs Jain began. Harsh's early interest in sports was undeniable. He did well enough academically to be considered a good student and had a fondness for video games when he was a kid. Harsh would often tell his mother that he was going to be a video game designer, but she would always laugh it off. She had no idea that he would be so true to his word. His mother, however, *had always had a sense that he was destined for great things*. She explained why this was the case by saying, *'He was a very street-smart boy. I promised my husband he would make us proud of him and he has. He will do something big.'*

From very early on in the interview, I realized that it takes a great deal of faith and confidence to let your child do what they want, and Mrs Jain had a tonne of it.

She said, *'I actually genuinely gave my children complete freedom. Both of them. I trusted them completely.'* Even when Harsh would go to school wearing skates and all the people would question her, she never stopped him from doing the things he was confident about. *'I never stopped my children from doing anything they were confident about,'* she said, 'but I was very close to them. I kept an eye on whatever they were doing.' How can one have full trust while still keeping an eye on the kid? 'I was more of a friend than a strict mother,' she admitted. *'You don't have to choose between being a friend and a parent.* Don't be just a mother; become a friend so you know everything that is happening in their life.' Her one big piece of advice would be to 'make sure your kids choose their friends wisely.'

She told me that she is a strict parent who never hesitates to tell her kids when they are wrong. She also stressed the value of a supportive social circle, 'I am that kind of mother who makes everyone feel welcome, which was great for my kids especially when Harsh's friends would come over. As a homemaker, I got to know my children very well. But I, like the rest of you, had my own hopes and aspirations that I wished to pursue. Yet I prioritized the kids over my passion for art.'

'I was always an artist, but I never took my career very seriously. For me, my children were my priority,' she said firmly and then admitted, *'but I wish that I knew at that time how to have balance between these two.'* However, she doesn't regret her choice. 'Married in a traditional Marwari family with a demanding social life, we didn't know all these things as well as you do today,' she explained.

As we continued talking, I brought up the topic of her notoriously not allowing Harsh to have a pet. She responded by saying that she and Harsh share a love for animals and that he was overjoyed to receive a dog as a gift when he was in eighth grade. However, they had to let it go as it started affecting his studies. 'I told him that we'd have a dog once he would graduate and I thought he would forget. But the day he graduated, he got his dog.'

This completely made sense as we delved into Harsh's qualities—*one of them being that he's a trier. He will keep trying until he succeeds and will always give his all*. It was surprising that he possessed these traits given that he came from a very prosperous family and had access to anything he desired. When I inquired about it, Mrs Jain said, 'He always wanted to do something of his own. He wanted to prove himself.' It's safe to say that his dad was his role model. At first, since he saw his mom paint, he told her he'd be a painter, but after seeing his dad work hard, he realized he too wanted to do something and prove himself to his father. His mom admitted, 'He finally created Dream11. I was not surprised because he had just combined his passion for sports and work. We never spoke to him about failure as it wasn't even a passing thought in our heads. The odds of him failing were, in my head, minimal because he was passionate about what he was doing.'

She also admitted that, at one point in time, he went bankrupt while creating Dream11. She said, 'We were thinking, "*Kya kar raha hai* [What is he doing]?" and even felt like *sab kuch doob jayega* [all will be lost]!."' But they supported him nonetheless. I asked them how they reacted when he initially told them about his plan, and she said, '*Whatever you want to do, try*. That is the best thing.' With his father being his role model, there was obviously pressure to perform well and his mom agreed, saying it was very natural that he wanted to be successful. 'For seven years, he struggled and then became successful. But he never gave up,' she recounted. She also remarked that he was always busy with something. Even when he got home from the office, he wouldn't stop working. Being a founder myself, I can visualize the situation and the difficulty involved. *But he never auctioned off his playtime with his son for it. That's commendable.*

Building something like that, something new, needs confidence more than hard work. And I think he got that from his mom, who so nonchalantly said, 'Actually, I always thought my children would go to the top universities,' when asked about their education abroad. This made me express my worry about my kids' university applications etc., to which again, in her calm and cool manner, she replied, 'You work hard and leave the rest to the kids.'

Mrs Jain's confidence in her kids really paid off. She told me an anecdote about how Harsh got admission to one of the best schools in London. 'He was questioned, "If you have to start a new newspaper, how will you do it?" And he replied, "I'd hire the best journalists and keep the price very low on the newspaper. The newspaper would be of good quality but it would also be low-priced, so people would buy it. And once the newspaper became popular, I would slowly increase the price." Before he landed back in Mumbai, he had secured a spot. I was absolutely not surprised that he was thinking like a businessman.'

I continued the conversation by asking how she kept them from going the wrong way and she said, 'I drilled in their minds that there was no smoking, no drugs and no drinking allowed.' Each time we would pass a hoarding while driving where we saw the back of a pack of cigarettes, I would just say, "This is what a cigarette does to you." It's not one day, it's not two days, it's years of conditioning. I warned him not to try it. That there would be no looking back if he did try it. Maybe it was his faith in me that he listened to me. There was so much freedom when he was away that he could have easily tried it. But that's the true test of values.' This was the one thing she relentlessly reminded them of. Then we focused on another important aspect.

I asked her how, with two really talented kids, she maintained the balance. '*Vo* qualities *jo achi hai, usko aap badhava do. Jo* qualities *achi nahi hai, usse* criticize *karenge toh bura lagega na* [You should encourage the good qualities. If you criticize the bad qualities, you will feel bad about it].' She further explained that since Neha (Harsh's younger sister) excelled in academics, she was very keen on her daughter's studies. However, Harsh was good at sports, so she saw to it that that area was developed in him. '*You have to see what your child is good at and you have to encourage that*,' she added.

Parenting is never easy, whether it's with the kids or even with your partner. Mrs Jain said, 'It was very clear in our relationship that where the children are concerned, I will take the decision, and actually, my husband never interfered. And where work is concerned, it is his cup of tea. But whenever I needed my husband's opinion, his help or anything else, he was always there.'

Mrs Jain was so graceful and calm that I wondered if the kids ever got scared of her. But she said, '*I believed in discipline. There has to be some discipline. And this can happen only when you become a part of your kids' lives. You have to show up.*' She described how she would accompany Neha to every dance class and watch every game Harsh would play: 'I have driven them to every class, it wasn't needed but I still did it. I waited outside all their classes so I could encourage them. I wanted to introduce them to everything, and then they could choose. In sports, Harsh was introduced to everything—football, tennis and cricket. Later on, he could choose what he wanted. But if he was not introduced, how would he know what was good?' Mrs Jain explained.

When I asked her how things were going for him now that he was a father, she said that Harsh still takes his son to school every day. 'He has a hectic schedule but still makes time for his family.' She maintains that it was her investment of time in him as a child and adolescent that taught him to prioritize his time with his children. *How your own parents parented you will have a profound effect on your own parenting style, both positively and negatively.*

When asked about how Mr Jain was with the kids, she simply replied, '*Actually, he was a weekend father. I don't blame him. He was also at a stage in his life where he needed to focus on work and only one of us could be in the driver's seat. I chose to be in that seat.*'

But they made it a point to have a family dinner together once a week and take a vacation together at least twice a year. 'On those holidays, we never took our friends or other family members,' she explained.

She remarked that Harsh is the person he is today because of his commitment, tenacity and 'never give up' attitude. And then she told me about the time a musician wouldn't stop playing his violin during Harsh's exam time despite his complaints that he couldn't focus. Mrs Jain gave Harsh Arjun's example. She advised him, 'Your focus needs to be like Arjun's. While others were distracted by the fish's surroundings, Arjun focused solely on hitting the fish's eye. Don't worry about the music and just focus on your notes.' Despite the short length of the story, it may have had a profound impact on Harsh's moral compass. As parents, we have countless chances to teach our children important life lessons. As a mom to a teenager, I've had the best conversations on walks, pick-ups, drops, school bus walks and while tucking them in bed. I would go wake them up with cuddles, kisses, sleep with them and they could ask me for anything. Make time for these.

He went abroad for college but returned to his home country as soon as he could. Mrs Jain's two children agreed that the US was a great place to go to school, but their work and family were more important. 'I never restricted them,' she said, 'If they feel like, "Oh my God, *vaha jate hi khit-khit chalu ho jayegi* mummy *ki* [as soon as I go back, mom will start grumbling for everything]," they will never come back.'

I am sure, as parents who send their kids abroad at a young age always worry, 'What if they go astray or deviate from their paths?' She answered by stating, '*Only faith works; only trust works.* And this trust is inculcated over time. In time, they will realize the value of it and then they will never break it.'

She went on to say that no matter how tough things get, we must never stop believing in our kids. She told Harsh's father, 'You give him how much money he needs, even when times are tough. I trust him implicitly. *Let him try at least till he himself gives up.*' Harsh sacrificed a lot for his career and worked relentlessly. But it is also the foundation of his being that helped him sail through and that's all a credit to his parents.

During the rapid-fire, I learned that Harsh's favourite food is anything with paneer, his favourite sport is football and he loves New York. He still fights with his sister and is a certified 'Mama's boy.' Mrs Jain has also allowed him to have four dogs now.

We ended with a sweet message for Harsh: 'He has to learn to create more family time with his busy schedule. Poor child, he is so busy that he hardly has time, but he tries his best. I think he needs to give a little more time.'

If you had a huge billboard on parenting, what message would it read?

'Khudi ko kar buland itna, ki teri takhdeer likhne se pehele, Khuda tujhse puche, bata teri raza kya hai. *[Make yourself so lofty, that before writing your fate, God asks you, what is your will.]*'

We asked parents on Instagram about their opinion on the following:

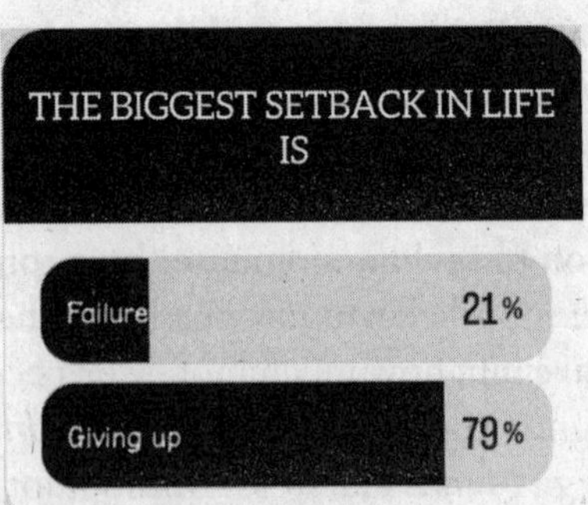

Learnings and Observations

1. Give freedom but within the framework of discipline.
2. You have to see what your child is good at and you have to encourage that.
3. Have confidence in your child.
4. Let them try everything and introduce them to everything.
5. Spend as much time as you can with them and it will go a long way.
6. Be a parent, but also a friend.
7. Know your child's friends.
8. Know how to find the balance between the things in your life.
9. One's concentration should be like Arjun. Unlike other people who got distracted with everything around the fish, Arjun just aimed at the fish's eye and he was successful.

18

Shivani Kalra

'Trust your birds and give them freedom.'

Instagram: @keepem.flying787
LinkedIn: Shivani Kalra

Shivani Kalra is an Indian pilot who currently works for Air India. She participated in Mission Ganga, an assignment to rescue 249 Indian students who were trapped in conflict-torn Ukraine.

Shivani's father, Mr Omkar Kalra, is a plant manager at a rubber factory, and her mother, Mrs Veena Kalra, is a teacher.

It's easy to be courageous, but it takes real guts to act boldly when no one else will. Shivani Kalra is a woman who owns this definition and has set an incredible example with her actions. In 2022, Shivani heroically operated the historical evacuation flight from Bucharest, Romania, to bring 249 Indian students back home to safety. Because I have two daughters myself, I couldn't help but wonder what kind of examples her parents set for their daughter. So, needless to say, I pounced on the chance to interview them the second it presented itself.

Seated comfortably on their sofa and humbled by their hospitality, we started from the grassroots—her childhood years. Mr and Mrs Kalra simply began by saying, '*We were just working parents. But it was our aim to give the best education to our children.*' Sending kids to the best schools is expensive, but they managed somehow staying true to their goal. But her mother continues, 'From the start, she wasn't playing with the dolls like other girls do.' This made me understand that Shivani was a bold risk-taker and did what she believed in even if it was out of the normal. As Indian parents, we always believe that education is the one weapon that will change the trajectory of our children's lives. Today, tomorrow and forever. Shivani's parents were no different. 'Coming from modest beginnings, we had no time to decide whether I should work or not. *Bas kaam karna tha. Bahut socha nahi. Bachhon ko bada karna tha. Unko* best *dena that.* [We had to work. We didn't think much about it. We had to raise the kids and we wanted to give them the best],' she stated with certainty.

Shivani was different, even as a child. I realized that she was focused when her mom pointed out that she had been the most regular child at her school and had barely skipped class even when unwell. This earned her a 100 per cent attendance certificate every year. Her mother vividly recalled a magazine story Shivani had written in the sixth grade about two friends who met in space while everyone else was busy coming up with jokes and short stories. 'From that moment on, we knew she would not grow up to be a typical girl or child. She will do something different,' her parents proudly stated. I probed a little more into this, asking if there were any other similar incidents, to which they replied, '*She was a daring child.* Unlike other kids, Shivani was fearless. Not getting lost in thinking about the end results, she did what she felt like. She was the only one who dared to go near the river bank on a trip to Gujarat while her friends quivered in fear. What is also important to note is that we allowed her to be fearless, to test the limits and to experience everything first-hand for herself. She never thought, "What if?." Of course, she was cautious and knew her skill sets, but the fear of something happening, which stops 99 per cent of people, was absent, and we were so glad.'

Her parents said, '*We always encouraged her to express her opinions and she grew into a confident young woman unafraid to try new things.*' On the academic front too, Shivani was a great student. 'She was good at academics but an absolute standout at extracurriculars. As parents of Indian girls, we always neglect extracurriculars but we never did that with Shivani. We valued it as much, so she would be encouraged to do better. Despite the financial burden, we encouraged her to pursue all her interests.' In my opinion, it's crucial for parents to provide both emotional and financial support for their children as they explore and develop their talents. Participation in different activities is not only for building or honing their talents but also for developing confidence and character. Extracurricular activities taught Shivani what academics could not. The ability to win, lose, wait for her turn, teamwork and how practice makes perfect.

'It wasn't easy. Even though it was pressing on us, she was never affected as all her demands were met. What can we say? She's our princess. We knew that every additional burden beyond academics was stretching us but you stretch for your kids. *Aur kiske liye* [For who else]?'

Mr Kalra said, 'Shivani learned how to drive a car in just one hour when she was fourteen. Maybe there was a scratch but that's about it. *And that's when it dawned on me that, given her keen eye for the road and undivided attention, she might make a good pilot*. This was what prompted us to ask her to get into the science stream and take physics, chemistry and math [PCM] after her tenth grade, so it would be easier for her to choose whichever career she wanted after twelfth grade. Parents should follow the signs of childhood. They are all speaking to us, if we observe. *We followed our gut and listened to our child*.'

Chatting further about her initial stages in the piloting field, I learned that she was sent to Miami to complete her pilot training at just eighteen years of age. When asked about how they were so confident as to send her abroad at that tender age, her mom replied, 'I was scared; it's not like I wasn't. *No matter how much you train your kids, you never know what will happen*. However, she is where she is today because of God's grace and the education and upbringing she received.' I was curious to learn more about this and the steps we can take as parents to ensure our children maintain their focus and avoid making poor decisions. They replied, '*Educate them in every area. If they aren't curious, you have to make them curious*. The most effective way to instil value in a child's character is to start early and work with them, answering their questions and keeping them focused on one thing at a time.' Honestly, we might feel like we are all sharing those values, but the key is to share them without being pedantic, especially for Gen Z. I often wonder if children remember or actually listen to us when we are speaking.

The interview progressed to the next phase, during which I learned about Shivani's upbringing and the challenges she and her family faced. Being between two brothers, she was raised with a lot of love. By the time Shivani completed her training and got all the documents and formalities done, like converting her American licence to an Indian one, the 2008 recession hit. *It was tough for the family who invested so much in Shivani to see her jobless, but even tougher for the girl herself.* However, this did not discourage Shivani one bit. Her parents explained how she never sat at home and always took up something or the other. She joined an event management company and did events. She also dipped her feet in the anchoring field and anchored for a good few shows, one for Amitabh Bachchan too. Her mom then confessed, 'I wanted her to be a news anchor, to tell you the truth. So, I gave her training from the very beginning for good and loud speaking skills. I would make Shivani stand in front of the mirror and keep practising.'

For Shivani, who ferociously wanted to be a pilot, even marriage wouldn't come in her way. At twenty-five, when asked about marriage by her parents, she replied, 'Not interested.' She continued to work and do odd jobs because she didn't want to be a burden on them. 'She was really harsh on herself in those years. She wanted to give us everything as a daughter and when she couldn't, it really frustrated her. She knew how much her parents had invested in the course and where that came from.'

I gasped when they informed me that each training session had cost more than Rs 20 lakh. It was a tough phase for the entire family. But as parents, how do we support our children in such scenarios? *By just being there for them and letting them know that they can count on you.*

They say, there's always a rainbow at the end of the storm. The rainbow in Shivani's life was an opportunity that she snatched with all her might, even with her own brother's wedding happening at the time. 'She didn't tell us that she had appeared for a test for Air India and had cleared it because she wanted to surprise us. She also didn't want us to be disappointed. Then, on her brother's wedding day, she went out in her uniform for the final interview, which no one knew about. When asked where she was going, she simply said, "*Shaam tak aa jaungi* [I will return by evening]." She gave her clothes and jewellery to her friends so she could come directly to the venue. We were all wondering.' My next obvious question was, 'How can you parents not get stressed about it?'

Of course, her parents were worried and confused, but they didn't stop her or interrogate her with a million questions. *This was trust echoing in the room.* The trust shared between a parent and a child. Mrs Kalra said, 'Everyone taunted, "Today she's gone, on her brother's wedding day?" but we held ground. On one side, there was the sangeet and dancing, and on the other side, I couldn't see Shivani. The will to do something and contribute to the house after deviating from her line was so strong in that girl. She had that *zidd* of wanting to prove everyone wrong and prove her parents right.' She continued, 'While she was away from the wedding we didn't think even once that "Shivani *kyun chali gayi* [why did she leave]?." We knew if she went somewhere, it had to be important. She had to do this to prove to us, herself, her God and to all of the people who doubted it.'

Later, when everything was revealed, people understood it wasn't her fault that the date of her interview just had to be her brother's wedding day. She made it for the *baraat* (procession) by changing in a mall and doing her make-up in the taxi.

Shivani's determination is commendable. And this is because of her parents' unconditional support. When I say 'unconditional,' I mean it. Her parents told me how many people reprimanded them for spending so much money on a 'daughter' but they never made any distinction between the sons and the daughter: 'We just said, whatever you want to become, you become that. We never forced anyone. One wanted to go for engineering and another wanted to be a pilot, okay with us,' Mrs Kalra said.

Shivani was the first girl to pass the test at number sixteen, with fifteen boys before her. I also learned that while Air India had initially paid for the expenses, they had stopped due to financial issues, because of which Shivani's parents had to pay for the training. 'I recall that the day we required Rs 15 lakh for Shivani's job and the licences and guarantees, was the day I got my gratuity. As you would know in a traditional Indian household, this money is your old age support. I gave it without a thought for Shivani.'

While talking to them, I realized that the sacrifices they made and the effort and hard work they put in, were at par with what Shivani must have gone through to become a pilot, despite the fact that they seemed so relaxed and laid-back while we were talking.

While discussing her qualities, without missing a beat, they said, 'Committed, focused and consistent.' And I think these three words perfectly describe Shivani's personality. Her mom continued by saying something very interesting: no matter the event she wanted to participate in since childhood—small, big, important, or whatever—they never said 'no.' And that is what shaped Shivani into the confident woman she is today. 'That's the training that it takes. It's not a one-day training,' her mom rightly stated.

This 'never saying no' point was proved when I was told that she didn't even ask or discuss it with her parents when she got the call for Mission Ganga. 'I remember when she got the call, we were shopping for my younger son's marriage and Shivani immediately said yes.' When asked about how she felt, her mom replied, 'I was scared, but I never said don't go.' She further elaborated on the mission and how they had to land in Bucharest and rescue some students. 'There was fear and I asked her if she wanted to go? She said, "*Yeh bhi koi poochne wali baat hai* [Is this a question to ask]?" It took 15–20 days as it was locked down and they had to work it out. But when she brought the kids back here, the smile on her face was bright.'

Shivani was independent and took her own decisions. *'But for her to become so daring, I had to sacrifice my worries,'* said her mom. *She had to say 'yes' even when she was worried about her daughter's safety.*

She explained how they still get worried when she's late from work. However, her parents are proud of their daughter. Shivani was the only one to say 'yes' to taking on this daring mission, and after this interview, I realized that no one else could have done it anyway. Her parents' 'yes' truly paid off.

As before, we had a rapid-fire and I learned so many things about Shivani—like her favourite food being anything non-vegetarian, 'lies' being something she despises and her sense of responsibility being a quality that her parents really admire. Actually, the whole of India should, for she really abided by her responsibility and completed it fearlessly.

We concluded the interview with this sweet message from her parents. 'Obviously, I would wish her all the best, or rather, all the very best, or excellence, in her coming life in the future.'

If you had a huge billboard on parenting, what message would it read?

'Trust your birds and give them freedom.'

We asked parents on Instagram about their opinion on the following:

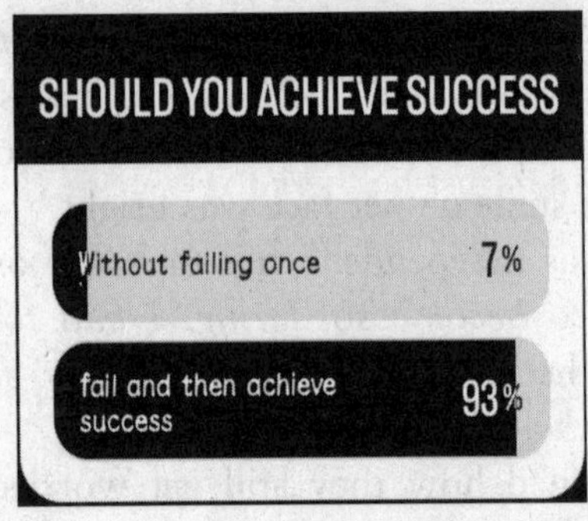

Learnings and Observations

1. Trusting your kids' ability to judge their capabilities is important.
2. Letting your kids fall and try everything and not wrapping them in a safety bubble all the time will help them become their own person and be confident.
3. We must allow our kids to make their own decisions and have a lot of faith in them.
4. Commitment, focus and regularity go a long way in shaping a person's life.
5. The greatest strength lies not in never falling but in rising every time we fall.
6. You should stay true to your goal.
7. Encourage your children to express their opinions and they will grow into confident young people unafraid to try new things.
8. You need to just be there for your children and let them know that they can count on you.
9. Sometimes, parenting is about following our gut and listening to our children.
10. No matter how much you train your kids, you never know what will happen.

19

Rujuta Diwekar

'It's not about how much time you give—it's about how you give your time.'

Instagram: @rujuta.diwekar

Rujuta Diwekar is India's leading nutrition and exercise science expert. She is also the author of three bestselling books, including *Don't Lose Your Mind, Lose Your Weight*, the country's highest-selling dietary book.

V.P. Diwekar, Rujuta's father, runs an engineering company in Mumbai, and her mother, Rekha Diwekar, is a retired chemistry professor from Sathaye College, Mumbai.

Rujuta Diwekar embarked on a career as a health nutritionist when it was not particularly fashionable to do so and succeeded beyond all expectations. I had to know what sort of support system it was that got her to the position that she has reached in her life today. Once we began our interview, it didn't take long for Rujuta's mother, Mrs Rekha Diwekar, to become one of the friendliest and most approachable people I've ever met. Being an ardent follower of her work, I have met her multiple times at Sonave, Rujuta's ancestral farm.

Something about her felt like home. And we started by going back to Rujuta's childhood days. With a smile that could melt anyone's heart, she said, *'Iska kuch nahi hoga, aisa toh nahi laga, leken iska kuch alag hoga, aisa zaroor laga* [I never felt that she wouldn't be able to achieve anything, but I did feel she would do something different].'

She went on to say that while there were many incidents, she remembered one very distinctly when Rujuta was in the eighth grade. 'She went to a school picnic in Kolhapur for Maa Ambabai Darshan and two or three girls had their periods. When they were forbidden by their teacher to enter the temple, Rujuta fought with the teacher. At that young age, she convinced her that girls should be allowed to go into the temples even if they are having their periods, that it is nothing wrong.

'So, after she came home and narrated all this to me, I said, "Rujuta, why are you going into all this discussion when they don't have any problem with it? Why are you there to fight?.' That was just how she was—*strong-willed and unafraid to advocate for the things she considered right.* Mrs Diwekar acknowledged that this characteristic occasionally gets her worried. But she understood that this attribute was what made her special.

I inquired more on this front. What did they, as parents, do to make Rujuta this confident and bold? She carefully said, 'I think we gave them freedom—that is the main thing. Because I remember, when they were small, painting *karana tha ghar mai* [we had to get the house painted], the contractors arrived and both my daughters were not at home. They were eight or ten years old. When they asked me about the colours and all, I said, "Wait, let my daughters come." He could tell I had young daughters just by looking at me. He laughed and said, "Why do you want to ask these things from them?" *We always used to take their opinions and talk about all these things*. Whatever was there, we used to talk about it. So, I think they also felt their opinion was very important.' I then turned the conversation a little towards Rujuta's choice of education. Rujuta studied PG sports science and nutrition at Shreemati Nathibai Damodar Thackersey Women's University (SNDT) College in 1999. I wanted to know what made Mrs Diwekar support this decision when sports science and nutrition were not so popular as careers back then compared to something stable and secure.

'At that time, it was not at all big,' she agreed. 'But we told her that "You have to first complete your graduation and then you are free to do whatever you feel like."' She then admitted that she has always loved the concept of health and nutrition. She told me, 'When I was young, like twenty-one or twenty-five, Malati Karvarkar was a nutritionist. She had 5–6 Marathi books on nutrition and I had all of them with me. I like this topic very much.' She went on to explain that teaching chemistry had helped her understand that people conduct experiments in the kitchen as well. 'I always found the similarity between the kitchen and chemistry interesting and whenever I was in the kitchen, I used to say that this contains this particular thing and this you must take.' As a working mother, Mrs Diwekar still made sure that lunch and dinner for her family were freshly prepared. I asked her how she did it, and she said, 'I think I had the advantage of being a teacher in college.'

She continued, 'In today's business world, even if you wanted to do that, you couldn't. When my daughters were younger, I would carry Ankita and take Rujuta to yoga class with me, holding her hand and doing the poses while listening to soothing music. I was able to do so because of the flexibility this job afforded me, as well as my interest in nutrition and health. And they witnessed me doing yoga. So, you doing something yourself should be stressed more than simply suggesting or commanding they try yoga or anything else. *Your actions only raise your children, not what you say.*' Truer words weren't spoken!

I inquired a little more about this topic. When asked how she got them interested in these activities, Mrs Diwekar said, 'Actually, I am lucky. I never had to force them because I believe that kids will pick up on the things you emphasize at home. These days, moms rarely cook at home. Instead, they constantly place mobile phone orders for takeout or delivery, to which their offspring inevitably respond, "Mom, I want what this other person is having." So, what you do has a significant impact on them. That's why you need to watch how you feel physically.'

That's a fact. We have a false impression that parents' only roles are to instruct, supervise and punish their children. But what about practising what we preach?

I steered the conversation towards Rujuta's academics now and how she managed to stay true to her roots in another country and live all alone.

'Actually, Rujuta is a very courageous girl,' Mrs Diwekar explained. 'Brave and fearless. Sometimes, I used to fear whenever she was going alone anywhere, but she never had that fear. She has gone to the Himalayas many times and has done that course for yoga as well. When she went abroad, I was worried, as all mothers are. I would say, "How will you eat there? What if it is too cold and you know no one who can help?" She was able to manage and do everything for herself, even though at home, children don't work that much. For the simple reason that they have so much going on with school, sports, etc. She prevailed despite my concerns, though. But *uska jo* nature *hai na, uske kaaran hi yeh hua* [But her nature is the reason that this could happen]. She isn't afraid at all.'

When I pointed out that Mr Diwekar had previously voiced concern about her being fearless, she shook her head emphatically and said, 'No-no-no, I never advise like this. I don't say things like "I believe this or that," because it is meaningless and accomplishes nothing. You have to act—what you do is the most important. When I was working in college, I was so sincere and hard-working, doing my best to help every child who was coming to me to learn anything. So, I think they have seen this work ethic. I've never had to tell them to be hard-working or anything else. Even my husband is very much the same. He is now seventy-four years old and still goes to his Vasai factory. Every morning, he is ready at 8 a.m. and sits in front of the computer. All this they see, so we don't have to say it.' 'Remarkable,' I thought to myself.

We kept talking and I eventually asked her how Rujuta copes with disappointments. It's inevitable that when you're a public figure with a sizable online following, your failures will get just as much attention as your successes. Mrs Diwekar insisted that 'we learn better and faster from our mistakes. No one ever learned anything without making some blunders first. Therefore, blunders are perfectly acceptable.' 'Okay, but what about competition?' I wondered. How does Rujuta deal with the competition in this space, especially now that it has grown exponentially? With ease, she replied, 'I always told them to compete with themselves. Because you don't know what the other person is going through. Two people will always be different and *har ek ka time bhi different-different aata hai* [everyone has their own time to shine]. So, it is not necessary that if you get this much percentage in the tenth or twelfth grade, you will be successful. It's not like that.' Now I understood where Rujuta gets her composure from. Mrs Diwekar is surely that 'cool mom' we all admire. She further stated that every person should do what they like. 'I think that is the most important thing. I used to like teaching so much that I was getting admission in a medical college but I didn't go there. I always wanted to be a teacher. Now, even though I have been retired for almost twelve years, I still teach in some way and take lectures or music classes,' she explained.

'So you always allowed them to do what they wanted?' I was surprised. 'Yeah, yeah,' she said enthusiastically, 'we must never impose our wishes on them.' Then she began to talk about how some of their relatives had disapproved of Rujuta's career path once they found out what she had decided to pursue. 'Our loved ones always asked us if we thought she could at least provide for herself in terms of food and shelter. We were confident about our girls, so we answered yes.'

She continued, 'You must foresee the future on your own, as everyone you know, including your parents, friends and even blood relatives, can lead you astray. They were encouraged to do whatever they could find enjoyment in. Life is about more than just money and having a comfortable financial situation.' When I heard this, I thought, 'Isn't this something we always miss? The bigger picture of life . . .'

She further revealed how many of her friends dreaded giving their kids freedom. *I would tell them, 'They are your children. A mother's inability to trust her own children baffles me.'*

On the contrary, she thought Rujuta was able to achieve her goals because of the independence she was granted. When I inquired about how the relatives reacted once Rujuta finally made it big, with excited eyes, she said, 'The relatives were shocked! I mean, when she made it big, they were happy, not out of any bad intentions, out of good intentions only. But they couldn't process that this could happen too.' Mrs Diwekar continued to say how Rujuta started as a gym trainer and slowly started to get high-profile clients. She said, 'And then obviously, when she got Anil Ambani and Kareena Kapoor as clients, then I was sure that we didn't have to worry at all. *But we never worried actually. I think that is our specialty,*' she laughed. *'We don't worry; we just say, see what you can do. That is our principle!'*

When I asked Mrs Diwekar if their family conversations had changed after Rujuta's rise to celebrity status on par with that of her clients, she replied candidly, 'See, for other people, she is a celebrity and all. *For a mother, she is a daughter only.*' Rujuta had started teaching her a few tech things, but other than that, not much had changed. She said, 'I am very confident now and it is all thanks to their teachings, like this Zoom meeting and all.'

We then discussed the impact that Rujuta's father had on her upbringing. 'In reality, my husband had his own work to do. Being an engineer kept him constantly occupied and he never bothered anyone. That's why he's always been there to back me and the girls up in our endeavours. One positive aspect is that he has always reassured me when I was anxious.' Mrs Diwekar shared a story about her kids from their school days: 'When Rujuta was in twelfth grade and Ankita was in the tenth, both of them decided to go on a trek without any formal permissions. they just gave their names and I was very upset. For me, they were a bit young, so I never wanted to send them. But then my husband told me, "Let them go if they want to," and then he went to drop them off in Delhi or wherever they were going. And then when they came back, Rujuta was like the leader.' Rujuta was a woman who spoke her mind and a strong leader, as evidenced by her actions in both the temple incident and the trek.

Having two kids, one of whom is a celebrity, must affect the other in some way unless we strike the right balance. I asked Mrs Diwekar how she managed to make both her daughters feel equal, and she replied, 'You should never compare.' She shook her head with a 'no' as if to put even more emphasis. *'Everybody is different. Everybody's work and attitude are different. So, I never said things like this. It has no meaning.'*

Then she opened up about something all of us working moms can relate to—mom guilt. She expressed how sometimes she felt she could've given more time to her kids and how she pacified herself by saying, 'Because I work, they became more independent at an early age.' She further added, *'It's not about how much time you give. It's about how you give your time.'* She continued by saying that they instilled the idea in their children that education is a lifelong pursuit and we need to always be expanding our horizons with new knowledge.

When I asked Mrs Diwekar what she thought made Rujuta who she is, she simply said, *'Hard work, thinking outside the box and being highly courageous.'*

I asked Mrs Diwekar if she had any advice to share with new parents and she said, *'Don't impose your wishes on them. Because you are a doctor, don't make your child think that he or she has to be one too! Let them choose according to their own tastes. Everyone has some particular ability, and in that ability, a person can grow well. It can be anything—dance, music or art. Now, the sky's the limit. There are so many different branches.'*

Finally, I wanted to know how Rujuta manages to remain so modest despite all she's accomplished. Mrs Diwekar responded immediately, 'You should always be grateful for what you have. *Because if you are grateful, only then, fear disappears and abundance appears.* Giving should also be there, it can't always be taking,' eloquently concluding her argument.

If you had a huge billboard on parenting, what message would it read?

Allow your children to fly. Don't bind them.

We asked parents on Instagram about their opinion on the following:

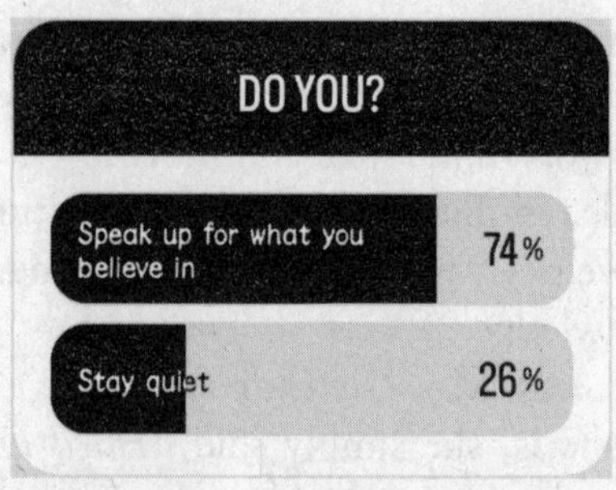

Learnings and Observations

1. Don't impose your wishes on your kids—let them explore their interests.
2. Actions speak louder than words.
3. If you are grateful, only then fear disappears and abundance appears.
4. It's not about how much time you give but how you give your time.
5. Education is a lifelong pursuit and we need to always be expanding our horizons with new knowledge.
6. Life is about more than just money and having a comfortable financial situation.
7. Let your children do what they love.
8. Value your child's opinion.
9. Always speak up for what you believe in.
10. Hard work, thinking outside the box and being highly courageous always pay off.

20

Radhika Gupta

'The apple doesn't fall far from the tree. If the tree is strong, the apple is stronger.'

Instagram: @iamradhikagupta
LinkedIn: Radhika Gupta

Radhika Gupta is an Indian business executive and is the chief executive officer (CEO) of Edelweiss Asset Management Limited, which is an investment and financial services company. She is the only Indian female head of a major asset management firm and has set up the country's first domestic hedge fund.

Her book, *Limitless: The Power of Unlocking Your True Potential* was published in April 2022.

Her father, Yogesh Gupta, is a former diplomat serving in the Indian Foreign Service (IFS), who is retired now and her mother, Arti Gupta, is a teacher.

As soon as the camera turned on, an eager and bright Mrs Arti Gupta appeared and asked me if the setting of the frame was perfect, and I saw a little bit of Radhika in her at that moment. Why did I want to know about Radhika's journey? She is the youngest CEO of the company and the only woman to hold such a position. I knew I just had to have her in my book.

I started with Radhika's childhood. 'Did you ever think she'd be the superwoman she is today?' I asked. With a small smile, her mother said, 'Every mother around the world thinks her kids are stars.' Mrs Gupta has been a teacher for twenty years, head of school for fifteen years and has taught in international schools across New York, Denmark, Rome and Nigeria. *'I always knew Radhika was special. She was head and shoulders above the rest of her class. Even though I didn't know she'd be the person she is today, I knew she would come up by herself. I'm proud of her,'* she said with confidence.

I asked if there was any instance or moment that made her go, '*Yeh toh kuch karegi* [This girl will do something]. 'She was born in Pakistan,' Mrs Gupta started. 'My husband was an Indian foreign officer and was posted to a new place every three years. So, for us, *it was a choice—to either thrive in chaos and change or not do well. We chose the former.* We would shift to and from different countries, which were poles apart in terms of education and culture, but Radhika has been brought up with Indian values. *No matter which part of the world they ended up in, the values of hard work, respect and regard for elders have been imbibed in her.* Now that she's the CEO, I don't know how much more she earns compared to me or her father. But this has never been in her mind. *Respect for elders and humility have always been part of her upbringing, and I think that's the backbone of her success.*'

But how does one thrive in chaos? Especially knowing that Radhika has a broken neck, how did they manage to make her feel normal?

And Mrs Gupta replied gracefully, *'The fact that she had a broken neck or that she was a girl child never crossed our minds. We raised her with all our love and passion and made her feel that she could touch the sky. We never raised her with this complex. She was our first child and she was very special to us.'*

Such a simple answer that had so many layers of complexity. There are many parents who are so concerned about their children's complexes that they are always worried about what society thinks.

I got curious about what Radhika's parents did to raise such a confident woman, and I got the wisest and most eloquent reply: 'We always told her, "You are what you make yourself to be." Radhika completed her high school and twelfth grade in Italy and Rome. In India, nerds are respected, but in Italy, they aren't. But Radhika still focused on her grades and education and that's what earned her respect. When she would be standing in the lunch line, the ninth-grade boys would look up to her and ask, "So you are The Radhika?" because she was the first to get a forty-five, which was a 100 per cent in all subjects.' Radhika grew up seeing her mom and dad work hard and she followed their course too. *'Even as a family, we do not care about what people will say—all we care about is what we think is right. That's our family culture,'* Mrs Gupta stated. This was really powerful.

We continued the conversation as I asked her about how she managed to teach Radhika to value things and, at the same time, make her realize that materialistic things aren't everything. And without missing a beat, she said, 'Her father and I are both self-made. We both come from very middle-class backgrounds. Her father is from a government school and became a foreign officer in the first go, while I attended St. Stephen's College and topped among the girls.' She continued, '*So, when I brought up my kids, both Radhika and her brother, I told them we are rich in education.* I made it very clear that it was because of their father's education and position that we could send them to these schools. *Another thing I emphasized was that nothing else matters more than values. So, we are rich in values.* The third thing was that we are a very close-knit family. I was an involved mother, even though I was very busy as a professional. And I ensured that they were confident.'

I couldn't agree more! Building confidence in kids and telling them the importance of their values and beliefs, and how they shape them as individuals is crucial.

Mrs Gupta recited an episode from Radhika's teenage years when she used to buy the material, design the dress, find a tailor and get it stitched since they couldn't afford any designer dresses. 'Radhika later confessed to me that it did bother her, but not to the extent that she felt the need to address it.'

At this point, we knew a little more about Radhika and how she had dealt with the many shifts in her life. Mrs Gupta said it was inevitable that they'd have to uproot their lives and move to a new, maybe less efficient country, every three years. '*You turn these adversities into opportunities for your kids. If you crib, they crib. But if you embrace, they embrace.*'

She said, 'We learned to settle down very fast. Radhika and I are very adaptable. When she took up the position of CEO of mutual funds, she knew nothing about it, but because of her upbringing, she picked it up. *She has learned this huge skill of adapting to any situation. What is given is given—what's not given, you ignore, and move forward to your goals.'* Such an important and relevant skill, especially in today's world where AI has come into play, is that our kids need to constantly up their skills, adapt to something and learn quickly.

It was time to get a deeper understanding of Radhika's upbringing. I asked, 'As a family and as parents, how did you instil this confidence in her that she is like any other girl? Especially at the adolescent stage. How did you let her know that it didn't matter? How did you do that without being very preachy?'

She chuckled. 'Well, it was easy for me, as I was a teacher. But we had these conversations where we were like, "You know, America is a great country, but we have a really great and strong culture too." Radhika wanted to attend an Ivy League college even though her father wanted her to be in the Indian Administrative Service [IAS], but he supported her anyway. She grew up eating Indian food, speaking Hindi and watching Bollywood movies no matter where on the planet we were.'

'She was the first from our family to study in America and at only seventeen! *There was no family there, but we were confident she'd rough it out and make a life for herself,*' said Mrs Gupta. This is so important—trust.

Now the most integral question, a thought that I'm sure every parent struggles with, is knowing that, as parents, we have done our job well. That the child will survive and stand on their feet no matter where they go. When she went to drop Radhika off at Wharton Business School, these were the things she had to be confident about as a parent.

'First, you have to be confident about the academics, which I had absolutely no doubt that she'd be able to cope with. Second, finance. Because, you see, finance for an international student coming from her background is limited. She had taken some financial aid and was getting some scholarships, but I was confident that she could manage with meagre resources.' And the last one she said was, 'When your child is studying in the United States, it's all about organization skills. They have to manage their interviews, their H1B and all that. Thankfully, she is incredibly organized and planned as a person. She had seen that in her house—in her father and in me.'

'But the most important thing, Mansi,' she emphasized, '*is the values. I was confident about the values I gave her. I told her that "This is the age at which you'll meet many boys, but what's important is that he should be a good human being*." So, she had that clarity and is a good listener. She values her parents and what we tell her. Of course, we have taught her to have a mind of her own. She has a very strong mind of her own, but she also has a strong background. I think she is proud of her parents too,' she concluded.

I guess this is why Radhika has grown up to be so confident about herself. Mrs Gupta explained that they have reached this position in their lives only because of their hard work and grit. It's this 'go-getter' approach that has been embedded in her. 'She has seen her father speak his mind and succeed. She has seen her mother speak the truth and stand for the values she believes in. And I think that has had a huge influence on her subconsciously. I don't remember having conversations about any of these values. It was actions, it was the obvious in the mundane. It was the norm, not an anomaly.'

I think it is also because of the quality family time that they've spent together and their openness to express their opinions and views about the world that they have nurtured this confidence. Since Radhika is so easily immersed in her work, Mrs Gupta admitted that the only piece of advice she keeps giving her is to prioritize her health and her relationships.

Success and failure are two sides of the same coin, and I wanted to know how Mrs Gupta acquainted Radhika with failure. Her composed answer was, '*Human beings are everywhere, in India and around the world. Their reactions are common. Radhika has seen her father, who is exceptionally bright, deal with failure without raising an eyebrow. We take success and failure in our stride. We never get overly excited if there is a big success in the family and never get too low if there is a downfall. We like to go with the flow.*'

Without missing a beat, I asked, 'How did you prepare them for competition?' As parents, we all know that the world today has left the rat race far behind and is now about the cut-throat competition of skill sets. With a small smile, she said, 'She has been a very focused and hard-working child from her primary school days, and has always excelled. But when we moved back from New York to Delhi, she was admitted in Delhi Public School, Vasant Vihar and didn't know a word of Hindi, which was a compulsory subject in the third grade. So, you know, I would lock her in a room and teach her Hindi for hours. And within one month, she had reached the same level as that of her peers. After Delhi, we moved to Regos, Nigeria, where she went to the American school. She had never seen the face of those computers in all her life till then and the first class she attended was a computer class. All the other kids were typing at whatever speed they could and she didn't know what to do, but she worked hard at it and conquered.'

Consistency is the key to success and Radhika truly abides by this definition. And her mother too, when she said, '*If it doesn't come to you naturaly, you get it by brute force.*'

As the conversation flowed, Mrs Gupta told me about how, *as a family, they face situations head-on. They deal with the problem and find the answer without brooding about the circumstances*. I also learned that Radhika has exceptional time management skills, something she definitely learned from her volatile life. '*Time management in a very organized way is also a key to success,*' Mrs Gupta pointed out.

She then expressed how she wanted Radhika to give back something to society now that she was successful. This prompted me to ask, 'How does she keep the balance between her son and her daughter?' And very firmly, she replied, '*We don't compare and we never have. We believe that everyone is unique and special in their own way. You see, my husband was an ambassador to India and I was a primary school teacher. If I compared my profession with his, I'd never be proud of my profession. Each one of us, whatever we do, is critical to the ecosystem of society. And we have to be proud of what we are doing, so there is no question of comparison.*'

But I probed further—'What if one came with a B+ and one with an A+?' She exclaimed, 'They both came with A+. I am blessed!' A laugh bubbled and then she continued with a beautiful thought, 'We tell her that the apple doesn't fall far from the tree. If the tree is strong, the apple is stronger.'

When someone achieves so much at such a young age, it tends to get their head in the clouds. Mrs Gupta explained that she always told Radhika that 'God is kind.' There are so many people who have the skills and yet, she got the recognition and it shouldn't be taken for granted. '*You have to be a good human being above everything else*,' she concluded.

Then we chatted a bit about the relationship that Mrs Gupta shares with Radhika and she promptly said, 'We talk about everything under the sun and can talk for hours! Everything from saris to Hollywood stars to relationships to my challenges as a principal is fair game for a conversation. As a result, our conversations cover a wide range of topics, which is beautiful.' While most parents tell their children to 'stop it' or 'you don't get it,' Mrs Gupta believes that, 'It's very important to not tell the children, "Don't do this." You should engineer it in such a way that you ask them the questions and they give you the answer you want.' This was the experience of a teacher talking, so I asked for an example, and she continued, 'When they were little kids, we lived in a house in Regos. In our building, we had a swimming pool where I used to go with the kids. They would be running on the sides and it would be a little slippery. Radhika was the one running more and she would get a toenail nicked and all. So, one day, I sat with them and asked her, "What were you doing?" and she said, "I was running." I didn't tell her, "Don't run." My next question was, "Do you think that was a good choice you made?" and she was silent for a while. I prompted her to consider my question with, "What else could you have done?" "Maybe I could have walked," she finally mused. *So, you see, you can parent by asking questions. Children are very smart. You just have to get it out of them. I do think my being a teacher has helped me in parenting*,' she confessed with a smile.

Radhika was homeschooled until the age of five by Mrs Gupta herself. 'I was doing my MSE in education at New

York University and I tried everything I had learned on her,' she admitted with a laugh.

She then added that her kids still don't share their hurtful moments with her, fearing that she'd be more hurt. But she doesn't mind. When asked if she ever disagreed with her husband in front of the kids, she said, 'Never disagree in front of the kids.'

It was such a fulfilling conversation. I felt I could go on and on talking to Mrs Gupta and I was and am so grateful for this interview.

If you had a huge billboard on parenting, what message would it read?

To raise a good human being with good values and give them the skills to achieve the best. Give them the right values and the right attitude. Then they'll make a life for themselves.

We asked parents on Instagram about their opinion on the following:

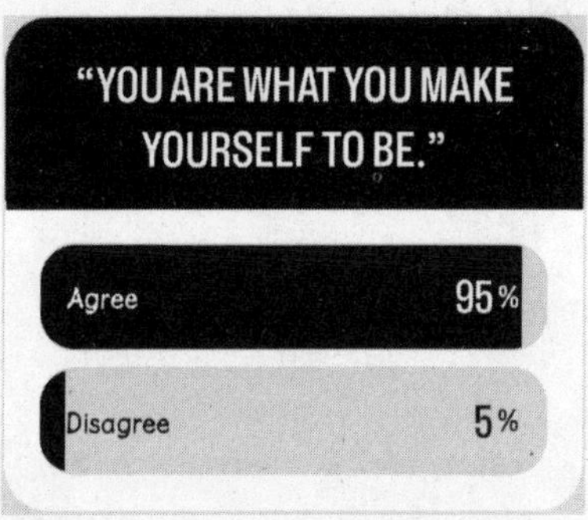

Learnings and Observations

1. We must start building value systems in our kids from childhood.
2. Having space for open-minded conversations is a must.
3. We must try making our kids' complexes into their strengths.
4. Time management and organizational skills are the keys to success.
5. One needs to constantly upgrade their skills, adapt to situations and learn quickly.
6. Instil strong values and boost your kids' confidence when they face problems in dealing with their complexes.
7. Every mother around the world thinks her kids are stars.
8. We can teach our kids how to thrive in chaos and change.
9. Respect for elders and humility should be part of a child's upbringing.
10. Our family views are more important than what the world thinks.

21

Abhishek Lodha

'Don't force or impose your views and expectations on your children. First, listen to them and if you feel they are wrong, correct them and guide them, but listen to them nonetheless.'

LinkedIn: Abhishek Lodha
Website: www.lodhagroup.in

Abhishek Lodha is the CEO of Lodha Group, a multinational real estate company headquartered in Mumbai that offers the best residential and commercial properties in Mumbai, Thane, Pune, Bengaluru and London.

His father, Mangal Prabhat Lodha, is an Indian businessman, politician and member of the Legislative Assembly representing the Malabar Hill constituency of South Mumbai. His mother, Manju Lodha, is an honorary doctorate in social work, chairperson of the Lodha Foundation, philanthropist, writer, poet, author, blogger and YouTuber.

Orchestrating this interview with Abhishek's parents seemed to be the easiest one. I spoke to his wife, Vinati Lodha, who managed to set it up in no time. As I walked into the gates of their residence, I saw a sprawling house overlooking the Arabian Sea and everything perfectly in its place, which only showed me that 'every piece about you speaks of you.' Their home was tastefully done and as Mr Mangal Prabhat Lodha walked down, I felt grateful for the few minutes he had taken to speak to me. Once he sat down, he patiently tried to understand what I was trying to do and how he could best answer my questions.

While we waited for Mrs Manju Lodha to arrive, he went on to conduct his next meeting. I saw him listen to a lady who was seeking his help with the same amount of patience so he could help her too. To me, this ability to listen so patiently was remarkable.

Mrs Lodha walked in with an effortlessly charming vibe. Just like any other Indian mother, she began with, 'Did they get you everything? How was the tea? What else should I order?' When I told her about the book and the idea behind it, she confessed that she loved to read and write too. Having Abhishek as part of the book was extremely important to me as I think he has transformed the way nuclear India lives. To me, his vision is as high as the tall buildings the Lodha Group constructs—he brought in the concept of community living spaces when he felt that people's ties to the joint family system were weakening. As a result of his initiative, senior citizens were given a new lease of life with a lot of self-respect and self-worth, as they began making friends at sixty and living an active life.

As we began the interview, I found many similarities between us and couldn't wait to know what this lady had done to nurture such a visionary. Like when creating a very tall building, we start from the foundation, similarly, we started from his childhood. His mother said he had always had an appreciation for finer things. His philosophy was, 'If I'm going to get it, I might as well get the best quality I can.' This made complete sense, as he now has some of the finest structures in the country. His mother reflected, 'When his dad and I moved to Bombay from Jodhpur, our lives essentially began again at square one, with just Rs 2000 and a tiny house measuring just 5 sq. feet.' Even though both she and Mr Lodha came from wealthy families in Jodhpur, where she grew up, and their home had thirteen bedrooms, they didn't bring any of their wealth with them. They started anew. 'In 1979, Abhishek entered our world. Abhishek has always been a dogged worker—once he sets his mind to something, there's no stopping him. And when something was not getting done, I used to tell him, "Leave it," but no, he wouldn't stop until he completed whatever he put his mind to,' she said proudly.

She then informed me about his academic performance: 'Abhishek was always good in studies, especially in general knowledge, in which he bagged several gold medals and certificates. He was very much involved in general affairs too, always watching the news and reading newspapers. He was very stubborn as well. If he wanted to do something, he would do it. And I always feel, *Har insan ka zindagi mein lakshya hona bahut zaroori hai* [It's important for every person to have a goal in their life]. Abhishek and his brother Abhinandan have an exceptionally warm and loving relationship,' Mrs Lodha continued, and told me about his enthusiasm for celebrating his birthday, 'Every year he'd want to get a cake and call all the building kids. There was a cake shop nearby on our way to school, so after school, he used to say, "Mummy *apko cake leni hi padegi* [Mom, you have to buy me a cake].” He wouldn’t walk ahead without a cake,’ she said with a smile. She went on to say, ‘He always wanted his friends to come over to his house to play with his toys. In the evenings, we’d head out to the garden for some free-range fun on the swings, slides and sandbox. I used to tell my kids stories about patriotism and he knows many patriotic songs too. We learned them from my father-in-law, so whenever we used to travel, we used to sing all these songs. This is the way Indian families pass on their learning from one generation to the next.’ I then asked about his favourite childhood toys, reflecting on the fact that such details can reveal a lot about a person and she said, ‘He played all the games and sports. He loved Lego.’

We chatted a bit more about his values and personality and what shaped him into the person he is today. She said, ‘These kids have been raised with so many values that they don’t even eat paan or supari. So when we sent them abroad, we never had this fear that they might do anything bad or form bad habits.’ She related an example from his wedding, ‘Even when he got married, when the grooms sit on the horse, they usually have paan, but that too he didn’t have. They had these values within them since childhood.’ She went on to say that her in-laws had never touched all these things because her father-in-law was in the RSS and her uncle was too. She continued, ‘When Abhishek used to go out to treat his friends too, he would clearly tell them that if you want to drink, do it with your own money, I won’t pay for anything except the food.’

When he was much younger and they were just starting out, Abhishek told his mom, ‘*Humare paas jo bhi hai, usme hum chalalenge mama* [We will manage with whatever we have, mama].’ *He didn’t like to ask or borrow from anyone.* When I asked Mrs Lodha how she managed to instil such strong values in her children, she said, 'They saw my husband and me struggle and make ends meet since they were children. During Diwali, they used to help me out with chores and the cleaning of the house. They would sit next to me and offer to shell the peas or wipe the bowls. So, since childhood, they've seen us working and helped us out with it.'

After hearing this, I started to wonder if we put too much emphasis on 'teaching' our children morals rather than setting an example and letting them learn from us by watching and listening. We stress the importance of raising good, helpful and obedient children. There is a lot of talking to them to get them to do these things, rather than just expecting them to come and help out of their own volition. 'They grew up watching their mother work, and so they also used to do it, and as such, it became a habit,' she went on to explain. She then spilled the beans on Abhishek's culinary skills and shared a sweet anecdote: 'On Sundays, these two used to say, "Mummy, *abhi aap kitchen ke bahar jao* [Mummy, now you go out of the kitchen]." Then they used to whip up a lavish five-star breakfast with one dish coming after another. When it would be time for them to give us a bill, they would write us a bill for "love". I don't know how many hours I spent cleaning the kitchen afterwards, but they loved cooking for us. And I never stopped them from doing what they loved." *How many times do we miss seeing the efforts our kids have put into something and can only see the mess they've made instead?*

She told me Abhishek was bright ever since he was a child, which prompted me to ask how she maintained the balance between both her children and made them both feel important. '*You are you and I am me. I never compare people.* Until the fifth grade, my younger son got good grades, but then he became a little careless. As for Abhishek, he used to ask me to ask him everything, all these questions and if he missed a line, he only used to tell me, "Mummy, *yeh* line *chuut gayi na* [Mummy, I skipped this linc right]?" She even complained to the principal when she learned that the teachers would compare her younger son to Abhishek. She agreed when I said that Abhishek comes off as a perfectionist, 'Yes, he was a perfectionist. As soon as he got up, he used to fix his bed and keep it neat. When he lived in America too, he was the same, so it formed a habit.'

Abhishek's dad, Mangalji, was busy making a life for them and was never really in the scene. Mrs Lodha told me, 'Till today, if I ask him, he says, "*Tumne hi unko akele bada kiya hai* [You have raised them alone]." So, I was constantly present and in exchange for him not being around, we used to go out and enjoy ourselves. But we used to spend Sundays with the kids. Even though Mr Lodha had a tendency to sleep early, the kids and I still managed to have a great time playing cards and ordering takeaway food,' she chuckled. Getting married at the age of eighteen had its own advantages, said Mrs Lodha. 'We were ready to make sacrifices. When we get married after a particular age and have formed our opinions, it is very tough to make compromises. In our case, however, we had no say and couldn't even voice our displeasure to our parents. We knew they'd say, "Take care of your house." Before I was married, I probably didn't even serve myself a glass of water, but it changed soon after we moved to Mumbai. But I was ready for it and I had a smiling face. There was a sense of ownership—this was my house—then everything became easy,' she expressed.

I now wanted to briefly discuss Abhishek's academic career abroad. Was there any clash of opinions? Were they okay with him going to an unknown place? 'No, we've always been there for him,' she responded, 'We never said no to anything. Abhishek wasn't even eighteen when he went abroad to study. He took an exam because of a friend and got into Georgia Tech. He told me, "Mummy *main jaana chahta hun* [Mummy, I want to go]." We thought about it for a while, which is understandable. *As parents, our primal instinct is to keep our children safe.* Sending them to a completely new and unknown place rings all the alarms in our brains." She explained, 'But he really wanted to go, so we all went along with him.' They were given a contact number through a mutual friend and his friend picked them up at the airport before taking them to their hotel. Mrs Lodha continued, 'We travelled to his university to finalize all the preparations, tour his dorm and store his belongings. I was crying a lot, leaving him alone for the first time. But one good thing that we had done was, through the internet, we had contacted a lot of people from the Jain community and had received a really good response. One of them even became his local guardian. Out of the fifteen days that we stayed there, twelve days we were in different people's houses having dinner. So, then it didn't feel like he was all alone. We felt reassured that there were so many to help him out and be with him. They even celebrated his eighteenth birthday over there!' she exclaimed with shining eyes. After hearing this, even my parental heart was at ease. *The role of communities can never be undermined in raising kids.*

Abhishek was a self-starter. He did everything on his own, from taking the exam to study abroad without telling his parents to deciding to major in photography in college. Mrs Lodha claimed that her son's success can be attributed to his inherited traits of perseverance and tenacity: 'Like I always say, I may not be intelligent, but I am hard-working.'

She proudly said, 'Even today, my two sons and my husband get up early and go to work.' The children's resoluteness and modesty are a testament to the stories of great people that Mrs Lodha would share with them every day and her attentive listening of their thoughts.

The Lodha group is well-known not only for its impressive architecture but also for its emphasis on community living. When I probed further into the inspiration behind Abhishek's idea, she simply said, 'He had this motto of giving the best and he gave his all because he wanted the best too. From childhood, he had this mindset and I think somewhere that has played a role in this. He didn't want to just build a building or a flat for people. He wanted to build homes, a place to live with the entire family and the community.' I could sense the immense pride the mother had for her son.

When I asked her what he thought about following in his father's political footsteps, she said that 'He should wait until he is fifty and has established himself before entering politics.' In addition, she revealed that Abhishek has ambitious plans for the company. He left a high-paying job to get started in this industry. It made me wonder why he joined a different organization in the first place, why not start with the family business?

'On the contrary,' she said, 'I feel, children should start working elsewhere and gain experience. They should start from scratch at the clerical level and climb the ladder, learning all the roles. If they work in their own business, they'll work like a boss and won't learn. Young people should get at least two years of work experience elsewhere. My husband too, put in his two years and learned the ins and outs of business. He was the first in the family to start a business.'

She continued, 'I feel, learning is very important and we must be open to learning all our lives. *Zindagi bhar aap shishya banke chaloge na, toh accha hai. Guru banne ki jis din humne koshish ki na, humara sikhne ka samay khatam ho jata hai* [All your life, if you live like a student, it will be good. The day we try to be a teacher, our learning time is over]. So, even as a child, we must learn and even when we become old, we must keep learning.'

It's probably because of this propensity that Abhishek still has a lot to do with the business—he's always trying new things and learning new concepts. Mrs Lodha went on to describe how Abhishek gets along well with the elderly, meets so many seasoned people, and takes what they did right and puts it into practice.

It's natural to feel a little puffed up with pride after building such an empire. But if you meet Abhishek, you will see no hint of it. When I asked Mrs Lodha how she instilled in her children a sense of humility, she said, '*I always say this and my mom used to say the same thing: "Ahankar toh Raja Ravan ka bhi nahi tika, jinki Lanka hi sone ki thi* [Even King Ravan's arrogance didn't survive and his kingdom was made of gold]." What are we then but just pawns in this game? There are bound to be low points in anyone's life, but it's especially important to be humble to everyone when you're on top. Because the same people will be the ones to come to our aid if we ever hit hard times.'

She added, '*Vriksh jitna badhta hai na, utna jhukta hai chaya dene ke liye* [The more a tree grows, the more it bends to provide shade for everyone]. I've always explained this to my kids. So, I think it has stayed with them.' It has, of course. Every one of these details has stuck with them and is now an integral part of who they are.

Mrs Lodha's life's anecdotes made me really think about how she has passed on these little nuggets to her kids through play, stories and poems. This conversation only reaffirmed my faith in what I always say and that is *children are not shaped in a day*. It's the everyday things that matter.

Then our conversation took a lighter turn as I asked what Abhishek does for entertainment, 'He loves to listen to music and songs,' she replied. However, ever since he got into business, she thought it must've worn off, until she took a car ride with him and Abhishek sang along to all the songs. Mrs Lodha then asked him, 'Abhishek *tereko pure-pure gaane aate hai* [Abhishek, you know all the songs]?' I couldn't help but laugh. 'I feel music and reading are his two passions,' she concluded.

I guess Abhishek's 'normal' way of life, no matter how successful, comes from Mrs Lodha's constant reminders of '*Jab tumhari ek gaddi thi tab aap kaise rehte the, abhi das gaddiya hai, fir bhi vaise hi raho* [When you had one car, how did you live? Now even with ten cars, we must stay the same]. She explained how studying in a *pathshala* where she learned about the *Santa Bhav*a impacted her tremendously and this had been passed on to her kids too. She said, 'I'm not the type to feel the need to collect materialistic things and I think my kids have imbibed that too.'

But I wasn't quite at ease even after hearing this. I mean, they can buy whatever they want, how do they just happen to be satisfied with what they have? I got a calm answer, 'I think it has to come from within. They should learn to acquire the ability to donate.' She further told me, 'Like all my grandkids and my daughters-in-law too—when it's Diwali, we say "Let's make sandwiches and distribute it to the poor." Since we are a part of this community, we owe it to this community to do our part. Like I shared earlier, the seeds of togetherness and community living were sown early on, and that has helped Abhishek extend it to his business even more.'

When I inquired if Mr and Mrs Lodha ever disagreed on anything, she cheekily said, 'I think, *har* husband *aur* wife *mai chattis ka aakda hota hi hai* [Every husband and wife have a bone to pick with each other]. We never argued much. I always feel that when one person is angry, the other one should be quiet. No matter if you reprimand them later, at least they will listen then. But when two people argue, it just keeps growing and neither wants to listen. Men have a little ego too, so they won't listen. But if you speak later, they will listen and say sorry too.'

A large part of Abhishek's success can also be attributed to his love of leading projects, like organizing a funfair in his building or taking charge of class projects at Georgia Tech. Abhishek was a bright student naturally—he never studied hard but absorbed everything he heard in class. Now that he's a parent, he also pitches in with his kids' homework and other projects.

Mrs Lodha said that she feels very confident in the way Abhishek and Vinti, his wife, are raising their kids as well. While they don't splurge on materialistic things for the kids, they do take them out on vacations a lot, spending quality time as a family, which is more important.

When I asked Mrs Lodha if she thinks she's done anything wrong, she said, 'I must have.' *But she did everything she could in the situations that they were in.* I then asked, 'Are we, the new generation of parents, thinking too much about parenting?' to which she answered, 'Maybe. It's fine if both parents are working, but make sure you're still paying attention to your kids. *A child who comes to you with a question deserves your undivided attention.* Don't give them the cold shoulder or promise to hear them out later. If your kids want to tell you something, you listen to them. Listen to everything they have to say *and trust your child. If your kid complains about something or someone, inquire about it.* I see so many kids today are sad because their parents don't listen to them. You've left the kids with the nanny, do you know what's happening? *The nanny is there to support you with chores, not take over your role as a mother.* So, when your kids are telling you something, listen to them. No matter if you can't give all your time, whatever time you can give, be with them, love them and it'll be fine.'

There are many sacrifices that Abhishek had to make to accomplish what he has. He works 10–15 hours every day, even now. But when people come and praise Mrs Lodha and tell her how amazing her son is, her heart swells with pride.

'We gave them the right values since childhood,' she said, 'and I always believe in two things, *bhagya* [luck] and *purushartha* [efforts]. He has his good deeds, and as a mom, I did what could do, but whatever he is today is because of his good deeds and his hard work.'

She described how their relationship has evolved. 'Now he talks less because he's busy, but before, I used to live with him in America. We would stay up all night, *duniya bhar ke gap-shap karte the* [we used to gossip about everything under the sun]. I used to talk to him about everything—my friends and all. Sometimes I tell him, "*Beta abhi toh tu ekdam hi change ho gaya, kitna kam bolta hai* [Son, you have changed so much. You talk so little now]." He says, "Mummy, *vo din aur yeh din mai bohot fark aa gaya hai*

[Mummy, there is a lot of difference between those days and these days]."

When I heard this from Mrs Lodha, I realized that, as parents, *your relationship and the time you spend with your kids evolve with every new chapter of life and accepting it is tough. You need to know as a parent that with every passing year, you will spend less and less time with your children. It is this realization that causes so much turmoil and insecurity in a parent's mind at various stages.*

Since we were discussing time, she emphasized the significance of 'time investment.' She said, 'They will repay your patience with their own when they're older if you give them some now. If you don't, they'll say things like, "*Bachpan mai apne kaha time diya, toh budhape mai kya* expect *karoge* [You didn't give us time when we were kids and you expect us to give you time now that you're old]?" *Toh samjho aap abhi* fixed deposit [FD] *kara rahe ho* [So, think of it as an FD that you are investing in].'

I was concerned that she might have abandoned her own ambitions in favour of raising a family, but she assured me, 'Quite the opposite, actually. I feel that because my kids encouraged me so much, I am who I am today.'

She confessed that she grew up with the kids, and even today, they support her and tell her if there's something she wants to do, she should do it. She said all those sacrifices she made were something every mother does for the kids, '*Yeh zimmedari bhi nahi hai aur zabardasti bhi nahi hai, yeh pyaar hai.* [It's neither a duty nor a compulsion, it is love].'

I asked her if she advises Abhishek in terms of parenting, to which she said that she lets him bring up his kids however he knows is right. 'I feel he's smarter than me. *I don't say much, just that "It's good to keep the kids in a little bit of adversity, as it was for you, too, when you were a kid. Don't make everything easy for them. Make your kids understand the value of things.*" That's very important.'

I asked her what advice modern parents should follow, and she responded, '*Just trust your kids! Always be there for them—never abandon them or say anything detrimental to their self-esteem,* like "*Tu yeh kar hi nahi sakta, tere andar toh yeh hai hi nahi* [You can't do this, you don't have what it takes]." We parents say this sometimes to our kids, that "You are useless, see other kids . . ." Don't compare them with others. Especially with people close to you, because it really affects the kids.'

What stands out most to me about the parents' words of wisdom from the earlier chapters is the unwavering confidence they have in their upbringing and the solid trust they have always shown in their children.

Somewhere, we fall into this comparison trap unknowingly for ourselves and extend it to our children. We ought to constantly remind ourselves that *every person is born with a unique set of abilities. Instead of forcing our children to do things, it is our responsibility as parents to recognize their strengths and encourage them to develop them. Even though the world has become ten times more competitive, we shouldn't push our children too hard.*

Mrs Lodha concluded by saying, '*Don't force or impose your views and expectations on them. First, listen to them; if you feel they are wrong, then correct them and guide them, but listen to them nonetheless.*'

I asked Mrs Lodha to share a few of Abhishek's habits and she told me of his love for Rajasthani food and how he still bites his nails.

When asked if they had a message for Abhishek, they said, 'Keep working hard and keep prospering. And whatever mistakes you make, you must keep them in mind too. See your successes, but at the same time, make a list of your mistakes too. Others shouldn't have to tell us our mistakes, we should know them on our own.'

I felt like a little girl again while we talked, learning so much about life. Mrs Lodha's friendly demeanour and easy-going nature put me at ease. Her wisdom and candour impressed and motivated me. Her poems and Hindi quotes will stay with me forever. It was such a blessing to have this opportunity.

If you had a huge billboard on parenting, what message would it read?

'Apne bacchon pe vishwas karo aur unhe pyaar karo *[Trust your kids and love them]*.'

We asked parents on Instagram about their opinion on the following:

Learnings and Observations

1. Learning never stops at any age and we should constantly be learning. The day you try to become a teacher, you will stop learning.
2. Even if you are riding high on success, be humble and grounded, and try to uplift the people below you.
3. Practice simplicity and be content.
4. Let your kids experience difficulties and don't give them things easily.
5. Adversity teaches you what success and prosperity fail to.
6. Investing time in your children early on is like an FD. It will yield results slowly but surely.
7. Trust your kids and listen to what they have to say.
8. As parents, we must embrace the limited time we have with our kids and be fully prepared that we cannot be the lead character in every chapter of our child's life.
9. Taking care of your kids should not come from compulsion or duty, it should always stem from love.
10. As you grow, give more to people.

22

Joshua Karthik and Joseph Radhik

'As parents, you have to let your kids swim in the depths of the water sometimes, knowing that they are finding it very hard to stay afloat.'

Instagram: @joshuakarthikr and @josephradhik
LinkedIn: Joshua Karthik and Joseph Radhik
Website: www.stories.josephradhik.com

Joshua Karthik and Joseph Radhik are the co-founders of Stories by Joseph Radhik, an international award-winning team of photographers. Joshua is also an award-winning photographer who was the recipient of the PX3 Paris, Tokyo International Foto Awards and more.

He has clicked the wedding pictures of Priyanka Chopra–Nick Jonas, Katrina Kaif–Vicky Kaushal, Varun Dhawan–Natasha Dalal, etc.

Their father, Harish Rallapati, is an expert at instrumentation systems for large-scale factories around the world and mother, Srivalli Rallapati, is a senior manager, human resources, and taught economics at the MBA level at Osmania University and Andhra University all through the 1990s.

Joshua and I met a few years ago at an event in Singapore when he had just shot the Virat–Anushka wedding. In fact, that is how I had saved his number on my phone too. Post our meeting in Singapore, I continued to follow him on Instagram and definitely wanted to learn iPhone photography from him because his pictures are poetry. We stayed in touch and as I saw the space of professionally shot pictures emerge for just about everything, I saw how his team had the passion and the vision to build and create something special. I then heard a podcast with Joseph as a guest and that's when I decided that they must be in the book—two great human beings who are both outliers.

Joshua and Joseph's family is from Vishakapatnam and they live in a joint family. Their mom is a highly educated professor who used to teach at an engineering college. At the start of our conversation, she said, 'While teaching at the college, I would go and read at the library, and there was a psychologist there who encouraged me to pray while I was pregnant. I prayed every single day, "Lord, give me the strength to bring this child up in true honesty and gentleness and they should obey me as I don't have that much capacity because of all these domestic problems. Please see that my child is able to get my point and immediately obey me, so that bringing him/her up becomes easy for me." You can choose to believe me or not, but the raw materials that have been given to me by God in the shape of these children are so nice. They are so obedient. Even before they had completed two years in age, people would call them unique. Maybe because they didn't cry for anything.'

She continued, 'I didn't have the time to manage anything beyond housework, my professional life and their studies. I continued to work as we were living in a joint family with thirty-three people and there were a lot of responsibilities.

Once their dad's job was set and we moved to a nuclear family set-up, I could focus on my children and hire some house help. I spent a lot of time teaching my children. I knew that to be anything, they needed to be good at their studies. Even to get into a coaching centre, they had to be good to get in. I still remember that day when the newspaper carried Joseph's photo because he topped.'

As the conversation went on, she told me a little bit about all three of her kids. 'Joshua and Joseph have an elder sister who is currently in the US. I had my children back-to-back—three kids in three years—and they just took care of each other. My husband would leave at 6.30 a.m. and be back late evening at 10.30 p.m. while I would be busy with the three kids, their studies, the house and all the paperwork. Even if my youngest one, Joseph, cried, his elder sister would just say "Mama has work to do, even if you cry, she will not take you."'

We often feel the need to do everything for our children when they are young and forget that that's the age their brains are the most active and they learn fast. They observe and understand everything. *'I used to talk a lot to my children. They knew their mother was with them, but she also had to do other things. There was no confrontation. There could not be,'* she confessed. She then told me about their hardships when they lived in a joint family set-up. 'Our purse strings were very tight living in a joint family and with the in-laws. So much so that I never bought syrups for my kids as they were expensive and used to give them pills. *There was no pampering them by crushing/grinding the pill or running after them. Where was the time for that? I would just show them how it is to be taken practically. I didn't give them a choice.* My kids studied in the kitchen when I had too much work. Joseph couldn't sit properly for long, so I would support him with pillows and make him sit. I shared all my hardships with my kids, made them understand why I was doing what I was doing. If they could understand what my difficulties were, they would co-operate better. *Communication is very important in parenting. Never lie to your kids and give fuzzy answers or not address their curiosity. That will extinguish their inquisitiveness or zeal for learning. When they start walking and touching objects, speak out the name of the objects instead of saying "don't touch." We should answer their questions, no matter how many things we are handling.*' This is so important to note. Today, as working parents, we feel guilty that we are not spending enough 'quality time' with our kids, but what we need to understand is that our kids don't want quality time, they just want our time.

Mrs Rallapati had a hustler's aura, who had always made things happen for her children and herself. While she was preparing for her MBA lectures, her kids studied management books at the age of nine. She shared, 'Joshua would say, "I find this so interesting, Maa, give me that positive motivation theory or this parrot theory. I should stick to that. The other one is better for *anna* (big brother) and *akka* (big sister), I think." Our weekends were as simple as our weekdays. Our weekdays were very busy, and since my husband was travelling and he hadn't been in India for the last three decades because of work, I was pretty much managing the kids on my own. On the weekends and holidays, I would wake up early, cook some tomato rice, finish cooking and cleaning, and head out with the kids and my house help, taking them around all the popular places in Hyderabad. Sundays also meant going to the church. We are very religious and spiritual.'

She went on to say, '*I never broke the promises I made to my children. They knew maa would always try her best to keep it. I never set goals for my children. I used to ask them, even when they were very little, to make their own goals*. Also, we treated our kids equally given we were both middle children. No favouritism, nothing. Everyone was and is equal.'

She then gave me a little background of their childhood. 'My first child was brought up by my very sweet, gentle and mild mother and father for 5–7 years. My second one also, Joshua, though he was with me, is very soft, gentle and filled with so much empathy. He is very bright and never gave me any trouble. My daughter is very helpful so she used to help me even when she was 8–9 years old. There was so much work she used to share with me. But that is a girl's nature. The boys didn't know how to organize and everything so their sister only taught them and led them. Your child's capabilities will never be equal to their focus. You will always feel as a parent that "My God, he has so much potential, why is he not pushing hard?" but that child who has the potential is very aware. The child who struggles and works hard to be consistent is the one you should be happy for. Because nothing can beat that.'

We then discussed a little about their academics. 'Our kids went to army schools and Kendriya Vidyalayas as we could only manage that. They managed all their entrances by themselves. My children, once they decided to do one particular thing, would rest only after they had completed it. I would guide them, but I never chose the courses for them. I used to ask them what they wanted,' she explained.

She added, 'God and destiny were very kind to us. We couldn't buy a house back then and lived as tenants at a gentleman's house. This gentleman worked as a scientist in

Washington, DC, and upon seeing Joseph's paintings, said, "Your child is really gifted, but let him study. With only art, he will not be able to fend for himself." We blindly, without even using our minds, stopped Joseph and took all those art things away from him. He used to ask us for them, but we used to say, "First study, then we'll give it to you. No, this is not the time, no art nothing." That child did not say anything and listened to us. But look, while he was working with Colgate, he started getting that zeal again for art, paintings, photography and all these things that we couldn't imagine.'

Then, the tough decision of leaving a well-paid job came along, as she described, 'I said "say a prayer and if it is His will, then you decide if you have to leave, but think twice before you leave this." I didn't ask him "Where do you want to go?" because I didn't know. I used to pray only. Then one fine day, he said he was out on the roads with his camera for three to four months. It was difficult for him also but he lived with it and later his brother and me. We used to send certain things but for some time only. Then later on, God blessed him and he could pick up the tab on his own.'

As the conversation flowed, she admitted, 'My children were a godsend—they sensed my anxiety and knew I was a single parent in India. One day, I took their computer in the bathroom to check what they were watching. I couldn't understand anything. Joshua saw me later and sensed that I was nervous. He came home from school that day and said, "Maa, all okay? Is your health okay? You are spending so much time in the bathroom." I told him I wanted to know why they were spending so much time on this screen? He showed me how to check the browser history. Which children would actually do that?'

She added, '*Coming from a middle-class background, we instilled the value of money very early on in them.* If they didn't get good grades, I would tell them, "I am not paying for anything. You take extra classes and pay your own fees." They actually started doing that. They gave tuitions and earned money that they would then come and give it to me. Once they learnt the value of hard work, I told them "Okay, now you know how hard it is to earn, now focus on your studies." *I think they realized that "Our parents can be with us and help us but they can't do it for us. The 'doing' is only in our hands."*' What a thought.

She then talked about her husband's reaction to Joseph leaving his job. 'My husband felt so shocked that he started shivering. He couldn't believe he was giving up a steady job, a good position and chasing nothing. He told him, "You are about to become a deputy general manager (DGM) and you are thirty. Soon you will be general manager (GM)." The folks at his company, Asian Paints, felt so bad that they said "Whatever you want to do, you do it from here but don't quit." They even told him, "Go wherever but if you decide to come back, we will welcome you."'

Talking about when Joseph was facing financial difficulties after leaving his job, she said, '*As parents, you have to let your kids swim in the deep end of the water sometimes, knowing that they are finding it very hard to stay afloat.* But my boy had so much perseverance and endurance. When your child wants to do something, they have a different discipline and grit and that is very precious.'

I then got to know the difference between Joseph and Joshua. 'Kids come with their own temperament and needs. Joshua, like me, needs some basic plans and he can't do without those. Joseph, on the other hand, goes with the flow. If he won't get a bus, he will take a lorry. He doesn't care,' she revealed.

His mom then went on to tell me that sometimes, as parents, we turn into hypocrites ourselves. We tell our kids to be and do a bazillion things, but we don't seem to practise them ourselves. She said, 'Kids observe everything. How you are acting and reacting in any situation. *It's not only about how we are bringing them up but actually how we are living as well. Even though we are the direct models for them, kids learn certain things from friends and society also.*'

Later, we talked about how we all tell our kids that 'if you respect others, you will earn their respect in return,' but in today's world, even we parents are aware that sometimes, this is not the case. She then told me about her daughter who is in the US and still asks her, 'Mama, you said if you are fair then the other person will be also but it doesn't work, I don't see that happening.'

I asked her how she balanced out the praise, or rather, made all her kids feel they are equal even with their different measures of success. She simply said, 'I never praise *na*, that's the thing. I am happy and content. I tell them to thank God for everything and remember that whatever they have been blessed with is not theirs alone. So, they also never boast about anything much.' She told me that having a listening ear is very important and further revealed that 'People and my relatives used to say, "Look, your kids are on the TV or the newspaper. You should buy it and read it." I never used to, though. I just used to praise and thank God. And you know na, a mother's *nazar* [evil eye] is not good for the child. So, I don't swell my mind with their success.'

But I saw the pride in her eyes that she had for her kids. She shared how the boys had magazine cut-outs of cricketers all over their rooms and now are able to meet the same people in person.

We then spoke a little about their qualities as she listed some that she felt had really cemented their personalities. She said they are 'obedient, honest and whatever they say, they stick to that. They are also meek and gentle—they don't try to boast or anything. They don't try to have a big show. They are very hard-working and empathetic. They are highly pious.'

I asked her about any disagreements that she and her husband may have had when it came to parenting and she told me that it had happened because she wouldn't give the kids things just because they could afford them. She used to send them places by auto, even though they could afford a car and didn't get them cell phones, even though all their other friends had one. She didn't want her kids to stop working hard, thinking they would get everything, or to make friends with only that class of people who owned these things. She said that one evening when the kids were discussing the topic, she asked them, '"What is meant by rich?" When I looked at Joshua, he was around 11 years old and he said, "Whenever we go to the school canteen, if we are able to take Rs 100 from our pocket to spend, then we are rich." Then I looked at Joseph, who said, "The one who can buy ice cream and also Cadbury's chocolate at one time and then give it to his friends. That is being rich."'

When asked if she had any advice to share with the parents of this generation, she said, 'There should be a balance—if one parent is stricter, then the other should be more liberal. But they should be loving and strict at the same time.'

From the conversation, I learned that Joshua and Joseph both love non-veg.

I asked if she had any messages for her kids, and she said she'd like them to spend some more time with family and take time out for themselves too. Do a little meditation and give time to prayers.

If you had a huge billboard on parenting, what message would it read?

'Walk the talk. Only say what you mean. Children are very keen observers. Whatever we do, the way we walk, the way we behave. Any principles you have in your life, don't only speak but put them into practice and they will reciprocate too.'

We asked parents on Instagram about their opinion on the following:

Learnings and Observations

1. When your children learn to live in other people's homes, they will be disciplined, respectful and humble.
2. Communication is very important in parenting. Never lie to your kids and give fuzzy answers or not address the curiosity.
3. We need to make our kids realize that we can be with them and help them but the 'doing' is only in their hands.
4. As parents, you have to let your kids swim in the deep end of the water sometimes, knowing that they are finding it very hard to stay afloat.
5. Walk the talk. Only say what you mean. Any principles you have in your life, don't only speak them but put them into practice and your children will do the same.

Conclusion

In writing the introduction and first few pages, I probably assumed that these children would be highly motivated, talented and clear about what they wanted to accomplish. Their parents were likely to be very dominant figures who had prioritized raising their children above all else, to the point where they may have abandoned promising careers. Most likely, there was a well-defined plan for their children's futures that included activities by the hour, like music, art, dance and language study. It turns out I was incorrect. The chapters I recorded proved me wrong. You can't follow a formula. Each and every child is unique. True, their parents might have prioritized them, but that didn't mean they gave up on themselves.

We're always trying to find the right balance of ingredients, but the *things that make people truly stand out are not taught in school but rather absorbed through exposure to the world and interaction with its inhabitants.*

They are not people who are crafted differently, they are people who respond differently. They have each paid a price and it's not a free ticket to success.

Outliers can be built in environments of abundance or scarcity. Trust, freedom, support and unconditional love are the cornerstones upon which outliers are made.

As parents, we constantly worry that we're not providing our children with enough. Are our noes more than our yeses? Will my kid hate me tomorrow for setting limits today?

It's easy for us parents to feel like the clock is ticking, that now or never is the only option and that tomorrow will inevitably be too late. When the time is right, the children will surpass themselves. Even within the constraints of family and society, they can forge their own path. When they're ready, the world will take notice and they'll stand out.

When I heard certain quotes, they revealed epiphanies such as:

'They don't need to defy or abandon; they sometimes need to obey and abide.'

'Every single thing that stresses you out as parents in this moment will always seem silly in hindsight.'

This book also gave me a visual that success is not a finite finish line. In these interviews, I met parents of high achievers who typically valued other things in addition to financial success. I was able to see the characteristics and personalities of each of the outliers who had been so successful. Education plays a critical role in any parent's life. We always believe it is that single factor that will change the trajectory of our life and that of our child. Each parent in the book strove to provide their child with the best education. *With this mindset as parents to Gen Z and Gen Alpha, it will take a lot for us to unlearn that education is no longer the game changer and our kids will choose paths that may not be built on the foundations of a formal education system. They will learn differently and they will embrace learning styles that are best suited for them. Their role models will also evolve and it may not be someone who is brilliant in one field like academics, sports, Bollywood or politics like it's always been.*

As parents, we label those qualities as *thanda* [chilled out], *dheela* [incapable] and *ziddi* [stubborn], but these are the very same qualities that drive them to their goals and their universe. Like my mom always said, 'If your child has never hated you, you haven't been a good parent.'

For the sake of ourselves, our kids and the rest of the world, we all need to stop obsessing over whether or not we're good parents. *We must remember that we are merely the vehicles through which they are empowered on their journeys. Nothing we do today will protect our children from the storm they will face tomorrow, but we also know that everything we teach them today will equip them to weather that storm more effectively.*

Trust will be broken, lies will be spoken, but we can just hope and pray that the values stay intact in our children, and that whenever they are at a crossroads between choosing right or wrong, the values echo in their ears and help them decide their path with or without us being around.

Something I observed in these stories was that the trust was built at a very young age. In the cases of Suhani, Jemimah and Anuj, to name a few, I saw parents who sent these kids alone on public transport and gave them the house keys when they were just kids. This makes me wonder—are we being overprotective of our kids today? Are we raising responsible kids? Are we showing them enough trust?

Each parent eventually had to distance themselves from their child, realizing that their presence was vital without overwhelming the young person. This passage from the Gita (Chapter 2, shloka 62) makes complete sense for parents going through all stages of parenting:

ध्यायतो विषयान्पुंस: सङ्गस्तेषूपजायते |
सङ्गात्सञ्जायते काम: कामात्क्रोधोऽभिजायते || 2.62||

dhyāyato viṣhayān puṁsaḥ saṅgas teṣhūpajāyate
saṅgāt sañjāyate kāmaḥ kāmāt krodho 'bhijāyate

The man dwelling on sense objects develops attachment for them; it springs up desire, and desire (unfulfilled) bursts into anger.

Tight, conditional love can be suffocating. Imagine a situation where a bird had landed on your balcony, and you put it in a cage to admire it. But it would eventually want to be free and that could irritate you. But setting him free would be the right and most natural decision. Similarly, a mother instantly falls in love with her newborn child and for the first ten years, that child is the centre of her world. *The dejection and his flight for freedom will make her pull him closer to her and strangle him in the name of affection.*

Nature is said to love us all and be unattached, and the Gita advises parents to do the same. In the exact same way, we need to love our children without any strings attached. It is the only way to keep a healthy relationship.

If you loved the book or have something to share, please reach out to me on Instagram (@mansi.zaveri and @kidsstoppress) and check out my website (www.mansi.zaveri.com) for exciting future updates!

For extended conversations:

If you scan the QR code below, you'll be able to watch the exclusive conversations that are the foundations of these chapters.

My Notes

As someone who takes copious notes, I felt compelled to create a section that I'd like to see in more books—a summary of key points and concepts with doodles, notes and thoughts scribbled all over by the reader.

Here, I'd like you to make a note of your favourite profiles and the page numbers where you found the most insightful quotes or suggestions for positive change.

Making this index will allow you to quickly find your preferred passages.

If there's a particular quote you really like and want to put into practice, for instance, you could add it to your index and, ideally, include a next step.

It's only natural that different people at various points in their lives will find different parents to be particularly meaningful. I'd love to know what you're taking away from this book! Feel free to snap a photo and send it my way on Instagram (@mansi.zaveri) if you're feeling generous. I see and respond quite a bit.

Happy note-taking!

Mansi
13 September 2023

Acknowledgements

To ensure a wide range of perspectives, I was eager to have a diverse number of contributors from different backgrounds participate in this collection. I'd like to express my gratitude to the illustrious parents who agreed to contribute to this volume despite their busy schedules and recognized the importance of doing so. I can only imagine how frustrating this was for the first-timers among them who were attempting to share their thoughts and experiences with the world.

The finished product is here now and I hope it inspires parents all around to communicate their ideas and put pen to paper more frequently.

To the parents: you are the driving force behind the exceptional and as your children win so many awards, you deserve special recognition for your boundless encouragement, sleepless nights and unwavering faith in them when they doubted themselves. Many people will try to emulate you because of the examples you have set.

Without the dedication and support of my colleagues at Kidsstoppress.com, this book never would have been written. A big thank you to my friend Sheetal Dharia who has lived every chapter, every guest, every connection and my most audacious dreams. My friends, Rajiv and Khushboo Poddar, and Mithun Sacheti, who helped me think of ideas, put me in touch with relevant people and brainstormed with me at every leg of the book. What can I possibly write to show my appreciation to Manish Pandey? Manish has been a rock for me and a veritable directory of contacts. I told him about the book on a Zoom call well over a year ago and his enthusiasm about it helped make this into a reality.

Thanks to Anupama Chopra at Film Companion for always being prompt, accessible and providing insightful introductions and feedback in a matter of minutes.

Thank you, Viren from Olympic Gold Quest (OGQ), for making it possible for me to include an Olympian in this book.

My dear friends Kamna and Bikash Chowdhary, who are more like family, got me unstuck when I was at a loss of motivation.

I owe a thanks to the (Jindal South West) JSW sports staff as well for supporting my ideas.

To all those managers who did not respond to my several follow-ups—I hope the talent you represent read this book. You made me think beyond myself and I am grateful for that.

I would like to thank the entire team at Penguin for making this book a possibility. My editors at Penguin, Gurveen Chadha and Aparna Abhijit, were patient with me as I changed deadlines and they gave me a free hand with this book. The endless follow-ups and stringing together very different stories could not have been easy.

A thank you to Tanya Lemos, who helped me through it all with her usual cool competence.

To my mom and mom-in-law, two powerful women who show the world how mothers can shape the lives of their children and communities—I want to thank you for your support and for excusing me through all those tasks and conversations that I missed to meet the deadline for this book.

To my sisters Neepa, Priti, Bijal and Nisha for supporting me and brainstorming with me through every milestone. I would like to express my deepest appreciation to Aanya and Akshata, my two harshest yet most insightful critics, who continue to be pillars of support and a source of motivation for me. They became my accountability partners and constantly asked, 'Maa, how many more chapters to go?'

This endeavour would not have been possible without my husband Nakul, who encouraged me to aim higher and acted as my devil's advocate throughout the writing of this book. He helped me see the big picture at every turn and it was through my conversations with him that I made the difficult transition from wondering to doing. None of my hopes, plans or ideas would be taking shape so rapidly without his audacious and authentic presence in my life.

A thank you to the most valuable members of the Kidsstoppress.com community—the readers, followers and supporters. This was my #SecretProject and I want to thank you for reading, sharing and engaging with me for the last ten years at Kidsstoppress.com. Your constant feedback and faith that 'if it's parenting, it's got to be Kidsstoppress.com and if there's anyone who can do this, it's Mansi' has held me accountable.

Scan QR code to access the
Penguin Random House India website